Indigenous Mexico Engages
the 21st Century

Dedication

Dedicated to the memory of my friend and compadre Encarnacion Velazquez who along with his wife Concha Duran welcomed me into their house in 1972. To the people of San Jerónimo Amanalco I owe a debt I can never fully repay.

Indigenous Mexico Engages the 21st Century

A Multimedia-enabled Text

Jay Sokolovsky

Walnut Creek, California

Left Coast Press, Inc.
1630 North Main Street, #400
Walnut Creek, CA 94596
www.LCoastPress.com

ISBN 978-1-62958-174-3 hardback
ISBN 978-1-62958-175-0 paperback
ISBN 978-1-62958-177-4 consumer eBook

Cover Designed by Jane Burton

Library of Congress Cataloging-in-Publication Data

Sokolovsky, Jay.
   Indigenous Mexico engages the 21st century : a multimedia-enabled text / Jay Sokolovsky.
      pages cm
   Includes bibliographical references and index.
   ISBN 978-1-62958-174-3 (hardback) —
   ISBN 978-1-62958-175-0 (paperback) —
   ISBN 978-1-62958-177-4 (consumer ebook)
   1. San Jerónimo Amanalco (Mexico)—Social conditions.   2. Indians of Mexico—Mexico—San Jerónimo Amanalco—Social life and customs.   3. Indians of Mexico—Mexico—San Jerónimo Amanalco—Rites and ceremonies, 4. Globalization—Social aspects—Mexico—San Jerónimo Amanalco.   5. Anthropology—Fieldwork—Mexico—San   Jerónimo   Amanalco. I. Title.
II. Title: Indigenous Mexico engages the twenty-first century.
   HN120.S25S64 2015
   306.0972´52—dc23

                                                                    2014047037

Printed in the United States of America

The paper used in this publication meets the minimum requirements of American National Standard for Information Sciences—Permanence of Paper for Printed Library Materials, ANSI/NISO Z39.48–1992.

About the Cover

"Rays of Light," the beautiful mural on the cover, was created in 2014 by Sergio Pérez Méndez, a resident of San Jerónimo Amanalco who is studying Visual Arts at the Autonomous University of the State of Hidalgo. His work covers an outside wall of the *delegación*, the community's main public administrative building. The mural was created in association with a new cultural center and community museum recently inaugurated in that building. The artist has graciously given permission to use the image here and on the book's web site. Check chapter 10 on the web site for links which illustrate how the mural was created, the meaning of its nine panels and a video highlighting the new museum.

About the image at the top of each chapter

This image is called Nahui Ollin. In the Nahuatl language it means "4-movement" and is important in Mexican cosmology. According to the *Handbook to Life in the Aztec World* (Aguilar-Moreno 2007), the Ollin symbol represents the sun's movement and the world's dynamic life.

Contents

Illustrations

Figures

Table

Using this Multimedia-enabled Book

Set in the rugged mountains overlooking Mexico City, *Indigenous Mexico Engages the 21st Century* fuses text with a range of digital media to explore the contemporary lives and culture of San Jerónimo Amanalco's residents. Our understanding of the community and its people, culture, and region is enhanced through Power Point learning modules and archival documents, audio, and video gathered through ethnographic research over the past forty years. These materials are not mere adjuncts to the written page but rather learning tools integrated into the fabric of the text.

A companion website at *www.indigenousmexicobook.com* enables print readers to access all the digital materials. Readers of the e-book edition can simply click on icons embedded in the text to gain access to these materials. Print edition readers can see the embedded icons but will need to log on to the website to have access to the digital materials. Such resources can allow readers to visually walk through Amanalco on Google maps, ⊕ witness a *quinceañera,* ◼ listen to the sound of an Aztec Band ◿ and explore the activities of an exciting new cultural center, *Centro Cultural Miyotl,* with a Power Point module. P There are also "Added Value" resources such as a video tour of the pre-Hispanic archaeology of the town of Huexotla ⬆ southwest of Amanalco. Within the website some chapters will also have questions for readers tying together the print and digital materials, such as in the last slide of a Power Point learning module concerning Amanalco's fading archaeological heritage. P

Each icon allows readers of the e-book direct access to the digital resources and guides readers of the printed book to the website for access to those same resources. On the website, banners, with corresponding icons, alert readers to specific resources..

A special note to e-book readers: if any link in your book does not work, go to the website for that chapter and access the link there.

Icons used in this book

Video Icon ◼	Power Point Icon P
Audio Icon ◿	General Link Icon ⊕
Added Value Icon ⬆	

Fieldwork is always full of surprises and renewed excitement if one sticks with it for the long run. When I left Amanalco in 2010, I was somewhat pessimistic about the vitality of the community. The central plaza was in a sad state, and more so than in previous years, people seemed to be grumbling about a sense of perceived disarray and disunity. Emails I received several months after I left lamented the lack of state support for a Nahuatl Cultural Center which had been planned since 2003. As readers will learn in the book's last chapter, this started to turn around in late 2012 with the renewal of the plaza and as the community developed its own small version of a cultural center. Just as important as these changes, on August 1, 2014, Amanalco opened its own "Community Museum of Nahuatl Men, Women and Children." As I was following the progress of all this through email, Facebook and phone calls, I was delighted to see a renewal of the community spirit and pride I first experienced in the early 1970s.

On November 10, 2014, as I sat at my computer a message flashed on the screen from someone trying to set up a Facebook video chat with me. After a few moments of missed connections the screen resolved and to my great surprise it revealed a young man from Amanalco whose picture I had seen recently on Facebook. It was Sergio Pérez Méndez, the artist whose mural adorns the cover of this book. While I knew his parents and likely saw him as a young child, this was my first opportunity to talk with him as an adult. Over the next hour we shared the excitement at the opening of the community museum in August 2014 and his commission to create the amazing image at its entrance.

I reflected on the fact that I was just his age, 24, when I first lived in Amanalco, and how differently his age peers experienced life back then compared to today. It brought back a flood of memories of both the fear and excitement of entering into another people's world and culture and inching towards some understanding of how their lives were made meaningful. It also helped me feel more confident that Sergio's generation could create a cultural space to celebrate the lives of their elders, but also to realize the need to positively transform their community as a key to engaging the future.

As I returned repeatedly to Amanalco and began to witness the kinds of rapid change that had occurred there since the 1970s, I began to conceive of a different approach to producing a document about what was happening to the community and its residents. In doing so, my hope is to provide readers, including those in Amanalco, a multifaceted learning experience beyond the written word. This is among the challenges of anthropology and the ethnographic approach: to enable a rendering of other people's lives in as many dimensions as possible. I hope this book is a step in that direction.

St. Petersburg, Florida,
December 19, 2014

Acknowledgements

There are a multitude of people who helped made this book possible.

First and foremost is my wife Maria Vesperi who as a partner, fabulous editor and anthropologist has helped me better understand our shared experiences in Amanalco.

In Amanalco itself there is a multitude of people and households who made this work possible. Most important among the residents of Amanalco are the members of my *tochantlaca*, Buena Vista, especially Dona Concha Duran, Juan Velazquez, Anastacia Dias, Emirihildo Velazquez, Juan Bernardo Velazquez (Gordo), Rosalba Velazquez, Elizabeth Velazquez and their respective husbands Herardo and Cirillo.

Of the other people and their families I especially want to thank, there is the community nurse Hipolita Espinosa who was a constant source of support, friendship and critical knowledge. I was also helped by her brothers Nicholas and Trinidad, as well as their father Rafael, who related many tales to me. Especially important was my neighbor, friend and Nahuatl teacher Juan Duran who always watched over me and taught me many things, such as how to age with dignity. Joyous thanks to Miguel Arias and the memory of his wife Anastacia, and all their many children, who always welcomed me into their house and made me return often with their laughter and joy for life. Special thanks to the many people in the Tlaxamulco household, especially Raymundo Juarez, his wife Jeronima, and their sons Salome and Alex who showed how to combine their traditional culture with the 21st century.

A memorable thanks to Jose Duran Duran for teaching me many things about the campesino lifestyle and for pulling on me the linguistic joke described in chapter 1. My neighbors Jose Lopez and wife Catarina Hidalgo will always be remembered for their easy ways and generous spirit. Many thanks to Vicente Hidalgo Duran, a former delegado who helped me understand some of the evolving complexities of heritage preservation. Just as important to me are Ramon Arias, his wife Maria Cruz Peralta, and their sons Marselo and Trinidad, who were very special supporters during my first year in Amanalco. In a similar way, neighbors Lydia Espinoza and Delfino Duran taught me their indigenous language and deep traditions. In more recent times, I have a debt to Miguel Osario Baez and Sergio Pérez Mendez who have contributed important information and images that help me understand what is happening in Amanalco since I was last there in 2010.

Other people in Amanalco I would also like to thank are: Severino Dias; Ambrosio Velazquez, that difficult man, but good friend; Delegado Joel Aguilar; Delegada Berta Dias Rojas; and Presidenta Maria Trindad Espinoza; Jose Alfredo Perez; Eduardo Duran; and high school teacher Edith Martinez Loera. Although he no longer lives in Amanalco, I met Dr. Miguel Maldonado Avila when he did his medical service there and have continued to gain insights from him on health traditions in Amanalco.

To a great extent this work would not have been possible without the long-term support of the anthropology program, faculty and graduate students at Iberoamericana University who let me use their field house in Tepetloaxtoc and for forty years provided encouragement, intellectual stimulation and inspiration. I am especially indebted to Roger Magazine, David Robichaux, Angel Palerm, Carmen Viquiera Landa, Patricia Torres Palerm, Carmen Bueno, Dubravka Mendek, Marisol Perez Lizaur, Marta Aceves, David Lorente Fernandez, Clorinda Cuminao, and Teresa Ochoa. I have a great debt of gratitude to Guillermo Torres and López Manuel Moreno, young anthropologists from that program who worked side by side with me in 2006 and 2010.

For understanding the region outside of Amanalco, I thank Tomas Martínez Saldaña and Ana Orozco, who is also doing the Spanish translation for this book. In Mexico City, Lourdes Baez Cubero, curator of the Nahua room at the Museo Nacional de Antropologia, helped me understand the Nahau tradition in its widest historical depth. I was also helped by Karen Lipman with the video and detail planning of our participation in Rosalba's Quinceañera.

This book greatly benefited from the review of various versions of the book manuscript by Serena Nanda, Ella Schmidt, Tony Andrews, Erin Dean, Roger Magazine, Alan Sandstrom and Janice Stockard.

Closer to home, Narciso Hidalgo and Nayvi Hernandez of the University of South Florida St. Petersburg were of great help with translating some of the video materials. Liz Southard served as my editorial assistant during much of this project, and John Stewart has continued to assist with cross-checking materials and undertaking the index. Thanks go to Lucas Cannistraci for help with digitizing, editing and translation. I also greatly appreciate the following students who were brave enough to make important comments about chapters they read: Lauren Munim, Delaney Parsons, Russell Heller, Thomas Tarantola, Courtney Robinson, and Kyleigh Cobett.

At Left Coast Press, Inc. I want to thanks especially Publisher Mitch Allen and Anthropology Editor Jack Meinhardt who encouraged the production of this new kind of book. At the press Ryan Harris and Jason Potter made copy editing and production a comparative joy.

A special thanks to David Latham of the Reed Foundation is necessary. David assisted in me receiving a Ruth Landes Memorial Research Fund grant which gave me the time to begin writing this book.

Finally, the website could not have been possible without the design and digital skills of Dan Coffman, who stuck with me through a long process of web creation and production.

CHAPTER ONE

Never say "Chou-chou ley" to an Aztec!

Tepetloaxtoc, Mexico: First Field Encounters

I was nervous enough about moving into Amanalco for my first stint of real anthropological fieldwork. I did not need Monolitón to tell me his definitive story about the ferocity of these mountain folk. Monolitón, age fifty-two, maintained a university field house in the rural Mexican town of Tepetlaoxtoc where I had been living during the fall of 1972. Using this house as a base, I ventured throughout the region learning about rural life in a variety of nearby communities. The night before I was to move into the indigenous village of San Jerónimo Amanalco, Monolitón came over to dissuade me from making the move, saying slowly but firmly, "But, Jay, my dear friend, I cannot let you do this."

Puzzled, I said to him, "You seem very upset. Why are you saying this?"

I noticed Monolitón was drunk and swaying, and before he replied, his powerful peasant hands grabbed hard on my arms, as much to emphasize his seriousness as to steady himself. "I know you have been there a number of times, but you do not know them," he said.

> These *Indios,* they will seem polite, bending to kiss each other's hand and saying "*compadrito, compadrito,*" but when your back is turned they will stick a knife in it and throw you in a ditch. Listen, a few years ago some forest workers came to look at Amanalco's woods, and the people got nervous. The *delegados* [mayors] ordered some men to find these strangers, and with shotguns they killed them like dogs and dumped them into a *barranca.* This is the kind of people you are going to live with!

Knowing Monolitón, I was immediately dubious about this story. Like others in Tepetlaoxtoc, he frequently directed ethnic slurs toward any inhabitants of the four indigenous communities hugging the mountain wall a mere thirty-minute drive from his own *mestizo* village. In his community residents no longer spoke *Nahuatl,* the indigenous language then widely used in Amanalco. At a very deep level I was also afraid to find out whether Monolitón's story was true and never inquired further about it until four months into my residence in Amanalco.

I wanted to think the best of the people I was about to live with, and for the most part Amanalco's residents had so far been generous and kind to me. My initial contacts with the village produced some suspicious reactions and serious practical jokes to test my nerve. Yet I had regarded these events as something I might have done in their place. For example, the third time I came to the village to examine the soils used for different types of crops, a large extended family invited me to a festive lunch. Leaving the house with a group of men who were also at the meal, I asked what would be a special way, in the Nahuatl language, to thank the several ladies of the house who were standing at their doorway waving good-bye. One man, José Duran, paused just a moment and, with a very serious look, said, "Tell them *chuchule*." I turned to the women, smiled, and shouted, "chuchule!" The ladies shrieked in unison and ran into the house. I turned to José, who was laughing so hard he had actually fallen on the ground in hysterics. He looked up at me as he stood and said, "No, no, you must say it faster like this: *chuchule, chuchule*." Stunned and thinking it was just my poor pronunciation, I complied with a call toward the house. Again, unpleasant shouts rang out from the women inside, and José had once again fallen, doubled up in a hilarious state. It finally dawned on me that I had said something very stupid or worse. In my embarrassment and anger I stormed away as Jose's seven-year-old nephew caught up to me and tugged at my sleeve. As I bent down he whispered intently in my ear, "Sir, why did you say 'fuck off' to the ladies?"

Over the course of that year this same boy, Juan Velazquez, and his family were to become the key to my survival in Amanalco. They taught me how to kick away attacking dogs, speak their village's dialect of Nahuatl, show proper respect and generally become a person in the eyes of other villagers. ◼◀ A month after my mortifying experience I ended up moving into their home, called Buena Vista, a few doors away from where I performed my linguistic disaster. Little did I suspect that over the course of the next forty years this family and I would nurture a relationship that went far beyond anthropology.

2010 Realities: From an Indigenous Peasant
Village to a Globally Connected Town

Flash forward to the twenty-first century. I am making the eighth trip to Amanalco since my initial fieldwork. By now this research has spanned four decades, across which community residents have experienced—and I have witnessed—enormous cultural and economic transformations. In my prior visit in 2006 my wife, Maria, and I participated in the wedding of our goddaughter, Rosalba. Then, in November of 2009, our *compadres* called us in Florida to ask whether we could attend the marriage of Rosalba's younger brother, Gordo, to take place the following month. Although we could not make this event, I promised to send some money to help with expenses and visit during the following summer. The family was pleased with the timing of our visit because it would be just before the birth

16

of Gordo's child. They hoped that my wife could participate in her role as *comadre* in a new ritual just catching on there, called "el baby shower."

So it is now a warm, hazy, and dry morning in early June 2010, and before traveling to Amanalco I am spending my initial few days in chaotic, exciting Mexico City. I am thinking of the materials I want to gather for writing this book that could add to my decades of attempts to understand village culture and its transformation. One day was spent in a very productive visit to the magnificent National Museum of Anthropology discussing with a curator the newest exhibit and research on Nahuatl culture. I also decided to travel somewhere I should have gone many years ago, to the beautiful village of Tepoztlán, a ninety-minute bus ride from the southern reaches of Mexico City, in the state of Morelos. The community has a mystical aura to it, teeming with colorful birds, surrounded by exotic semitropical vegetation and overlooked by a high mountain Aztec-era temple to Tepoztecatl, the god of *pulque* (an alcoholic beverage made from the sap of the agave cactus). It is here that anthropologist Robert Redfield, from 1926 to 1927, gathered data for his PhD work and used this to publish, in 1930, *Tepotzlan: A Mexican Village—A Study in Folk Life.* This book about a Nahuatl-speaking people became a touchstone for a multitude of other works in Latin America and elsewhere examining the impact of modern life and urbanization on a peasant community. Redfield's book, written in accessible language, described the patterns of Aztec heritage such as their rituals of personal respect, the elaborate *fiesta* system, and women's use of *temazcals* (sweat baths) for promoting health. Hidden within these idealized descriptions were the emerging ruptures in community life and the nascent rejection of indigenous culture.

Four decades earlier, in preparing for my own PhD research and in eventually writing up my results, I poured over Redfield's book and a controversial restudy of that village in the early 1950s by Oscar Lewis (1960). Lewis's study was much more sophisticated and found that the earlier work had oversimplified the complexity of peasant life and the dynamic relation to urban zones. In my own work I was to find this approach to analyzing peasant communities a key template for perceiving the dynamic reality people experienced in their daily life. In June of 2010 I experienced Tepoztlán as a highly regulated tourist town with boutique spa-hotels, Chinese and Indian restaurants, and jewelry-gift stores catering to international tourists. Yet there is also an underlying feeling of a people well in control of what cultural traditions remain, especially in terms of religious rituals and, as JoAnn Martin illustrated in a recent book, the ability of the community to resist usurpation of their lands (2005). As I found in my work in Amanalco, the ability to aggressively and quickly respond to perceived threats to environmental resources has been an effective protective mechanism of community rights in a political system severely tilted toward vested elites.

The next day, back in Mexico City, the annual rainy season had not yet started in earnest, and air pollution was giving me daily, pounding headaches. This was my cue to take off for Amanalco with a Mexican graduate student assistant, Manuel

Moreno, and pick up a rental car at the airport. We use the highway shortcut, the Via Corta, which passes across the dry hardpan bed of a once grand lake system and, within thirty minutes, reached the outskirts of the city of Texcoco (see figures 1.a and 1.1b below).[1] This is the capital of the municipal district that bears the same name, and Amanalco is one of twenty-seven *pueblos* (rural villages) in the far eastern edge of the area politically led by Texcoco. In 1972 Texcoco was a sleepy regional capital of twenty-five thousand, but by 2010 its population had swelled to about two hundred thousand. It is here that inhabitants of Amanalco must come to register titles to land, obtain a civil marriage license, pay their electric bills, or complain about an injustice that their own authorities cannot handle. This urban center, with its banks, appliance stores, movie theaters, medical clinics, technical colleges, Volkswagen and Nissan car dealerships, Domino's Pizza delivery, Home Depot, and one of Mexico's newest Walmart superstores, serves as a juncture for the diffusion of Mexican national culture and increasingly international ideas and consumer goods. ▉◖

The Acolhua people settled this ancient urban zone in the twelfth century and, along with the Tepanecs and the militarily dominant Mexica, eventually formed a powerful "Triple Alliance" of extraordinary imperial power of what Europeans eventually called the Aztec Empire. Texcoco came to be known as its seat of intellectual life, especially under the long reign of the fifteenth-century poet-king Nezahualcóyotl. Amanalco's early history was most influenced by its connection in the pre-Hispanic period to what anthropologists call the Northern Acolhuacan domain. This was a state centered in urban Texcoco that ruled several dozen communities and extended over three major environmental zones, bounded by Lake Texcoco in the west and the Sierra Nevada mountain chain in the east. Today a massive modern

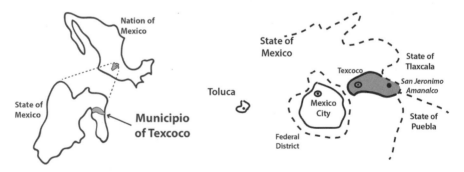

Figures 1.1a and 1.1b   The map on the left sets the Municipio of Texcoco in the State of Mexico and the one on the right locates the community of San Jerónimo Amanalco in the eastern mountains of the municipal unit of Texcoco. A link here shows key communities mentioned in Chapter 1. 📄Ⓟ *You can then "google map" the community of San Jerónimo Amanalco,* ⊕ *and at this map, even take a "street view" stroll through the residential areas of Amanalco.*

statue of Nezahualcóyotl, with pointing arm, beckons drivers eastward onto the Mexico-Puebla highway. Drivers pass junk yards, dairy farms, the huge Rockefeller International Agricultural research center, tire repair businesses, simple restaurants, and the occasional soccer field, all of which edge this busy roadway.

Lying at seventy-two hundred feet above sea level, this is the flat eastern portion of the valley of Mexico, a region crucial to the history of Mexico and all of the Americas. Due north is the town of Tepexpan, where in 1948 there was found a late Pleistocene (about 9000 BC) female human skull and the oldest human skeleton then yet known from North America. Despite such early habitation, it is today a very sleepy town known only for one of the country's few Chronic Care Hospitals. Just further north are found the famous pyramids of Teotihuacan. ⊕ From the third until the late eighth century AD the New World's first megalopolis developed at this site, eventually spreading out over eight square miles and housing a quarter of a million urbanites.

Of more contemporary vintage, the town of San Salvador Atenco on the northern edge of Lake Texcoco gained more recent global notoriety when, in 2000, a group of armed farmers firmly rejected the federal government's offer for land payment in order to make way for a new international airport. They not only imprisoned the town government but also kidnapped a national official who was sent to negotiate. The federal government eventually gave in and decided not to build the new airport after all. Activists in this community have formed an organization, the People's Front for the Defense of the Land, which continues to support other communities who have tried to resist such things as the building of Walmarts across from the pyramids of Teotihuacan or at the site of a flower market on the outskirts of Texcoco.[2]

For the past two thousand years this high fertile valley has been a flash point for regional competition and conflict and has witnessed the florescence and collapse of numerous pre-industrial indigenous kingdoms and states. The best known is certainly the infamous Aztec state, dominated by the Mexica peoples who had migrated in the early fourteenth century to this region, which was already highly populated and controlled by a series of contentious chiefdoms and city-states. By the later part of that century the Mexica, through alliances, intrigue, strategic marriages, and military prowess, came to control the entire region. They built their capital, Tenochtitlan, in the middle of a shallow lake system, and it developed into a canal city of perhaps 250,000, with the watery elegance of Venice and the regional power of early Rome. The Mexica are known to the modern public for their use of human sacrifice in public rituals and their starkly powerful art, displayed in major museums around the world. Lesser known was the sophistication of their agricultural, engineering, and scientific knowledge. This produced a complex system of food production and trade that sustained an urban-linked empire spreading throughout central Mexico, from the Pacific to the Gulf coasts and beyond. ⊕ Amanalco itself was established as a formal community in the early fifteenth century when the ruler of Texcoco sent engineers there to create a large irrigation system, which is still operating today, flowing from ten springs in the rugged mountains above the community.

Central Mexico has been the source of much anthropological research and imagination from the discipline's inception. Edward Tylor, credited with the first anthropology textbook published in 1881, earlier in 1855 wrote *Anahuac,* a travelogue that included culturally detailed descriptions of Texcoco and some of the surrounding communities and peoples. It is particularly interesting to read about his discussion of the varied Europeans elites and their relation to the indigenous peoples he encountered. It provides an idea of the human face of Central American colonialism in the middle of the nineteenth century. ⊕

The road from Texcoco toward Puebla gradually slices higher through foothills of a piedmont area and past signs for mestizo villages such as Tlaixpan, Purificacion, and Tlaminca. In this region is also found the archaeologically and symbolically important mountain called Tetzcotzingo. Here, in the fifteenth century, King Nezahualcóyotl created temples, waterworks, and a ritual setting within one of the world's first botanical gardens. This green space sought to preserve flora and fauna from the breadth of the Aztec empire (Avilés 2006). ◀ The mountain is dramatically visible from certain vantage points in Amanalco and still figures in some of the myths recounted there. However, villagers in the piedmont zone surrounding Tetzcotzingo have long discarded the Nahuatl language and cultural traditions that Amanalco is now struggling to retain and integrate into their current lives (Ennis-McMillan 2006). The piedmont zone between the valley area, at a seventy-two hundred feet elevation and the "sierra" zone past eighty-five hundred feet, offers a wonderful climatic zone with pleasant weather much of the year and has attracted some urban elites to build vacation houses in this region. It is also an area transformed prior to the twentieth century by rapacious colonial capitalists who established large agrarian plantations called *haciendas,* usurping large portions of prime community lands. Although much of these lands were regained following the Mexico Revolution of 1910–1920, villages in this area compared to those in the higher sierra zone were forced at a much earlier time period to have residents leave their homesteads to sustain themselves economically.

Further east and just past the exit for the town of Tepetlaoxtoc, a paved turnoff pierces the lower edge of a high mountainous zone leading to Amanalco and the region's few other Nahuatl-speaking communities. Quickly passing by the small village of Santa Inés halfway up the mountain, I pulled the car over to glance back toward Mexico City. Although hills obscure this urban behemoth, a gray ring of smog crowns the area as if to anoint the king of pollution. Taking a deep breath, I smiled, realizing the eye-irritating ozone and potent odor of diesel fuel has been replaced with the intermittent whiff of cow manure and wood-burning stoves. I relaxed and thought, *I am almost back home.*

On the left side of this road the area almost replicates what can be seen in my photos from 1972—a highly eroded, dusty beige landscape dotted occasionally with scrub bushes, prickly pear cactus, and electric power towers marching up the mountain. [P]   On the right I searched fruitlessly for the Aztec-era house mounds and associated potsherds that once dotted the landscape and had survived into the early 2000s. For the past two decades farmers in Amanalco and Santa Inés have plowed these under as they attempted to reclaim this once-barren wasteland for agriculture. Limited corn and wheat fields are sprouting where once there was little else but rock and assorted cacti. Ironically, as these material remnants of an Aztec past were being obliterated, some of Amanalco's citizens were adopting a broader sense of their heritage, amplifying positive aspects of history and their native language, Nahuatl, still spoken by over a million people in Mexico. Most now object to being called an *Indio* (Indian) but have embraced the term *indigena* (person of indigenous origin) or sometimes refer to themselves as *Nahuatlaca* (the Nahua people). In doing so they reject the long-standing negative and racist connotations of being called an Indian in Mexico. Instead, they identify with the larger body of indigenous peoples in the state and nation who have been working to reclaim civil, political, and cultural rights stimulated by the successful insurrection of indigenous Maya speakers in Chiapas, Mexico, began in 1994.

Importantly, those pushing hardest to retain an indigenous identity are often residents with the most education, including a collective of college students and graduates who, in 2008, formed a group called *Ollin Amanalco Pilhuame* (sons of Amanalco Moving Ahead). ◼️   Part of an emerging strategy was not only to integrate newly designed Aztec heritage cultural events into the cycle of ritual events but also to develop plans for a local Nahuatl Cultural Center in conjunction with a Polytechnic University in Mexico City.

Returning to the car, a five-minute drive took me to a fork in the road—San Jerónimo Amanalco to the left and Santa Maria Tecuanulco, another Nahuatl-speaking community, straight ahead. In the distance toward Tecuanulco I saw that a large greenhouse has sprung up as part of new horticultural efforts in the region begun in 2000. I turned left and quickly swooped down a hundred feet from the eroded lands via a road bisecting the verdant zone of Amanalco's central residential community and irrigated lands. To my right I passed waving stalks of young corn on a terraced set of fields named Mashala. It is owned by the family of my close friend and elderly neighbor in the village, Juan Duran. He was the community leader during my first fieldwork stint and is now one of the most respected elders in town. I was encouraged by how well the fields are tended, as this may mean that Juan is back to good health since I last saw him a few years ago.

I immediately noticed that the paved road into the village has more speed bumps but was starting to show its age, having last been redone in 2003. That year, when I drove into Amanalco, the renewed road bed was barely a month old, and lampposts were topped with political banners proclaiming this new construction effort as part of that year's political campaign. At that time a parade of local politicians would barnstorm through the center of town, giving presentations and passing out favors such as pens with "Vote for . . ." emblazoned on them.

The Reality of "Never More Campesinos"

Driving through the community's central artery in 2010, I can hardly believe this is the same indigenous village I had first lived in four decades earlier. 🄿 Yet the changed landscape I was about to witness had been unfolding before me over the past two decades. During that time I would hear directly or implied the idea of *campesinos nunca más*, "never more campesinos"; that is, people are no longer so intensely focusing on working the land. Said as a declaration by the young and as a lamentation by the older generation, the notion of "never more campesinos" enters into ideas of self and community in a complicated way. This idea, as explored in future chapters, references transformed notions of work, gender, ethnic identity, and Amanalco's increasingly globalized context. It also provides an emotional touchstone to the village I first saw and the lives people lived in the 1970s.

Unlike in those days and despite the lush fields of Mashala, I pass many other plots of land that lie fallow. This observation was quickly connected to what I saw next: a young male teen zoomed by on a skateboard, and a passing car was full of older teens, one of whom had spiked purple hair and facial jewelry similar to that seen on many of my undergraduate students. Just past a newly opened Jehovah's Witness temple, with a sign in both Spanish and Nahuatl, lay the side of a fresh cement wall sporting a garish gang signature, "los destroyers." In a small building on the side of the road, opposite a tiny, Protestant church named Salem, the village's first Internet center has the added feature of alcohol sales marked by dual eight-foot-high plastic beer bottles. Internet service was started here in 2003 by a twenty-one-year-old female technical school graduate, with the help of her father and his kin. Looming up ahead is a cell phone tower, erected in 2006, that sits on the edge of a corn field across from the colonial-era church. What I am experiencing is a former village grown into a globally connected town of over seven thousand residents whose young citizens largely reject the campesino cultural script centered on farm work that had dominated the life of older generations. ▮◀

Driving slowly with the windows open, we hear an overlapping mixture of songs coming from radios, a new music store near the center of town, and the distant blare of an off-key trumpet being practiced. In the 1970s the village had a half-a-dozen fiesta bands and two Aztec bands that played locally and in regional villages, mostly for religious celebrations; some of these musicians also played in military bands in Mexico City. In the intervening time music as an occupation and preoccupation has exploded among the male population, with some becoming well-known music teachers and even recording artists. Different types of popular music bands have proliferated and had become a powerful occupational niche for well over a third of the households in the community. In 2010 Amanalco seemed like "garage band" central and youth under twenty sounded almost as familiar with current songs as many of my students back in Florida. An example of one of these new bands is Vientos del Cerro (Mountain Winds), and

I was able to video a practice session in a converted store front in the middle of Amanalco. ◼️📹   You can interact with and follow the exploits of the group on Facebook or by subscribing to their channel on YouTube. ⬆️

Recent stays in the village led me to suspect that engagement with nonfiesta music was one of those subtle but powerful forces that was becoming a catalyst, fueling bursts of globalization. Incredibly, in 2009 the world-famous performer Yanni had somehow heard about Amanalco, came to visit one of its bilingual schools, and was so taken with the musicality of the Nahuatl language that he flew a group of community children to Acapulco for a music video starring these kids singing in their indigenous language! ⬆️

Everywhere my eyes wandered I glimpsed a certain level of material prosperity and population explosion marked by diverse commercial establishments and a multitude of new houses crowding onto former cornfields. Many are two- and three-story cement and brick houses, even some with castle-like turrets upon which are mounted water heaters for showers and satellite dishes for global TV and Internet service. These structures are sprouting up next to traditional adobe structures, some of these decaying past usefulness. Passing along the main road, I was stunned by an array of new stores: a Veracruz-style fish restaurant and establishments for tire repair, rotisserie chicken, hardware, cakes, city clothing, music CDs, and cell phones.

Reaching the still-sleepy central plaza of the village, I passed a store owned by a man who had spent the year 2000 working in California. I saw a faded sign advertising hamburgers and pizza for a restaurant he had hoped to open in 2006. This never really panned out, and I saw him sitting in a car waiting for passengers by Amanalco's new central taxi stand, one of three that had just begun to operate in the village. Ringing the central plaza are several very modern, card-based phone booths, a general merchandise store, and a couple of places advertising music video sales and Internet service. A contrast to this explosion of commercial enterprises is the sad condition of the central plaza compared to my memory of just four years ago. Its previous shrubs and flowers were replaced by small gray stones, with paper and plastic garbage floating about and looking quite barren and uncared for. This is puzzling, as the adjacent colonial-era church courtyard is more beautiful than I have ever seen it, with a new garden and tree plantings. This is a puzzle I tell myself to unravel quickly. I was soon to learn things that were even more perplexing and unexpected, especially as I have stayed in frequent contact with the community since this last face-to-face visit (see Chapter 10).

I had to squeeze my car past a huge Coca-Cola delivery truck and intercity buses coming and going from Texcoco. Although the paving now continued halfway up the mountain side, with some interesting-looking new stores set fast by the road, I passed these up and turned by the church toward Buena Vista. Just before getting there, I waved at the son of Juan Duran, who was digging in the household garden behind his house. I shouted to him in a mixture of Spanish and Nahuatl, saying that I will visit with the family later. He shouts back, "Si, si,

Figure 1.2   Pizza Tlamapa opened in Amanalco in 2010. (Photo by Jay Sokolovsky)

moustla"—yes, yes, tomorrow. I was especially curious to learn about the new sign "Pizzas Tlamapa" adorning one end of their large residence.

Arriving at Buena Vista, I honked the car horn, and several young children came bursting out of the courtyard, greeting me with shouts of "Ché! Ché!" their version of my first name. We were soon shyly hugged by Ana, the very pregnant wife of my newly married godson, Gordo, who was working that day at another village house making clothing. He and his new bride both live in Buena Vista. Gordo's dad, my compadre Juan Velazquez, is in the middle of his multiday shift driving the family's minibus in Texcoco. His married younger brother, Angel, living across the courtyard, is off selling flowers, his main occupation these days. A dignified salutation was given by Juan's wife, Anastacia, and his elderly mother, Concha, who is minding her ten-month-old grandson, who resides in this house compound. After the women and I exchanged gentle hugs I introduced everyone to my research assistant, Manuel. Anastacia said with a soft, broad smile, "Welcome, compadre and Manuel. Thank you for visiting. I hope our comadre [my wife, Maria] will be arriving soon, as we have your room ready. Please come in and have something to eat."

Over tortillas, beans, boiled chicken, and rice soup we caught up on family and community events that had transpired since I last slept in Buena Vista in 2006.

CHAPTER TWO

Orientation to This Book

The first chapter detailed some of my early encounters with the community in 1972 and offered a glimpse into the dynamic cultural landscape I experienced during my last visit in 2010. This latest entrance into Amanalco sparked many questions in my mind: What was a Veracruz-style seafood restaurant doing in the middle of the village? Why had the plaza fallen into disrepair? Why the sudden presence of urban representatives in the town? Puzzling out the answers to these questions is part of my adventure with ethnography to be shared in this book.

In exploring such issues I suggest that the community is important to study because, by the late twentieth century, it had largely succeeded in confronting, on its own terms, the powerful forces of globalization now impinging on every corner of the earth. However, steady increases in population, the demise of a campesino lifestyle, the rise of teen gangs, and adult alcoholism may be pushing the community past the capacity of its indigenous culture to adapt positively. In what follows, the citizens of Amanalco and its region will be examined through print, web-embedded, and e-reader-enabled resources. These include archival images and documents, original photographs, audio recordings, and extensive video gathered through my ethnographic research in the region over the past four decades. I will also incorporate the responses of community members to my research through social media and e-mail, especially comments on video about their lives that I have posted on YouTube. *Indigenous Mexico* attempts to represent the changing worldviews of the people of this region who actively contest the meaning of their lives with outsiders and among themselves. From this perspective I hope to avoid the stance of the distant anthropological observer who interviews "informants," replacing it with the idea of "cultural interlocutors," a term that places representatives of a cultural system on equal terms with those who study their way of life. In this manner anthropologists can carry out a dialogue with community members removed from the privileged assumption of a superior Western knowledge of the world.

In June of 2010 I had two meetings with Amanalco's elected community leaders about this book project. At that time I presented them with a DVD filled with new photographs and videos I had collected. Prior to my stay in 2006 I received permission from individuals to place on YouTube videos I had made about them, and I showed some of these to the assembled group. We agreed that I would continue to put more video on YouTube after getting permission from the people involved and that after the book was published I would use a portion of the royalties for a project to benefit the children of the community.

This book brings into the discussion research of other scholars who are studying varied aspects of Amanalco and nearby communities. Importantly, anthropology faculty and graduate students of IberoAmericana University in Mexico City have accelerated their research in this region (Magazine and Martínez Saldana 2010). This includes studies in Amanalco of demography, marriage patterns, nutrition and personhood, fiestas, teen gangs, and indigenous identity. Throughout this book I incorporate their findings, especially those of two graduate students with whom I worked directly, Guillermo Torres on teen gangs and Manuel Moreno on indigenous identity. I also connect my work with the scholarship of university students from Amanalco, one who has already published articles about mythology and his indigenous language and another who is studying linguistics and doing research on the contemporary use of Nahuatl.

The Focus of This Book

Indigenous Mexico focuses on a seeming paradox that emerged around the time I began to study the community. In 1972, when I first entered Amanalco, it was recognized regionally as having the strongest ties to an Aztec cultural heritage. Yet as I was to find out, these traditional cultural features coexisted with a series of locally initiated, modernizing changes that also made the village the most rapidly transforming of the indigenous communities in the area. Some changes, such as village electrification and the construction of a new elementary school, had been completed a few years before I arrived. Others transpired during and within a decade of my initial research stay. These changes included construction of a passable dirt road, the creation of a potable water system, the opening of a state-sponsored medical clinic, a high school, and a bilingual Nahuatl/Spanish elementary school. In 1988 Amanalco finally acquired its own resident priest and became the Catholic parochial center for the other nearby mountain communities. By the beginning of the twenty-first century the community had an expanded paved road, very regular bus connections, a health clinic, a cell phone tower, and Internet cafes. With the assistance of the state and federal government they had built two preschools, a bilingual elementary school, a secondary technical school and a high school.

Amanalco is indeed a community undergoing a profound transformation from a peasant, farming village of self-described campesinos to a largely proletariat, wage-earning populace that is stretching the limit of a traditional cultural system to contain its globalizing circumstances. Anthropologists generally think of peasant communities as rural agrarian places that, although linked politically to states and economically to urban markets, focus on subsistence agriculture and/or craft production. Their local life is centered in kin-based labor exchange, with social bonds revolving around life course ritual and public celebrations such as fiestas. The word campesino translates as "person of the country." In thinking of how it applies to personhood in Amanalco, it would fit William Roseberry's basic definition as "relatively poor, predominantly rural dwellers with strong ties to agriculture either as producers, laborers, or more frequently, both" (1993, 362n). It is also noted that in most discussions of the term, farm-based labor is focused on the subsistence needs of households and is typically supplemented by the sale of surplus crops, local raw materials, animals, short-term labor, and sometimes artisan manufacture of items such as pottery or textiles.

In Amanalco, for those who think of themselves as campesinos, there is a deep, central identification with forging a life connected to learning about, extracting resources from, and nurturing the *milpa*[1] (field) and the *kwautla* (mountain forest). In contrast, rural folk who are talked about as proletariat have a core economic dependence on selling their labor or the fruits of their work outside of their home community. Today, if you spend a while in any of Amanalco's house compounds, you will encounter young and middle-aged adults who work in an urban store, perform music, sell flowers in a city market, style hair, teach in a school, drive a bus, or make clothing. Although they likely think of their elder parents and grandparents as campesinos, they talk about themselves in relation to their employment as a *musico* (musician), *maestra* (teacher), *comerciante* (market seller), or *chofér* (bus driver).

It is interesting to note that in 2010 three-quarters of the elder campesino men and women lived in multigenerational extended-family house compounds with their mostly proletariat offspring. These older adults are involved with a delicate balancing act of managing their expectations for late life and the potentially difficult handing-down of a cultural legacy in a world few expected to encounter in their lifetimes. This is far from a unique situation, as research in places such as India, China, and Ghana is demonstrating (Sokolovsky 2009).

Within Amanalco you can encounter newly installed speed bumps, teenage gangs, DVDs of pirated Hollywood movies, adolescents wearing Metallica T-shirts, elders donning Hard Rock Café jackets, and microbuses running every ten minutes to the nearest city. Yet it is also still possible to hear and see the face of tradition holding a very tenuous sway against the winds of modern urban life sweeping rural Mexico. It can be viewed especially in the eyes of young children as they approach an older relative and bow to plant a respectful, ritual kiss on the uplifted hand. It is observed also in the public fiesta dances, where a child of eight might share the same dance platform and ritual significance with a man or woman of age forty, or even sixty. Such multigenerational engagement in performances, though greatly reduced in frequency, are still embedded in familial and public domains. This gives both youth and aging adults a place in their society that transcends simple platitudes such as "We show respect to our elders." These symbolic acts counter the recent claim by many elders themselves that "these days the young don't treat us like they should."

Fortunately for youth and elders, Amanalco through the late twentieth century had largely renegotiated this paradox of tradition and change. Their culture remained quite traditional—within the context of rapid change—by relying upon and eventually transforming the most customary aspects of belief and village organization to pursue the goal of community transformation. However, the accelerated levels of community change and the dramatic expansion of Mexico City into one of the world's largest metropolitan centers have created new challenges that are beginning to test the best of local intentions. In the context of such changes the framework for the path through life is being written from a more diverse and complex script.

The Life Course in Cultural and Global Context

It is critical to understand that Amanalco was not a passive receptor of change but rather has sought through its collective initiative to recast itself in terms of local concepts of a "civilized" or "modern" place. These changes in educational, transportation, and health infrastructure were literally happening in front of my eyes. This was dramatically demonstrated in how the life course of individuals altered in response to both internal and external change, especially globalization. In returning to Amanalco on a regular basis since 1989 I have increasingly focused on how these transformations are altering the cultural dynamics I had experienced decades before. At the beginning of the 1980s I had conducted research in rural Croatia and observed that under conditions of rapid change, state supports for shifting patterns of multigenerational engagement and the economic utility of older adults could play a vital role in positive community development (Sokolovsky 2002). Jason Danley and Caitrin Lynch propose a compelling reason for a focus on the life course in anthropology, stating that a life course approach

> recognizes that as individuals age, their lives unfold in conjunction with those of people of different ages, and that all of these actors, who occupy different and changing positions and multiple cultural and physical environments over a period of historical time, are shaping and influencing each other in important ways. A focus on the life course, therefore, helps us to see not only the possibilities for individual development and maturity, but also how intergenerational conflict, cooperation, and contact can reconfigure values and redistribute roles and resources. (2013, 3)

In this book I examine how the interwoven life course is connected to created cultural scripts, cultural spaces, and a rapidly transforming ethnoscape enacted within the realities of twenty-first-century globalization. Framing the book through these constructs enables readers to better understand the similarities and contrasts with their own lives and cultural contexts.

Cultural Scripts, Cultural Spaces, and Ethnoscapes

My use of the term *cultural scripts* comes from work by Kalyani Mehta in Asia (1997). In studying ethnic Chinese, Malays, and Indians in the multiethnic city state of Singapore, Mehta shows that contexts and cultural dictates affect the enactment of broadly similar scripts for the life course and late adulthood. For example, late life migration to the city places kinship ties in a highly altered cultural space. Although elders might have a married son and perhaps grandchildren in the local environment, they would not have siblings or many other age-peer relatives around for support. Within this environment different implications were found among Hindu Indians and Muslim Malaysians in the script of late-life women who experienced the death of a spouse. For Indians in Singapore widowhood was stigmatized, and such women were strongly discouraged from remarrying. Widows practicing Islam, however, were not stigmatized, and remarriage of females was strongly encouraged. The comingling of the situational and the cultural can be particularly powerful for older women, especially in the urban immigrant situation in which supportive homegrown institutions and networks may not be in full flower or even exist.

As is happening in Asia, cultural scripts for rural indigenous Mexicans that are focused on filial devotion enacted in multigenerational households are being short-circuited. Multilocal and transnationally "outsourced" sons and the competing demands of educating children are key factors in moderating elders' authority. In Amanalco to date there has been only limited international migration. This contrasts with other Mexican regions, especially in the state of Puebla or Oaxaca, where one might find equal numbers of villagers in Brooklyn, New York, as you do in their Mexican home town (Boehm 2013; Smith 2006).

Yet since the 1990s Amanalco has become a truly multilocal community, with 60 percent of households having one or more persons working or being educated in nearby urban communities or regional market centers. Counterbalancing this, local occupational niches, especially textile production among young adults, have expanded rapidly and fostered a growing equality in generational relations while promoting continued extended family patterns. At the same time, the cultural spaces for experiencing older and younger parts of the life course are becoming more divergent. For the older population this is clearly seen in the age-peer communion of a new club for elders begun in 2006. Among youth, neighborhood gangs, popular music bands, and city-based work networks have emerged since the 1990s. The final chapter of the book *The Many Meanings of Never More Campesinos* explores the capacity of indigenous culture to build bridges between these diverging worlds.

A powerful change in the past two decades is that enacting scripts of multigenerational engagement in household cultural spaces has become distinctly more egalitarian, and this has caused some elders to seriously gripe about the loss of respect. In the public spaces of community—religious, ritual, and civic authority—a different change has emerged, as elders are shifted from active participants to audience. Just since 2006 a striking change in gender relations has also emerged, with women inching into available leadership roles in the public spaces of both politics and religion.

29

Cultural Spaces

By *cultural spaces* I refer to the physical and social landscapes where key elements of the life course are carried out. This includes domestic and public domains as well as zones for employment and entertainment, whether in agricultural and animal grazing areas or a bus route driven to a city. Most elemental for the domestic domain is the Nahuatl word *tochantlaca* (people of my place), which has a powerful dual meaning. First, it identifies the people who are connected to one's natal house compound, which is named after the piece of land it is on. People get to know you as "Juana de Ashushko," or Juana from the house compound called *Ashushko,* which, in Nahuatl, means "place of many frogs." Most houses are named in the indigenous language, but some, like "La Santisima" or "Buena Vista" are in Spanish and relate to more recent subdivisions of land. More expansively the word tochantlaca can be used to refer to the closest kin relations of both a husband and wife. In essence, the term encompasses the core network of bilateral kin to whom people turn for support. The remaining kin network is collectively referred to in Nahuatl as *iwamuchi tochantlaca*—literally "the remaining kin connected to this place."

Especially in terms of the kinds of rapid changes in domestic work life I have been observing in the twenty-first century, there remains the expressed notion of belonging and laboring in collaborative effort and sentiment to sustain unity of the tochantlaca. Although I discovered in the earliest periods of fieldwork that the ideology of the tochantlaca could be short-circuited by the realities of life, the deep sentiment of connectedness to this entity provided the core building block of this society.

In Amanalco, similar to what both Catherine Good and James Taggart found working in other Nahuatl communities, the concept of *tequitl,* or "working together," was a critical cultural value that linked family systems to community (Good 2011; Taggart 2008). It expressed a powerful connection among people through collaborative effort not only in homesteads but also through giving of time and money for public rituals and the labor necessary to maintain the local infrastructure. The residents of Amanalco also use a more specific Nahuatl term, *nechpalewiko* (reciprocal help), to synchronize the campesino economic system primarily based on the mutual assistance of those in the furthest reaches of kin networks and other persons in one's immediate neighborhood.[2] For example, during the 1970s virtually all major agricultural tasks such as planting and harvesting of corn were done via the concept of nechpalewiko. At the broader community level there is also a system of organized collaborative work, called in Spanish *faena* (labor). This is a critical function of the local political system that tasks households, on a rotating basis, to take care of regular infrastructure maintenance or repair, such as widening roads, clearing the irrigation canals, or repairing pipes that provide drinking water.

These actions of work tether people to the cultural spaces of the central plaza, adjacent Catholic church, main streets, and the irrigation system as well as *la milpa* (agricultural fields) and *kwauwitl* (the mountain zone). They encompass the traditional zones of material and spiritual sustenance in which the campesino life course was enacted. Now these spaces are competing with other zones embodied in an enhanced school system, gaming parlors, urban malls, gang territories, a transportation workers' union, a rodeo riding group, and a club for elders. Understanding these new spaces is critical to examining the response of Amanalcanos to the dramatic changes that have occurred over the past four decades and the changing formation of their Indio identity.

Ethnoscapes

The twenty-first-century construction of indigenous identity in Mexico and elsewhere should be understood in the context of the global political economy. It also involves deterritorialization of culture as it digitally moves across national boundaries. This is perhaps best understood within the framework of what Ajun Appadurai calls *ethnoscapes,* a shifting cultural landscape forged by a network of people associated with one another by history, kinship, and other varied forms of social interaction that are tied together by webs of mutual understanding (1996). This construct of ethnicity does two important things. First, it places the idea of ethnic-based cultural formations in a truly global context. Second, it acknowledges that the cultural landscape created by the enactment of ethnicity is a fluid, creative phenomenon and not a fixed, unchanging heritage linked to the past. When I first arrived in Mexico in 1972 the urban middle class treated "Indianness" as an icon of connection to an exotic, pre-Hispanic past. This is still exemplified in the performances of nonindigenous "Aztec dancers" in central Mexico City and similar groups that work the Native American pow-wow circuit in the United States.

However, in the Indio community I was to study, that ethnic marker served as a highly ambivalent symbol of their perceived marginality. By the twenty-first century some of the prominent material features of Indio traditions were dying out. Yet on a broader level identity as an indigenous people with history and value was being amplified, especially by more educated members of the community with more experiences beyond its borders. In fact, the nature of Amanalco's ethnoscape has always been shaped by its relation to the outside world.

Some of the earliest modern anthropological studies of rural peoples in Mexico, in the 1920s to the 1950s, involve ethnic Nahuatl-speaking communities (Gamio 1979; Madsen 1960; Redfield 1930). Beginning in the late 1960s and 1970s anthropologists, including myself, would undertake what was to become multidecade research in Nahuatl-speaking regions of Mexico. These include James Taggart in the mountains of northern Puebla, Alan Sandstrom on the coastal tropical forest of northern Veracruz, Catherine Good in Guerrero's Balsas River Basin, and David Robichaux and Frances Rothstein in Tlaxcala, just east of Amanalco. Each of these researchers has been similarly surprised by the

31

resiliency of these communities to adapt ethnic cultural patterns to extreme economic downturns, regional violence, and emergent globalization (see especially Berdan et al. 2008; Taggart and Sandstrom 2011).

Globalization and Cultural Landscapes

"The local is not transcended by globalization, but rather
. . . the local is to be understood by global relationships."
(Savage, Bagnall, and Longhurst 2005, p. 3)

Imagine the following scene: scantily clad "natives" peer through the window of their hut as geeky-looking visitors in pith helmets and Abercrombie and Fitch jungle attire arrive by canoe at the shore of their jungle village. The people inside their house are holding an assortment of fancy electronics and, in a panic, one shouts, "Anthropologists, anthropologists!" as they attempt to secret away these markers of modernity.

For anthropologists today this *Far Side* cartoon by Gary Larson provides an apt metaphor for our attempts to take into account the local-global nexus within twenty-first-century realities. The cartoon uses humor to illustrate an optimistic perception of benefits for "less developed" peoples of an accelerated movement of consumer goods, people, and capital across once-inaccessible boundaries. It also obscures the fact that overall, the enduring economic and social benefits from the explosion of "free" trade pacts, privatization of governmental functions, and Internet accessibility end up mainly helping small, affluent sectors of national citizenry, often those who needed it least. Along with VCRs and DVD players, in places like Mexico or Kenya has come "structural adjustment," imposed by the IMF or World Bank in order to liberalize markets, stimulate foreign investment, and end government support for basic commodities and services. Such imposed reforms have often resulted in the loss of jobs to local citizens and resulted in more expensive and less effective goods and services.

When I began research in Mexico in the 1970s the primary model for considering how massive worldwide change would affect rural communities was "modernization" theory. This model tried to predict the impact of change from relatively undifferentiated rural, traditional-based societies with limited technology from modern, urban-based entities. This shift was said to be marked by four main factors: modern health technology, economies based on scientific technology, urbanization, and mass education and literacy. Third-world countries were said to "develop" or "progress" as they adopted, through cultural diffusion, the modernized model of rational and efficient societal organization. In the last two decades of the twentieth century this came to be linked with a "neoliberal economics" model of development, promoted by Western governments. This approach stressed deregulation and privatization of previously nationalized industries and services, free trade across national borders, and, in general, an enhanced role of the private sector in a nation's economy. Robert Reich calls this "super-capitalism," stressing the radical expansion of communication technology, multicountry agreements such as NAFTA to promote the unimpeded flow of capital across national borders, and shifts in the location and nature of production of goods and services (2007). Such changes are but the most recent wave of globalization emerging since the 1970s.

In my first decade of contact with Amanalco I witnessed the implementation of various modernization projects. Some of these had distinct benefits, especially in terms of the provision of electricity and improvements of schools, better roads, and local health resources. These were changes requested by the community and similar to modernizing efforts that were unevenly occurring in rural Mexican communities being studied by other anthropologists.

I also observed the beginning of more subtle but pervasive globalizing impacts, especially in the area of food. In 1973 I watched as a representative of the Ciba-Geigy multinational corporation touted the benefits of using both chemical fertilizers and pesticides to improve corn production on some villager's test plot. The twenty campesinos watching the presentation were not particularly impressed. Afterward they wondered aloud, "Why should we pay for fertilizer when we get it free from our animals and the pesticides they are pushing would kill the weeds we feed to these livestock?" During that same decade Nestlé corporation began heavily marketing its baby formula in many countries, including Mexico. Fortunately this did not catch on in Amanalco, although the antibreastfeeding campaign did cause an increase in infant deaths in some rural areas and sparked a large boycott action against its advertising practices (Newton 1999).

Other kinds of inputs from global companies are epitomized in the photo below from 1978. Figure 2.1 shows an image of products in the small store off the central plaza where one found Twinkies, Wonder Bread, baby formula, Bic pens, Alka Seltzer, and a variety of soft drinks. [P] Sodas such as Coca-Cola became readily available and problematic for long-term health; due to less regulation they contained even more sugar content than similar products sold in the United States.[3] This is but one reason why by the 1990s diabetes began to rise in Amanalco and, by 2010, it had become the most prevalent chronic disease in Mexico (Everett and Wieland 2013).

Frances Rothstein's book *Globalization in Rural Mexico* (2007) discusses the various ways the term *globalization* is applied. The historian David Harvey sees it as a hyper-compression of time and space (1989), whereas others focus on the rapid flow of commodities and the building of transnational communities (see also Schmidt 2007, 2012; Stephen 2013). Ajun Appadurai, who gives us the term ethnoscape, intriguingly stresses how the movement of media and people over national borders stimulates the global flow of ideas and the blooming of cultural imagination (1996). As Jonathan Inda and Renato Rosaldo sum it up, globalization implies the accelerated movement of "capital, people, goods, images, and ideas across the world" (2002, 9).

Figure 2.1   Central general store in Amanalco, 1978. In the web site a PowerPoint file directs you to the some of the global products mentioned above. 🅿 *(Photo by Jay Sokolovsky)*

Yet as all of these authors note, a central feature of twenty-first-century glo-balization is the unevenness of winners and losers within and across nations. In 1970 the difference in GNP wealth between the poorest and wealthiest nations was 88 to 1; in 2010 this differential had risen to 263 to 1. Mexico provides an interesting example. Although this nation's implementation of neoliberal poli-cies has helped it produce the world's wealthiest man, Carlos Slim Helu, worth $80 billion in late 2014, for average Mexicans this period was disastrous. This is best indicated by brutal economic realities: during the last two decades of the twentieth century there was a drop in real wages of two-thirds, and by the end of that period 43 percent were living in extreme or intermediate poverty (see Moreno-Brid, Carpizo and Bosch 2009).

Since the 1980s Amanalco experienced the significant decline of its relatively stable agrarian economy as large numbers were forced to work in urban markets to feed their families. In this new millennium they are also facing an impending collapse in community unity, rapid increases in chronic diseases such as diabetes, and the rise of teen gangs and alcoholism. Yet an examination of the changes in Amanalco during this time also reveals an improvement in child health profiles, greater access to education, and more opportunities for women to take on more varied and high-status roles in the community. By 2006 phone texting and Inter-net service has become more commonplace, but even in 2013 consistent access to such globalizing services was spotty at best and is very far from penetrating the daily lives of residents as it has in the United States or urban areas in Mexico.

The past four decades of life in Amanalco provide a critical time period in which to consider the interaction of modernizing projects and globalization on its cultural landscape. In doing so we encounter what many anthropologists over the past decade have begun to experience, the edges of the global digital platform described by journalist Thomas Friedman in his controversial book *The World Is Flat* (2005). Experiencing this "flat" world, even rural folk in places like China, India, or Mexico may engage the global telecommunication revolution in cell phone, Internet, and social media linkages that has been tied to the broader process of globalization. Through the late 1990s it was almost impossible to communicate directly by phone or even mail with people in Amanalco; now I just need to dial the cell phone of my compadres to find out what is happening in their lives.

Does this really mean the world is truly flat as Freidman suggests? To date, the evidence seems very compelling that it may be more beneficial for these societies' powerful elites, who can more easily use global communication for their economic advantage (Domosh 2010). As we will see in Chapters 4 and 10, it is also an advantage for anthropologists who are trying to keep in "virtual" contact with the communities they work with. It does not, however, put young adults in villages like Amanalco on comparable footing with, for example, my students in Florida. In the final chapter we will find that productive engagement with the twenty-first century must rely on adapting some of the most traditional aspects of community life with changing circumstances. But first, the next chapter looks at the historical and cultural context to explore these issues.

CHAPTER THREE

Historical and Cultural Context of Community Transformation

The deep history of the highlands of central Mexico is shrouded in mythology, dramatic archaeological remains, and recreated pictographic documents crafted after the Spanish conquest of what came to be known as the Aztec Empire. As Eduardo Douglas notes in *In the Palace of Nezahualcóyotl* (2010), the term *Aztec* literally means "person of Aztlān," with *Aztlān* referring to the mythological homeland of the Mexica peoples before they migrated to the central valley of Mexico sometime in the thirteenth century. ⊕

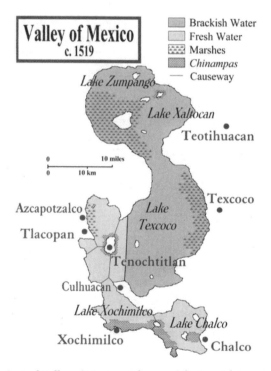

Figure 3.1   The Central Valley of Mexico at the eve of the Spanish invasion, circa 1519. (© Wikipedia Creative Commons)

Indigenous Mexico Engages the 21st Century, by Jay Sokolovsky, 37–54. © 2015 Left Coast Press, Inc. All rights reserved.

By 1430 the militarily aggressive Mexica had formed a "triple alliance" with two other adjacent and older kingdoms: the Tepanecs, who centered in Tlaco-pan (now absorbed into the Tacuba district of Mexico City), and the Acolhua people, with their capital of Texcoco, still an independent city on the expanding eastern edge of Mexico City (see Figure 3.1). The Alcolhuan domain refers to the state in the eastern part of the valley of Mexico ruled by Texcoco. 🔼 A set of early colonial documents, the Codex Xolotl, ⊕ the Quinatzin, ⊕ and the Tlohtzin ⊕ maps were created in the 1540s to depict the preconquest history of Texcoco, especially its royal dynasties. According to Douglas, part of its purpose was to assert the right of its colonial patrons, who were, in fact, "descendants of rulers, whose achievements they commemorate and extol" (2010, 162). His analysis of these manuscripts shows that although appearing artistically and culturally similar to pre-Hispanic historical documents, they fuse pictographic and literary elements of indigenous ancestors and their colonial Spanish masters with whom they are trying to assert rights to lands and authority. (By connecting to this 🔼 you can access key resources for understanding pre-Hispanic and early colonial documents.)

In a similar manner some aspects of material culture I initially documented in Amanalco, such as back-strap looms or sweat baths, are virtually identical to pre-Hispanic prototypes. Yet many behavioral and ideological aspects of "indigenous" culture represent a different relationship to the deep past. These were born in the multilayered and unequal meshing of social orders set in motion by the Spanish conquest, which took place within the harsh consequences of massive population loss and the imposition of new religious, economic, and political frameworks. One result was a reordering of social relations and transformed cultural practices. Largely developed in the seventeenth and eighteenth centuries, these *syncretic* cultural patterns range from forms of music, such as the contemporary Aztec bands, 📎 🔼 to fiestas celebrating Catholic saints, ideas about sorcery, and constructs surrounding health practices. Such cultural practices are anything but static, and some are either withering away or, more likely, being adapted into a form more appropriate for contemporary life.

A prime example is the system of civil-religious hierarchies, also called the *cargo* (burden) or ladder system, which anthropologists have studied in dozens of campesino communities throughout the highland regions of Mexico and Guatemala (see especially Magazine 2012). Although it was initially thought to be an ancestral indigenous trait, this model of political and ritual organization was in fact largely a colonial-era creation. Following the conquest of the Aztec empire in 1521, the new Spanish rulers implemented the "Law of the Indies" fif-teen years later. 🔼 This edict sought to consolidate the dispersed and greatly diminished indigenous population into a tax-paying, town-dwelling peasantry. Such concentrations of people, known as *La república de los indios,* served as the historical basis for what anthropologists such as Eric Wolf came to call a "closed corporate community" that sought to retain as much political and religious au-tonomy as possible within a harsh colonial system (Wolf 1955, 1986).

This did not mean that such communities were completely isolated but instead that they tried to regulate control of their limited resources within their village boundaries and resist cultural change being imposed from the outside. Especially in highland Latin America, the remaining indigenous elites often collaborated with the new Spanish rulers in fostering the cargo system that allowed a certain amount of local autonomy while enabling exploitation by indirect rule.[1] Dozens of studies from the 1950s to the 1980s of cargo systems described a hierarchy of local political and ritual roles that rotated among households and gave increasing status as persons took on more important tasks requiring more time and monetary resources. As discussed more fully in Chapter 8, underneath the surface Roman Catholic ceremony of Mass and the veneration of saints is the pre-Hispanic cycle of agriculturally linked ritual that previously focused on a panoply of deities. Although civil and religious hierarchies were separated by Mexican national law, in the 1970s they were still unified in Amanalco under a single moral order. For example, it was the political leaders who helped the annually elected religious stewards collect monies for fiestas or who ordered skyrockets to be lit to scare away hailstorms brought by Mexica water demons called *ahuake*. No person could hope to be elected political leader of the community without having successfully shouldered one of the major sacred sponsorship positions. More fundamentally, Roger Magazine argues persuasively that cargo systems, even when carried out in communities that have long rejected an Indian identity, are tethered to an indigenous-based construct of work and giving of the self that only has profound meaning when it is done with others in the context of community ritual (2012).

Regional Connections

As a rural agrarian community, Amanalco has always been incorporated to some degree within larger political spheres. It was founded in the fifteenth century when the king of Texcoco developed an irrigation system from the springs located in the mountain forests overlooking the contemporary village. This gave it strategic importance and connection to the downstream communities that depended on the maintenance of water flow. Access to the large mountain forest zone above its residential area favored the specialty of raw materials and finished products derived from the trees and pastures. Some items, especially charcoal and firewood, were sold as far away as the Mexica capital, Tenochtitlan (now Mexico City), with the rest being traded in the large pre-Hispanic market in Texcoco or bartered for different specialty items in other peasant communities. Lying just thirty miles east of contemporary Mexico City and thirteen miles away from Texcoco, such general entrepreneurial patterns continued into the 1970s as a key economic strategy for the majority of three-generation households.

Amanalco was established near the sacred peak of Mount Tlaloc, named for the powerful god of rain, a prominent deity throughout ancient Central America. At the summit a temple with an icon of Tlaloc had once stood, surrounded by smaller

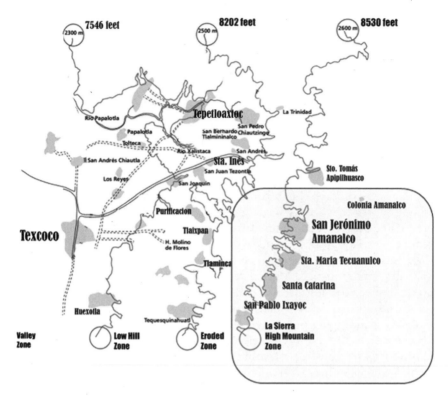

Figure 3.2   Ecological zones of the Texcoco Region. (Adapted from: Marisol Pérez Lizaur [1977].) P

images representing the hills surrounding the mountain. Regular ceremonies of child sacrifice to this rain god were held here, especially when draught threatened to cause famine. It was thought that the dying children's tears would provide an irresistible plea for Tlaloc to unleash the rains. Still today, in effecting certain cures, traditional healers must walk five hours to the peak and provide offerings to Tlaloc's helpers, the ahuakes, when they are thought to have caused a villager's illness. As seen in Figure 3.2, P Amanalco is one of a handful of communities situated in small valleys at the edge of the rugged high Sierra ecological zone. Along with Santa Catarina, Santa Maria Tecuanulco, and San Pablo Ixayoc, these are the only places in the area where Nahuatl is still spoken.

Ecology and Adaptation

This Sierra region starts at almost eighty-five hundred feet above sea level, and its terrain, compared to villages at lower altitude, is marked by smaller flat areas

40

for agriculture. In addition to the higher elevation and cooler climate, weather patterns present more chance of damaging crops. Farmers anticipate that every three years severe storms could reduce the harvest 15 to 20 percent. When I first lived in Amanalco the predominant campesino lifestyle was focused on the flow of three named seasons: *tlawakilisli* (time of dryness, field preparation, and planting of irrigated lands) from February to late May, *shopantlaticate* (time of rains, planting of nonirrigated lands) from June to October; and *tlasenwetiz* (time of hail and cold, harvest, and movement of cattle to high grazing lands) from November to January. To provide an idea of how I experienced these seasons at various times, in 1973 it rained once during the dry season, and when the wet season began it rained for twenty-seven straight days. That same year, in November, a hail storm with heavy winds toppled some corn fields before they could be harvested. In December 1998, when my wife and I sponsored the *quinceañera* of our goddaughter, the seemingly pleasant high of 70 degrees and low in the 50s the week before the event shifted to a high of 50 and gusty lows in the 20s at night when all the major celebrations were held all in a large open patio. No houses in Amanalco have heating systems, and it was the first time I ever went to sleep wearing six layers of clothing.

The indigenous name of the community derives from the Nahuatl word *amanali*, or "place of water." As I discuss in the next chapter, an origin tale links the current name to a Catholic saint called Jerónimo; it also notes that there was once a water pool adjacent to where the colonial-era church now stands. Archaeological surveys in the region show that certainly by the late Aztec periods (AD 1300–1519), a village just north of Amanalco's present location formed part of the Acolhua kingdom controlled by the city of Texcoco. Above its lands lie rugged mountain forests and ten springs that were used to create an important irrigation system during the reign of King Nezahualcóyotl in the early fifteenth century. These waters originally fed fields in more than thirty communities and were even connected by a viaduct to sustain the royal gardens on the hillside of Tetzcotzingo. Today these springs are used in only seven communities. Hydrological archive data I found show that the flow from most of the springs had reduced by half between the 1920s and the 1970s and that over the past several decades continued loss of forest cover has contributed to a steady reduction in flow.

Located so close to the main springs, Amanalco likely had some pre-Hispanic administrative control over part of the irrigation system, a position it maintains today. In the process of Spanish colonization of Mexico, the Texcoco region as a whole gradually moved away from irrigated corn farming. However, campesino communities in the Sierra mountain zone, where Amanalco is located, generally continued corn farming and traditional specialty production. The Spanish more intensively dominated the piedmont villages, with their flatter lands and warmer climate, while impinging much less on the lives of the people of Amanalco and the other four communities of the more rugged mountain zone. This fact contributes to the persistence of indigenous, ethnic cultural traits and identity in these villages and the turning to more *mestizo,* or urban focused, cultural patterns in the rural zones closer to the city.

From 1827 until the end of the Mexican revolution in 1920 Amanalco was subject to a *hacienda* (private estate) called Tierra Blanca (white land) in its mountain reaches that set up a glass-making factory and grew wheat on high-altitude fields. The village retained ownership of much of its irrigated lands, although control over communal forest, water, and grazing resources was partially lost. Other communities closer to the city of Texcoco were not so lucky; by 1910 many people there had given up subsistence agriculture in favor of wage labor in the city or on the haciendas and saw much of their traditional culture changed in the process. Some of the fiesta dances discussed in Chapter 8 and seen in an associated video dramatize the work of campesinos and, in one case, offer a humorous mocking of the hacienda owner.

After the Mexican Revolution Amanalco eventually regained much of its lost high mountain territory and water rights through the *ejido* program. This was based on Article 27 of the 1917 Mexican Constitution, which called for land redistribution in the form of land parcel grants to communities rather than individuals. A small residential settlement, called Colonia Guadalupe, formed in the rugged high mountain lands and today, with its own church, largely functions as an autonomous adjunct of the main community. The ejido law was altered in 1992 to expand the possibility of privatizing ejidos, and Amanalco responded to this by voting to allow sale of these lands only to community members.[2]

Seen below in Figure 3.3 is the rough layout of how the ejido lands are situated in relation to the rest of the community. The remaining territory, though referred to as *moncomun,* or communal, is composed of various types of ownership. These include both privately held land, shown in the dotted line around the symbol for the church, and communally owned territory. Lands owned by the community are at its entrance, including a cemetery; the schools; and extends east into the higher mountain zone. In this elevated area there are specific commonly held lands that the community agriculturally works and the harvest is sold to support both the schools and the church.

In the center of the town is an open plaza. As in most Latin American communities, it forms the central place for the most important civic, religious, and commercial activities. For residents this is the "face" of their community. Here the ancient church bells mark the day and call people to Mass or an important *assemblea* (meeting) to discuss and vote on public matters at the *delegación,* or the public administrative building. This is where the three elected mayors, *delegados,* politically rule Amanalco, settle disputes, and coordinate the work of committees that manage and support the infrastructure of the community, especially its roads, water supply, schools, and cemetery. At another edge of the plaza is the main public elementary school now bursting with too many children. Along the central artery leading into the plaza and above it on this major street one finds the greatest concentration of commercial establishments. In 2010 the plaza was

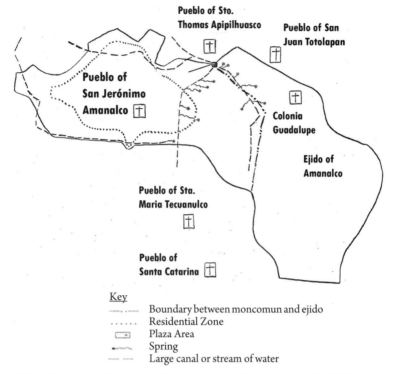

*Figure 3.3   The Lands of Amanalco. (**Source:** Adapted from Mexico, DF. 1973. Departamento de Asuntos Agrarios y Colonizacion. Estadistica y Cadrastro, "Amanalco.")*

in rather shabby condition compared to four years previous. However, on Sundays it became a vibrant market, ◼ with fruits, vegetables, made-on-the spot delicacies, music and video recordings, and household supplies.

The main road into Amanalco also serves as a rough dividing line between two named geographical zones; on the north is Santo Domingo, also called *Serrano* (mountain), and on the south is San Francisco, also called *Caliente* (hot).[3] P   I was told that as the population started to grow rapidly in the 1950s it seemed necessary to get a more equitable organization of alternating community service in the civil and ritual positions undertaken by citizens. All of the religious roles would be evenly split between the two areas, and similar efforts would occur with regard to balancing political roles. As it is culturally taboo to marry within one's male-linked kin lineage, and these are highly localized, this division also informally functions to regulate choice of marriage partners.[4]

Since 1990 the population has grown substantially, and the community's dual division no longer serves such a strong marriage regulation function. Up through the 1990s I was repeatedly told that this organizational device was purely to make things easier for sharing the burden of taking cargos but that Amanalco was one unified community. In the twenty-first century, as the population grew past seven thousand and the occupational diversity dramatically expanded, people have been less confident about Amanalco functioning as a unified place. The town is now big enough that, since 2005, there have been efforts to develop other administrative zones called *manzanas* (block of houses). However, I have heard many people voice concern that this will further undo the community's strong unity.

Land as Resource

From the relatively flat central zone of the plaza, fields gently undulate north and south, providing the majority of the best irrigated agricultural lands. It is in these fields—or milpas, as they are called—that the majority of corn, beans, and squash are still locally harvested. Most house lots will also have a small garden growing flowers for the household altar or sometimes for market sale as well as five or six medicinal herbs. Spread around this landscape are small groves of fruit trees, especially plum, pear, apple, lemon, lime, and tangerine, which are used for household consumption and occasional barter or sale in nearby communities. In 1972 and 1973 I spent much of my research time learning about and participating in the process of planting and harvesting a proper milpa filled with huge stalks of corn towering over the beans and squash sequenced in the furrows (see Figure 3.4). Today this has become a legacy that most youth know about but rarely see as their calling.

Figure 3.4   A father and two teenage sons removing weeds from their growing corn field, May 1973. (Photo by Jay Sokolovsky)

Figure 3.5   Large mountain spring, May 1973. (Photo by Jay Sokolovsky)

Looming above these fields lies an even higher region containing a multitude of natural resources, from varied woods, nine types of edible mushrooms, dozens of medicinal herbs, and strong grasses for making household brushes and brooms (see Figure 3.5). There are still some skilled campesinos who can grow corn at nine thousand feet, but agriculture at this elevation is mostly potatoes, wheat, barley, and haba beans. Here in these rugged elevated areas of deep forest are life-giving water springs, small valleys for grazing, and a habitat for eagles, coyotes, bobcats, and very elusive mountain lions—known in myth as *huey mistli* (big cats). Perhaps most vital in people's minds are the mountain springs. These not only allow early planting of corn before the cold autumn months but also, since the mid-1980s, have been the source of clean water piped to over 90 percent of the households.

This high zone ascending toward the sacred peak of mount Tlaloc (also called El Mirador) 🔝 at 13,615 feet is a key cultural space where the magical imagination of residents takes flight. Many stories that I heard began, "I was working up in *Kwoutla* [the mountain forest] when ..." These tales might entail seeing dangerous tiny beings called ahuake in water ways or noticing colored lights of the blood-sucking *tlahuelpuche* dancing among the hills. Elders recalled the exploits of the god-king Nezahualcóyotl as he challenged the devil to impossible feats within this domain (see Chapter 9).

The high Sierra lands, although not very agriculturally productive, contain a multitude of resources that have fostered the viability of extended household organization and community solidarity by maintaining traditional agrarian pursuits and providing the raw materials for some new patterns of economic adaptation. Especially for land-poor residents, this zone has provided a margin of survival, and protecting its resources against outsiders is an obsession of the community. At times it has provoked extreme measures.

Struggle for the Forest

Archive materials document a constant battle over mountain forest resources both during and after the Mexican Revolution. As early as 1912 Amanalco began to request return of its lands from the hacienda Tierra Blanca, but the hacienda's owners reported that men from the community were sacking the hacienda, and federal troops were sent in. Prisoners were taken, and one man from Amanalco was sent to jail in the far southern reaches of Mexico. Murderous attacks by hacienda workers on villagers continued, resulting in the revenge killing of the hacienda manager in 1923. A serious conflict continues with the successor family to the hacienda; in the late 1990s the community accused them of clear cutting forest land they claimed to own. This greatly reduced the flow of water from a spring upon which Amanalco relied. The community retaliated with the arrest of the son of the land owner, but he was eventually released, and some community officials were arrested, charged with and convicted of kidnapping.

This ongoing fight over key resources puts Monolitón's story (Chapter 1) about the killing of the forest workers in the 1960s into powerful context. His tale about this event was validated in my discussions with Amanalco's residents, but archive documents and an eye-witness account I recorded give it a different meaning. During the 1950s men from a lumber company in the area of Tepetloaxtoc had begun illegally cutting wood in a remote part of Amanalco's forest and harassing any villager who protested. According to the eye witness, the day of the incident some women ran to the delegados and said they had seen men from the lumber company beating up some young boys and taking their collected wood. The group of villagers who arrived at the spot on horseback claimed to have seen the boys being held captive by armed men. When approached, the interlopers tried to run but were shot as they tried to escape.

The community continues to regard the mountain woods and water as its life's blood. I was in the Amanalco in 1973 when a lumber company executive arrived with state officials who were pushing the sale of forest lands. This came with the promise of sufficient monies to not only improve infrastructure and the irrigation system in the ejido lands but also to begin paving the main road into Amanalco. Although a minority was in favor of this deal, I listened intently as a community assembly in the plaza voted for the majority sentiment: it is not worth losing the forest patrimony, this inheritance for all their children (see Doane 2012, and this Added Value link). 🔼

More recently I was told that in the early 2000s a company in Texcoco did testing for purity of the spring waters in Amanalco's highlands and floated the idea of establishing a water-bottling plant at one of the major springs. The community quickly got wind of this and sent a delegation to Texcoco's municipal president. He was told in no uncertain terms that he would have to kill every man, woman, and child in Amanalco before that would happen. The project was dropped. Although the region as a whole has a reputation for defending its ecological resources, members of other communities repeatedly told me that Amanalco was regarded as the toughest of them all. Readers will learn in the concluding chapter that, as a community, local residents will not hesitate to harshly defend against perceived attacks on newer economic interests unrelated to their environment.

Adapting to the Late Twentieth Century

My study of Amanalco's traditional corn-farming production showed that by the 1950s steady population growth had already exceeded the capacity of the land to feed all the villagers. However, access to the mountain forests and irrigation waters stimulated the development of two economic activities that helped families resist the wholesale need for full-time laboring in industrial zones, which already had disrupted household integration in villages closer to the city. The first involved producing sturdy wood crates that were welcomed by Mexico City fruit merchants, who purchased all the community could produce. This work drew upon indigenous wood-working knowledge and allowed for teams of fathers and sons or brothers to gather the wood and make the crates on simple machines in their own courtyards. Crate making had the additional advantage of allowing land-poor villagers to resist permanent migration or factory labor. At about the same time, villagers began to convert parts of their irrigated fields for the cultivation of decorative flowers, which family labor would gather and sell in urban neighborhoods of Mexico City (Figures 3.6a/3.6b).

In 1973 I found that almost two-thirds of extended-family households were producing at least one of these specialty products. Not only did these two activities provide a fair amount of cash, but the work also was best accomplished within a multigenerational domestic work unit. Moreover, the economic utility of the aged, especially males, was enhanced, as they were more likely to continue contributing to these cash-producing endeavors long after their effectiveness in other agricultural work had diminished.

47

Figure 3.6a   Picking flowers for market sale, 1973. (Photo by Jay Sokolovsky)

Figure 3.6b   Father and son making wooden crates for sale to wholesale fruit vendors in Mexico City, 1973. (Photo by Jay Sokolovsky)

Partly as a result of these factors, the village reached the 1970s as a highly integrated campesino enclave depending largely on patterns traceable to Aztec-era ancestors but shored up by new economic innovations. Yet the benefits from these changes were limited by an inefficient irrigation system, lack of a passable road for motor traffic, and the community's low level of education. Fortuitously, it was in the late 1960s and early 1970s that the state government, with Mexican federal assistance, began to selectively invest in improving rural infrastructure through electrification, road building, and, eventually, the expansion of rural education and health care services. As a start, the community combined its traditional communal labor system with materials and engineers provided by the state government to improve their irrigation system with a reservoir. They also built a small bridge over a ravine that had been a serious obstacle to motorized vehicles entering the community. With these initial successes in the 1960s Amanalco's leaders began to petition for the other "modernizing" changes mentioned above.

A McDonald's Nightmare: Back to the Future

I did not quite know what to expect in June of 1989 when, after an eleven-year absence, I drove my rented car toward Amanalco. I had returned for two brief visits during the late 1970s but had taken a decade of research detours in Croatia, England, and New York City. A week before my return I began to have nightmares. Some involved learning that children from the household I had lived in during the 1970s had succumbed to the high child mortality rate then still prevalent. In another dream the road up to the village was nicely paved and the Aztec-era house mounds lining that road were covered with condominiums, neon-lit strip malls, and American-style fast food restaurants.

Fortunately my dreams were only slightly clairvoyant. I was relieved to find that it was no longer likely that a third of children born would die before age five, and this new reality was starting to change how young adults and even the elderly felt about reproduction and intergenerational relations. Doña Concha,[5] the elder woman of Buena Vista, had lost four of six children prior to my first stay in the village in 1972. In 1978 I had photographed her house altar shortly after the Day of the Dead at the beginning of November (Figure 3.7).[6] Forever emblazoned in my memory are the candy skulls surrounded by ritual marigold flowers[7] the family had grown and a special bread they had baked to welcome back the dead children's souls. To my great relief, Concha's surviving children, Juan and Leticia, and their two siblings born in the mid-1970s were all alive and healthy.

Although a McDonald's was not yet within sight of village lands, global cultural influences were very much becoming a part of daily life. A Dominos Pizza franchise had recently opened in Texcoco, and the dirt access road to the village had, in fact, been newly paved a month before my return in 1989. While there were no fancy apartments atop the archeological ruins lining that road, Amanalco's farmers had plowed under many of the ancient house lots and began to arduously

Figure 3.7   Day of the dead altar, 1978. (Photo by Jay Sokolovsky)

reclaim the surrounding marginal soils along the road. Throughout the 1990s Mexico City metropolitan area was on its way to becoming one of the larger urban zones in the world, with a population of about 15 million inhabitants then and about 21 million in the metro area by 2014. Here families from Amanalco found new, burgeoning areas in which to sell local goods produced by extended family labor. This type of work was greatly facilitated by the improved village road and more frequent bus service. A majority of families who had previously grown commercial flowers began to buy them cheaply in other communities for resale in urban markets, some even having their own little stores or stalls in Mexico City or the edge of Texcoco for this purpose. At this time numbers of younger males and females began to seek employment in nonagricultural labor outside the village in nearby cities or large towns.

However, unlike in many other areas of México, relatively few residents (3 to 4 percent) actually migrated permanently away from Amanalco or attempted to cross the northern border to the United States. However, by the 1990s men in their sixties and seventies were having a hard time getting their urban-employed sons to work the fields during critical parts of the growing season. Despite this downward trend in agriculture, at the end of that decade a handful of families were beginning to construct large greenhouses. The National Agricultural School just south of Texcoco encouraged these efforts, and by 2012 about twenty such structures were producing commercial crops. With the abundance of irrigation water they could produce marketable produce for sale in cities.

Certain households were able to create new specialty products with extended family labor. I observed an excellent example in 1994, where wedding cake figurines

Figure 3.8   Men loading wedding cake figurines they made for sale in Mexico City, 1994. (Photo by Jay Sokolovsky)

made within one of the larger extended-family groupings in the village were transported for sale to a market area in Mexico City that specialized in matrimonial products (Figure 3.8). Smaller families would also go into the wholesale markets, buy food products, and then travel to other parts of the city to sell these items. More recently a small group of families started making seasonal and decorative folk art products from stiff mountain grasses such as animal figures (Figure 3.9).

Since the 1990s there has been a explosion of work options, particularly for men but also for women in the field of education (see Chapter 5). The man shown in Figure 3.10 was brought up to have all the campesino skills of his father, but as an adult he became a bus driver on the Texcoco–Mexico City route. His wife worked as a secretary at the Chapingo Autonomous University. Their nuclear family was part of one of the largest multigenerational house compounds in Amanalco. Here lives the elder parents, residing in a house with the eldest brother's family, and within enclosed walls are separate households of the three other married brothers.

Among the dramatic changes in community cultural spaces, especially after the mid-1990s, has been the development of a fuller public educational system. This now includes two regular preschools, a bilingual preschool and primary school,

Figure 3.9   Folk art objects made from stiff mountain grasses for market sale, 2014. (© Manuel Moreno)

Figure 3.10   A TV and U.S. cartoons join images of saints by the household altar area, 1996. (Photo by Jay Sokolovsky)

and a middle and high school. Prior to the 1980s, to go beyond elementary school, students had to pay travel expenses to Texcoco and also buy food and school uniforms. Many parents did not see the benefit of such expenses, and if the investment was made back then, it was likely only for a boy in the family who seemed to have strong academic skills. Most residents are very proud of having a new array of educational opportunities in their community, though from the start there was some ambivalence and anger over how teachers sometimes treated the children.

In 1973, for instance, I stood with a proud grandfather watching the elementary school graduation ceremony. As we watched his grandson perform, he expressed both pride in the accomplishment, given that he himself had only a third-grade education, and also anger that the school teachers were using physcial punishment to stop students from speaking Nahuatl. This is certainly not the only reason for the dramatic loss of full fluency in that language over the past forty years, but it is part of a complex community debate over indigenous identity that is explored further in Chapter 6.

Twenty-First Century: In the Shadow of a Megalopolis

It is interesting to note that a small number of students have gone on to higher education and professional schools in law, psychology, linguistics, music, criminal justice, art, and even anthropology. Yet the on-the-ground reality is that this is

Figure 3.11   The hyper-crowded eastern edge of Mexico City pressing toward the almost dry lake of Texcoco, June 2010. 📷 *(Photo by Jay Sokolovsky)*

still a working-class rural community. As in many ethnic minority communities in North America there is a very high dropout rate. In 2012 only 40 percent of students in Amanalco's high school came from that community. For the most part a majority of residents still do not see much use in even a high school education but cling instead to a postcampesino security of working for a wage, driving a bus or taxi, playing music, or making clothes, with any of these choices tethered to a secure home and backup agrarian work when necessary.

Only in the first decade of the twenty-first century have Mexico City and Texcoco drawn Amanalco's families deeply into its urban social and cultural fabric. This occurs through jobs, advanced schooling, and expanding markets for the community's goods. Reciprocally, urban markets are the preferred source for machinery, consumer electronics, and ritual items such as Rosalba's wedding dress (see Chapter 7). This was really driven home to me in 2010 when my wife, Maria, and I were asked to get some supplies for a new ritual, "el baby shower" party, to be held at Buena Vista. We found that the best place to find them was at Texcoco's newly opened Walmart, which was right next to a Sam's Club.

The frequent travel from small town to city lights has entrenched most of Amanalco's residents, especially the young, in a global cultural network of personal style, consumption of material objects, and ideas. At the same time, the outside world is establishing a presence like never before. In 2010 I counted five businesses owned by persons from outside the community selling food, cell phones, and tire repairs.[8] Amanalco and the surrounding indigenous communities have also experienced a dramatic increase in state and federal institutions entering their lives. This has included mobile health clinics, senior clubs, sanitation service and programs promoting child health and nutrition.

The vibrancy and strength of its culture and economy have enabled Amanalco to, so far, resist some of the worst kinds of potential social dissolution and exclusion that can result from globalization. How I set out to study Amanalco and its engagement with four decades of change is the subject of the next chapter.

"Hey, Mister Are You an Anthropologist?" And Other Mysteries of Fieldwork, Culture, and History

Monday, October 14, 1972, 2:15 p.m.: The day is sunny and very dry, in the upper seventies. I finally found the awful road into the center of the village from the main highway. I am driving on a rutted path of dirt, dust, and boulders up to a foot in diameter and on the right is a dry irrigation canal. Close to the road I notice slight rises of four to six feet above the ground with the only serious vestiges of greenery clinging to these elevations. ▶ I make a mental note to investigate these areas, as I suspect they might be Aztec-era house mounds. I keep the car in first gear for most of the uphill trip, and it takes about thirty minutes before I get to the turnoff to Amanalco's plaza.

In the center of this dusty village few people are stirring as my car emerges into a large dirt square dominated by an old colonial church, which looks identical to the 1609 building in a seventeenth-century document I copied last week. Across the plaza is some kind of two-story public building under construction and a school yard. This large plaza is also bordered by a one-story adobe building that looks like a simple store, with a dog sleeping in front and a boy loading some supplies onto a donkey. Before entering I approach several shoeless children and ask, in Spanish, "Please tell me, where is the delegado?" The oldest, about twelve years old, points toward the store. I decided not to flash my official permit for doing research in the area and cautiously entered the store. There were about eight men, in dusty campesino dress, ranging in age from the young twenties to midforties, sitting in one corner drinking beer. As soon as I entered, their conversation stopped and they stared at me for a few seconds before a short, tough-looking man, about age forty, shouted at me in Spanish, "What do you want here?"

Hesitantly, I replied, "Well, sir, I would very much like to speak to the delegado."

The man replied, "Ah, that's too bad, you see he is a very adventurous sort and recently went on a trip to China . . . but tell us what you want here!"

I replied, "I am an anthropology student who wishes to understand Mexica culture and learn the Nahuatl language. I have been learning about some things

Figure 4.1a   Driving into Amanalco's plaza. The store described in the text is at the center left of the image, October 1972. (Photo by Jay Sokolovsky)

from people in Tlaixpan and Atenco, but I think there is much to learn from the people here and would hope to find a place to live here so I have time to learn about your lives."

The same man shot back, "Well, I don't know anything about that, but you look strong enough, and these men here need some peons to work for them—

Figure 4.1b   Entrance to the store described in the text, October 1972. (Photo by Jay Sokolovsky)

they could use some help harvesting crops, so come back when you are ready to do this."

I thought of cavalierly saying, "Sure, sign me up," but, ignoring his remark, said, "I am thirsty—who would like to join me for some beer?" There was a mad dash for the remaining bottles in the barely functioning cooler, and soon we were clinking bottles and shouting in Nahuatl slang, "*Chantes huehues*," which I eventually learned meant—"drink to become out of control." Shortly we were dancing in a circle, toasting many things such as my success as a peon, and singing in a mixture of Spanish and Nahuatl. Before leaving I had an agreement to return in a few days to talk with the delegado if he ever returned from his trip to China.

May 20, 2003, 1 p.m.: My wife and I are driving into town in the early afternoon, with dark clouds and thunder streaking across the mountain tops announcing possible rainstorms to break the long, dry, and dusty season. We were last here in 2000 to visit our godchildren and to video that year's grand *fiesta del pueblo,* the largest annual ritual celebration (see Chapter 8). Every hundred meters or so we wave to someone who knows us or we hear a loud whistle and shouts of "Ché!" and have to stop at least a half-dozen times, get out to give greetings, quickly catch up on family news, and promise to visit soon. Despite the clouds it is hot and dry, and we decide to stop for a drink in a new *tienda* just before the church. Minding the store is a teenager who sells

Figure 4.2   Alex Juarez in his family store, 2003. (Photo by Jay Sokolovsky)

us two ice cold Cokes, but he is eyeing me curiously. After we start guzzling our sodas he shyly asks, "Hey, mister, aren't you an anthropologist?"

"Why do you ask?" I reply.

The boy responds more enthusiastically, "You are Rosalba's godparent right? I think you know my parents and my older brother? My name is Alex Juarez, and I want to study to be an anthropologist who specializes in tourism. I speak very good Nahuatl and can help you with whatever you want to learn. Please come and visit us at my parent's house, Tlaxomulco, in the next few days."

On one level it is all too easy to just talk about the obvious difference in these experiences separated by three decades. They illustrate how over time I have become embedded in the community not only by sheer persistence but also by being recognized as a member of the Buena Vista household and ritually connected to their entire lineage. After my wife and I became *padrinos*—the main ritual sponsors for Rosalba Velazquez's quinceañera, marking her fifteenth birthday (see Chapter 5), this established us as godparents to her and, more expansively, as *compadres* (coparents) to her parents and all the adults in their immediate kin network. Developing a compadre relationship is a quite common experience of anthropologists who work for extended periods in Mexico and elsewhere in Latin America. In the case of Amanalco this has also connected my wife and me to the other godparents responsible for managing the ritual movement of Rosalba through the entire life course, from baptism to death. Because of this we are expected, whenever possible, to have specific roles in key life cycle ceremonies, not only for Rosalba but for all of her siblings as well.

These vignettes also say something about the transformation of Amanalco into a multilocal community that was undergoing the loss of a traditional campesino cultural script. This also involved the emergence of new cultural spaces in which

Figure 4.3   Author with the small household then residing in Buena Vista, 1972. (Photo by Jay Sokolovsky)

to imagine a future not wholly divorced from a fading way of life. It is clear from my many decades of connection to the Buena Vista household that the generation coming of age in the 1970s was even then beginning to disengage from a campesino identity and could imagine using this identity as only a backstop to selling their labor and local products in urban places. Now generations living together in Buena Vista have adopted a working-class identity built around driving urban bus routes, selling flowers at city markets, making clothes for sale in their homestead, and occasionally fattening pigs and cows for market.

In contrast, high up a mountain road is the large Tlaxomulco house compound. By 2010 Alex could still be found there with his recent bride and an infant son. Across a dirt courtyard in separate houses lived his older, college-educated brother and sister, who are each married to people born elsewhere in Mexico. Alex's parents, a never-married uncle, and an unmarried sister also live there. In this sprawling compound, with elders in simple adobe structures and their sons in modern cement houses with wireless Internet, one can perhaps view the promise of positively fusing the 1970s campesino village with the realities of a globalized twenty-first-century world. Since meeting Alex as a teen, frequent visits to his household compound have provided a glimpse into multiple cultural scripts successfully coexisting—the campesino and postcampesino merged with a strong indigenous identity. Especially in 2010 I had extended discussions and interaction with Alex's elder campesino parents and coresident uncle. This clued me in to the need to look at the experience of adult maturity within a globalized context and how older citizens were using the flexible boundaries of extended family in their cultural game of life. As I will demonstrate in Chapter 6, contemporary life in Amanalco is embedded in a dynamic yet very contested view of ethnic identity that has changed from "Indio" to "indigenous" in the past several decades.

The workings of these two households is highlighted throughout this volume. On this book's website and in the digital version readers will be able to connect with daily activities and life-cycle rituals centered in Buena Vista and learn from interviews I conducted at Tlaxomulco on a wide range of topics. These discussions touch on teen gangs, bilingual schools, sorcery, and the mystery of *xocoleros*, the belief that when twins are born one becomes a sorcerer who causes spiritual sickness and the other is a healer who cures that illness.

In essence this chapter examines my anthropological fieldwork enterprise as I first tried to comprehend a seemingly classic indigenous peasant community encouraging certain kinds of change. In the continuation of my research over four decades I began to consider the rapid broadening of this cultural landscape under the impact of globalization. During the past decade I have adopted new visual and digital research approaches to document transformed cultural spaces and scripts that are dramatically altering family organization, work collaboration, mate choice, gender expectations, and shifting generational lines of power.

Necessary Prelude to Fieldwork: Preparing to Study the Village

In addition to advanced Spanish-language courses and graduate classes in Latin American culture and archaeology, my preparations for fieldwork in Amanalco focused on poring over the available books and articles on peasant life in the zone called MesoAmerica, dominated by studies in Mexico and Guatemala. As there was not a class anywhere in the United States teaching spoken Nahuatl when I planned to begin my PhD research, I opted to learn the language in the field. I did, however, manage to purchase a modern copy of a Nahuatl-Spanish diction-ary written in 1571 by a Franciscan priest, Alonso de Molina. This at least gave me a head start in learning some of the basics in grammar and key vocabulary. As was clear in the opening chapter, I had not learned enough from this resource to prevent some very embarrassing moments.

I took particular interest in reading the work of William Madsen on Milpa Alta, a Nahua community in the highlands south of Mexico City (1960). Profes-sor Madsen was gracious enough to reply to a letter I sent him before beginning my earliest work in Amanalco. I asked him to look at my research proposal and discuss the changes he had seen in Milpa Alta by 1972. In his letter 🔼 he detailed many of the things I was to find in my own research and foreshadowed transformations I was to witness in the coming decades. In trying to conceptual-ize the impact of the aftermath of the Spanish conquest, its new political bosses, and the imposition of altered political, economic, and religious orders, I was drawn to the work of Eric Wolf, who was writing in the 1950s and 1960s about the historical and cultural rise of peasant communities in MesoAmerica (1955, 1966). He also developed a model of such cultural entities as "closed, corporate peasant" communities thought to be emblematic of indigenous villages, which used subsistence agriculture and local craft production to survive largely outside of national institutions and class divisions. After my first field trip to Mexico I learned that Wolf had directly encountered the tenacity with which the people of Amanalco sought to control access to their lands. The first time I met Wolf in 1976 at his City University office in midtown Manhattan he regaled me with a story of how, in 1955, he was given a tour of the beautiful high mountains forest of Amanalco by a famous Mexican anthropologist. Unfortunately the Mexican colleague neglected to inform village officials of this. The interlopers were caught and had to spend the night in a makeshift jail until things could be sorted out.

More importantly Wolf was one of the first anthropologists to develop a dynamic model for understanding the mutual dependence and interaction between such communities and the ever-expanding urban centers (1982). His work provided an intellectual starting point with which to challenge an emerg-ing theoretical model proposed by people such as George Foster, who used a homeostatic model of Mexican peasant communities that ignored the role of national class systems and global economies in shaping the lives of campesinos (1965). Instead, Foster saw their culture dramatically damping down any real economic differences and their religious institutions as forming impenetrable barriers to modern life.

Instead of perceiving communities such as Amanalco as being totally closed and isolated cultural islands, Wolf showed how key institutions such as the religious fiesta system and the civil hierarchies running most villages were formed in the aftermath of the Spanish conquest and continued to adapt to the history of social, economic, and class relations connecting regions. Prior to traveling to Mexico, my master's research project followed some of the threads of Wolf's historical research. It showed that the fiesta system typically masked real local inequality but gave cultural cover to those differences. In my first month living in Amanalco, when I would ask about participation in the fiesta system and economic differences in the village, I would get proclamations of "*Somos todos indios y somos eguales*"—"We are all Indians and we are all equal."

However, even before I lived in the community my archival research documented significant economic differences that had persisted over the past century. It was clear that the fiesta complex provided a cultural space in which such differences could be managed in a socially acceptable framework. As I will indicate in Chapters 5 and 8, the fiesta as a model for celebration and social connection is flexible enough to embrace both the identity of adults with new employment activities and youth gangs who mark their territory through ritual dedication to particular saints.

My master's research, which examined the transformation of the governing civil-religious hierarchies of MesoAmerican peasant communities, led me to a focus on regional history during the first part of my early PhD work. Before moving into Amanalco I lived in Mexico City, where I examined documentary archives and talked with university professors and graduate students who had an interest in the area where I planned to work. This allowed me to develop a historical basis for understanding the paradox of Amanalco's rapid change in the context of traditional culture. 🔼 A couple of times each week I would drive out to the rural zone I was planning to study and casually talk to people about their communities. I also participated in a graduate seminar on peasant studies at the IberoAmericana University, which included students who had recently conducted research in that region. Before moving into Amanalco I was graciously allowed to use the university's field house in the town of Tepetloaxtoc as a base to conduct a side project for one of my professors and consolidate preparations for serious fieldwork in nearby Amanalco. 🔼

Observing the Lived Past: Ethnohistory in Action

Unfortunately the conquering Spanish and their priests destroyed virtually all of the codices, the original writings and iconographic documents, of the Mexica and other indigenous states like the Acolhua of Texcoco within several decades of the conquest. In urban Texcoco, famed for its library, the royal archives went

61

up in smoke. Even codices that were hidden to avoid this initial destruction were eventually put to fire in the 1530s as an inquisition by Bishop Zamarrago made it known that possession of such original documents was evidence of idolatry and sedition (Pomar 1941). Ironically, as this archival destruction was going on, other Europeans were commissioning codices in indigenous style to document both pre-Hispanic and early colonial life. Important documents about local history and the conquest were also created by surviving members of Texcoco's royal family who were eager to assert the importance of their ancestral line in the new social order (see Douglas 2010).

Although Amanalco's ancestral archaeological site yielded some linkages to the contemporary village, more salient connections provided a clear ethnohistorical path to some aspects of cultural life in the community. Ethnohistory fuses ethnography in living communities to a wide array of historical data from archaeological remains, pre-Hispanic and colonial texts, and mythology recorded in the field. One of the intriguing things about my earliest contact with the people of Amanalco was observing domestic activities and connecting them to depictions of daily life displayed in the early colonial reconstructions of indigenous society.

One such mid-sixteenth-century resource is the Codex Mendoza, ⊕ which includes detailed drawings of daily life in the general region where the village is situated. The codex illustrates such things as color renditions of women making tortillas and the production and weaving of a fiber called *ixtli*, extracted from the leaves of the *maguey* cactus (the century plant) and used for the fabric that clothed commoners. In Amanalco I observed these activities on a daily basis. P

During Aztec rule, laws stated that commoners could only wear garments of maguey fiber. In 1973 in Amanalco, ixtli fabric was still produced but exclusively for everyday carrying cloths used to haul items such as corn or household tools. In my first month living in Buena Vista I noticed that Doña Concha was beginning to spin some ixtli fiber when the clay spindle whorl she had bought in Texcoco broke. The next day I saw her working on the project with another spindle that looked very old; it turned out that early that morning she had taken a hike to the archaeological zone where her ancestors once lived and found one that was perfectly serviceable (Figure 4.4).

One of the key colonial-era documents I found that dealt directly with Amanalco was a 1609 colonial map related to a land dispute (see Figure 4.5). The document states that the new pueblo of San Jerónimo Amanalco was founded in its present location in 1540 (Mexico D. F., ATN, "Amanalco," 1912, 1). The illustration shown marks the completion of Amanalco's Catholic church, the designation of its Spanish governor, and the delineation of its territory in relation to surrounding villages. This was part of a legal dispute over land boundaries with surrounding communities, the kind of dispute that sometimes led to physical battles. The document states that the community of Amanalco petitioned

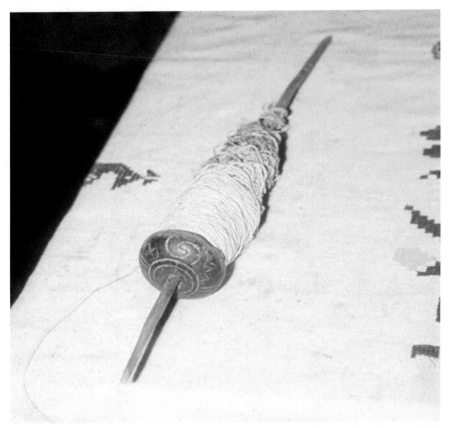

*Figure 4.4   Pre-Hispanic spindle whorl Concha found in the local archaeological zone, 1973. To learn more about the production of **ixtli** fiber access the following link.* ⬚P⬚ *(Photo by Jay Sokolovsky)*

to have its total territory defined because people in neighboring Santa Maria Tecuanulco were pasturing sheep in mountain lands that San Jerónimo Amanalco considered its own. This area is shown graphically in the accompanying figure, which indicates the boundaries, with distances marked off in *varas* (about .84 meters). One can also note in Figure 4.5 the central location of Amanalco not only in terms of other mountain communities but also with respect to villages in the lower piedmont. In 1973, when I shared this document with community leaders, who also had a copy, they told me about its continued use when other communities tried to infringe on their lands. In fact, they added, sometimes this resulted in armed conflict between villages, most recently in the 1960s, when at least a dozen people died from gunshot wounds.

*Figure 4.5   Colonial map showing the founding of Amanalco's church and delineating the boundaries of its territory, 1609. (**Source:** Mexico D. F., ATN, "Amanalco," 1912:1)*

Observing the Cultural Space of "Indio" and the Cultural Script of "Campesino" and ... Its Decline

In 1973, after my first few months of residing in Amanalco, people still looked at me as an oddity. I was later told that they had assumed I would just stay for a few days or at most several weeks and then leave. Eventually residents got used to seeing me every day as I talked to residents and sometimes carried out mundane practical tasks such as helping people haul supplies to fields, planting seeds, or harvesting crops. I would try my best to explain that anthropologists like myself study diverse ways of life and that I was particularly interested in how people in Mexico preserve their native language and their customs so close to Mexico City. Many individuals gave me a skeptical expression and walked away, but eventually key people realized that I was serious about learning their Nahuatl language and that I was trying to fit in as a regular member of the Velazquez lineage and the Buena Vista household.

Although in this chapter's opening vignette the delegado and other men joked about needing me to do agricultural work, I often willingly put myself in that position for a number of reasons. First, I wanted to experience the agricultural cycle as the people themselves were encountering it. Yet such actions only slightly began to reciprocate the many small gifts of food, information, and help received in pulling my car out of muddy ditches almost on a daily basis. In certain cases I would make a balanced reciprocal exchange of, say two hours of harvesting wheat for one to two hours of interviewing time after the work (see Figure 4.6). P   This gave me a basis for seeing, in the 1970s, both the framework of an Indio cultural space and the enactment of a campesino cultural script for the life course. Perhaps most importantly it helped establish in most people's minds that I did not place myself above them and was happy to work side by side with poor Indios.

The Indio marker remains a powerful issue: it still provides strong cognitive boundaries by which people are made to feel ashamed of their indigenous heritage. I learned very quickly not to pretend that I was a campesino from Amanalco, although with my farmer hat, old jeans, and dusty work shirt, a couple of times visiting officials made this mistake. Villagers instantly corrected the error, typically elevating my social status to a "professor from the USA." In that I was trying my best to fit in, I sometimes felt hurt that I could never be considered a member

Figure 4.6   Harvesting wheat in exchange for interview time, 1973. P   *(© Jay Sokolovsky)*

65

of the community no matter how well I learned Nahuatl or their customs. I discovered that it was important for residents to present me as a non-Mexican who not only had interest in their culture but saw it as something of importance. This aspect of research identity can be a tricky issue for fieldwork situations among marginalized people who can be appropriately sensitive to outsiders who pretend to be native or take some advantage by being in their community. People in this mountain region were particularly attuned to be wary about outsiders from more powerful sectors of society who might come to their communities and claim to be eager to better their lives.

These early encounters in Mexico helped me a decade later in doing applied research with homeless men in New York City. I avoided the temptation, sometimes tried by journalists, to get their story by staying out on the streets and pretending to be homeless. Such people were referred to as "poverty pimps," who sought to study the homeless only to gain some benefit for themselves. The key in both cases was to be honest and lay out the purpose of a study, what the researcher has to gain, and what benefits there might be for the community being studied. For the homeless project I was working with a hospital outreach group to help staff understand the best way to deliver a range of services to the older long-term homeless and improve the functioning of a small storefront center serving that age group (Cohen and Sokolovsky 1989).

In New York City, as in my Mexican research, I had to learn a new lexicon and worldview of people surviving undomiciled in a large and, at that time, very dangerous city. Besides spending limited time sleeping in parks and "flea bag" hotels, I also helped prepare and serve food at the storefront center and went with social workers and doctors to help people on the street. I also brought back lessons from this urban research for my return to Amanalco, particularly the understanding that I could never in my deepest personhood fully experience the daily reality of a homeless male or an Indio, and to think I could was an insult to them and a profound act of self-deception.

I learned two other things during the homeless study that reverberated in my Mexico research. One was that no matter how closely one studies a community's culture, it is not possible to understand how it changes without seeing connections or disconnections to societal structures far beyond its boundaries. I also came to understand that no matter how well meaning and neutral I thought my presence as an anthropologist was, there would always be some people who resented me being there and might act on that feeling.

You Can't Be Friends with Everyone: The Joys and Hazards of Fieldwork

I encountered this latter point in the third month of my first residence in Amanalco. Just as I was starting to feel really comfortable in the village I learned some information that put me on edge. My working-class Jewish upbringing in

Brooklyn, New York, emphasized an open, warm ease of social interaction that involved plenty of hugs with my male relatives, and this seemed to be playing well in the village. No matter how dusty their shirts or manure-laden their shoes, I eagerly engaged in the warm and often quite vigorous *abrazo* hug and back-slap greeting that males often give each other. I was even told that people were impressed with my feeling for residents compared to their recent interaction with an upper-class Mexican graduate student who had spent a few days in the village and let it be known through his mannerisms that he was better than the Indios here. Yet early one morning, as I was standing alone outside of Buena Vista taking photographs, an older neighbor stopped and cautiously looked around to see whether anyone else was listening. He said quickly, "Be careful. Last night I heard that Miguel was drinking heavy and said he just did not like having you in the village and meant to do you serious harm."

A few years older than me, Miguel was a sly individual who always gave me a suspicious look as I came near any group of people he was with. He was often dressed in a slick leather jacket and dress pants and gave curt answers to anything I asked, making it clear with facial expressions and body language that he was not interested in anything I had to say. Although not yet having witnessed any real violence in the community, Monolitón's tale of Amanalco's leaders ordering the killing of outsiders still clung to my mind.

Taking no chances, that evening I walked over to visit my neighbor Juan Duran, who had recently been elected head delegado and had taken as one of his tasks to school me in Nahuatl and village customs. I told him of my concerns about Miguel. He did not seem particularly worried about my imminent demise at Miguel's hands. Juan helped me to devise a plan using my slowly growing cultural and language knowledge to, at least, disarm Miguel's alleged lethal intent. The next morning I drove to Texcoco, bought a small gift, and had it neatly wrapped. That afternoon I saw Miguel talking with three other men, including Juan Duran. Cautiously I approached the group, greeting them by saying in Nahuatl "*Kentimetz tica?*" (How are you?) and shaking hands with all but Miguel. I quickly turned to my protagonist and addressed him, saying, "*Kenitmetz tica no tiouchkoawk?*" (How are you my older brother?). Then I gave him a traditional hug and, with a flourish, presented him with the gift. He looked at the offering and, with clenched teeth, constrained a snarl, while from behind Miguel the delegado nodded a knowing smile. Before Miguel could respond I proceeded to say, "I hope we can become friends and that I will be able to learn much from you during my stay. Many people say that although you are not an elder, you are an educated man who knows much about the community." He managed to politely thank me but then made an excuse to be somewhere else. My public ploy did not do much to soften Miguel's attitude toward me this first year. Through the 1990s and 2000s, as I began to return frequently to Amanalco, I always brought him and his family little gifts and emphasized a continued interest in indigenous culture. Eventually we forged a cautious friendship.

The Nitty-Gritty of Fieldwork:
Community Connection and Culture Shock

For my first year in Mexico I brought two large SLR cameras (one for color, one for black-and-white), a compact tape recorder (weighing two pounds), a Polaroid camera, a pile of notebooks, a typewriter, several reams of paper, and carbons for making copies of my field notes that I mailed back home on a regular basis. In 2010 my equipment included a high-resolution compact digital still camera that fit in a large pocket, a compact HD video cam that fit in a hip pouch, a tiny digital voice recorder, various notebooks, several thumb drives, and a two-and-a-half-pound netbook loaded with all my prior notes, hundreds of photographs, and more than thirty hours of video shot since 1998 in the village. During my latest research, besides backing up typed notes on a thumb drive, every few days I would e-mail the files to my university, using one of the several local Internet cafes or some houses with wireless connections (such as Tlaxomulco).

I remember the early phase of fieldwork as being alternatively exhilarating, frightening, and exhausting. While living at the lower altitude in Tepetlaoxtoc I would frequently have to battle with rather large scorpions, but fortunately the higher altitude and colder weather made them a rarity in Amanalco. However, the village was teeming with mean-looking dogs, and even though I had always had dogs as pets growing up, the experience at almost every house could be unnerving, to say the least. Upon my approach to the open door of a house compound two or more snarling, barking dogs, seemingly intent on ripping my guts out, would come at me in classic challenging behavior. I eventually solved this problem by paying the seven-year-old boy in Buena Vista to walk with me for a few days and show me how to deal with these mangy scourges. The key was to stand my ground, shout a sharp Nahuatl curse, and sometimes direct a kick at the hounds, and if that did not work, throw a small rock in their direction. Of course, much of the problem with dogs evaporated as I began to smell like other people in the community—as I ate the village diet, bathed once a week, and my skin and clothes became saturated with the fine dust of the fields. Nevertheless, I took to traversing the village landscape with a large walking stick and a light jacket with its big pockets filled with stones.

Early on, after walking miles through the village each day, often participating in various activities and hauling around my heavy, equipment-laden backpack, I would not go to sleep until I had fully turned my handwritten jottings into formal notes—actually I sometimes fell asleep while typing. Often banging away until early morning hours at my old typewriter, I recorded the events of the day and what Roger Sanjek refers to as "headnotes" (1990)—suppositions you can make based on field notes, but they had to be explored further to validate the ideas. For example, every day in 1973 I would observe formal ritual greetings and record notes such as the following:

Walking on a small dirt path leading up the mountain and I see Miguel V. just up ahead (about age sixty-five and who I met yesterday), with a hoe slung over his shoulder. Before I got up to him another man around the same age passes by him, and pauses in front of Miguel. They both slowly take off their peasant hats as they mutually bend to kiss each other's hands and I can hear that they say *nukne(we)tzin* (literally, respected brother). As the other man takes off away from me I approach Miguel and ask how he is doing and inquire about the hand kissing that I have seen each day. He says that "this is a sacred form of respect that we Indians use to only acknowledge close relatives on the father's side of our family in our part of the village. These are the people we depend on for all aspects of life." I ask about what they said while doing this respect gesture, and he said that the other man, Jose, "is my uncle's son and so in Nahuatl I use the same word for brother—*nukenew(weh)* and add *Tzin*, which means respected." I have seen this kind of respect gesture done many times in a day and as I am generating a kin map of many households. I think I am also seeing this performed with kin who are linked through female ties who each live in very different parts of the community. What does this mean? Is the system of kin-based support starting to change? (February 19, 1973, 4 p.m.)

As it turned out, after about four months of recording such encounters and talking to many elders, I was able to validate that a broadening of kin greeting ritual had recently begun. This reflected a change in some kin groups, which needed to recruit support outside of the traditional males-linked kin networks used to carry out key activities of agriculture production and ritual. Over the mid-1990s the actual performance of this respect greeting, especially between youth and their parents and grandparents, has changed in a way that reflects powerful social changes such as a sense of greater equality between generations. By then teens often greeted elders with the addition of a gentle kiss and more open display of affection in public. ◼️ By 2010 some youth were simply refusing to engage in hand-kissing gestures, although they often give a simple kiss on the cheek in greeting elders in their immediate family. Many elders perceive this as but one marker of a growing lack of respect.

One of the things I learned pretty quickly in going from connecting field notes and headnotes to grounded knowledge was to use information from varied people or even the knowledge of children, who often had fewer filters on the information they were giving. Children, especially females, were particularly helpful in ferreting out accurate information about kinship data. Listen carefully to a 2003 interview about household composition and aging with an elderly neighbor, who is minding a great-granddaughter while her husband irrigates their corn field. ◼️

I also had to make sure I was getting a holistic picture of the community and its dynamics to help me understand the seeming paradox of tradition within the context of rapid change. With the help of my host family and key individuals in the community who took an interest in my work, after about four months I reached a level of simple conversation in Nahuatl. Most villagers appreciated that I was serious about learning their indigenous language, especially as people in the city and nonindigenous villages, when they heard it spoken, harshly ridi-culed such persons as *"tontos del monte"* (stupid mountain folk). Each day I set about observing, asking questions, and recording information on kin relations, transitions in the life cycle, mapping the ecological zones of the community, and seeking out elder individuals who could give me their view of local history. As many anthropologists before me have found, by mapping kin relations and later placing them in a broader form of social networks connecting persons, households, neighborhoods, and communities, I was able to begin to have an understanding of the process of change.

Examining kinship data over time revealed some patterns that were otherwise hard to get at from interviewing alone. When they were spotted, such details al-lowed me to develop more realistic data when talking to people about social life in the community. For example, early on people made a point of emphasizing how principles of elder-respect, especially toward one's *tatzin* (father) and *tiaouchkowk* (older brother), minimized migration and kept brothers working together under all circumstances. Yet after completing about twenty genealogies and beginning to have longer term interaction within families, I began to see how life could alter these ideals. Two patterns in the kin charts stood out early on. First, when three or more sons survived into adulthood there was a high likelihood that one would migrate out of the community. Second, I noted that if the father died in the early part of the developmental cycle, say when one son recently married and the oth-ers were approaching social maturity, this could set in motion friction between brothers in the absence of the authority figure of the father. The problem here is a contradiction within a cultural system that stresses both age authority and fierce personal independence for adults.

I encountered both of these issues in documenting a bitter conflict between three brothers: Juan (age thirty); Angel (age twenty-eight) and Santos (twenty-one). The father of the three men was not particularly wealthy, owning a hectare of irrigated land associated with their house (see Figure 4.7). In 1969 the oldest son, Juan, had moved with his wife and two children to Texcoco, where he found a job in a fertilizer factory. One year earlier Angel had married, and his family lived in his parents' house and worked the lands with his father and brothers in good campesino fashion. The father died in 1970.

When I first began visiting their house in late 1972 Angel often took the role of the dominant father, ordering Santos to fetch firewood or run to the store for a soda or beer whenever I came to talk. Santos, at twenty-one years of age, resented this subordination, especially as he was planning in a few months time to bring his girlfriend into their joint household in a prewedding ritual called *robo de esposa* (robbing of the wife—see Chapter 5). On his own, the prior year he decided to plant a small plot of flowers on the edge of the cornfield and be-gan to sell them in Mexico City. He did quite well at this, but his older brother became angered and accused Santos of planting the flowers without consulting him or giving him any of the money from their sale. Santos saw this as a chance

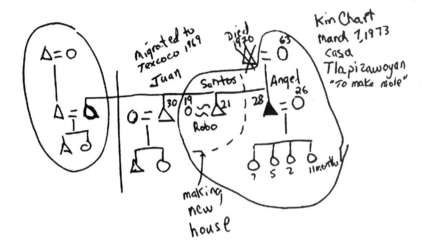

Figure 4.7   Kin chart. Focus on the conflict between brothers, 1973.

to assert his independence and convinced the city-dwelling brother to push for a new land-use arrangement. To formalize this sibling schism, Santos asked the delegados to serve as witnesses. I was there as his eldest brother, Juan, angrily plowed two lengthwise furrows in the irrigated house lands, demarcating a tripartite division of the soil and at the same time playing out a recurrent process of intragenerational family conflict.

Juan declared that previous arrangements were no longer in effect and that he would return in several weeks to plant his own corn crop. Angel was furious with his younger brother and told him to leave his house, whereupon he moved in with his paternal uncle and aunt living down the street. The rupture of this extended kin unit had occurred, and it would be some time before amicable relations would again ensue. Two months later the brothers were trying to reestablish the semblance of a relationship, and Santos quickly built an adobe house adjacent to that of his older brother for himself and Juanita, his girlfriend, whom he moved into that space.

Over the years I have frequently visited both of these brothers who, by 2010, were each grandparents many times over and heads of their own large, multigenerational households. Their mother, who moved into Santos's house after his first child was born, worked successfully with other kin to restore a viable relationship among the three brothers. The economic changes and globalizing context that drew one brother to the city, another to focus on the commercial sale of flowers, and the third to follow a classic campesino cultural script represent the kind of dynamic variation in the cultural space of family life that was emerging in the 1970s.

Culture Shock and the Boy Who Cried "Witch!"

In the process of initial fieldwork I recorded dozens of household and lineage genealogies and broader social network maps. I began to place that information in relation to the two sides of the community, land ownership, and the balance of power. Along the way I would get tales from elders about the hardship of their childhood during the 1910–1920 national revolution, the community's origins, miraculous myths of the god-king Nezahualcóyotl, and stories about encounters with malevolent sorcerers and harmful spiritual beings. Some of this knowledge was not disclosed to me during my first stint of field work but was gradually revealed in the 1990s and 2000s. It became clear that I was returning to the community on a regular basis and had established permanent social relationships with a lineage by accepting, with my wife, godparenthood obligations for children in Buena Vista. Probing into such difficult cultural terrain as sorcery required acquiring familiarity with the proper setting and context in which I, as an outsider, could address such issues. As is my nature, I sometimes jumped in too soon.

In 1973, after two months residence in the community, the new head delegado, who was also my immediate neighbor, finally allowed me to attend and record a meeting for resolving *tlatuli*, the Nahuatl word for "scandalous behavior." These were issues regularly brought in front of the three delegados for resolution. During the third case they heard that day one family accused a woman in another household of being a *tetlachiwe*—that is, of being a witch. The accusing family offered scant evidence of this, and the third delegado, an elder in his late sixties, quickly and judiciously dispensed with the accusation and cautioned the accuser about bringing such a serious tlatuli without any real evidence. This gave me a window into the difficult area of sorcery, and that evening, at the head delegado's house, I was able to ask him privately about the kinds of sorcerers and what they could do (see Chapter 9 for a full discussion of sorcery).

The next day at the plaza store, with some kids lingering at the entrance listening to elder men talk, I walked in and, after greeting people, tried out this new knowledge. Stating an interest in how the community handles tlatuli, I asked how often there are cases involving *tetlachiwe* accusations. This totally stopped the conversation as men looked at each other, figuring out who would answer. Finally, after a long pause, the eldest man there said, "Yes, I see you are learning a little of our language, but please can you tell me how do you say tetlachiwe in English?"

Clearly he was trying to avoid answering the question, and I replied, "Of course, we say, 'witch.'"

They all laughed and prodded me to repeat it slowly several times. It was agreed that "witch" certainly was a funny word. Quickly it became clear that in this kind of venue the subject was closed. I made a mistake in talking about a very sensitive topic in public when it was not already part of a discussion by community members. This really backfired, as the very next day, while walking through town, I observed that kids were looking at me in a strange way and loudly whispering to each other in Nahuatl, which I translated as "there is the 'witch.'"

This had an unnerving, emotional impact on me, and it also happened that the day after being tagged as a witch I got extremely sick with 104-degree fever and uncontrollable vomiting. Both the illness and name-calling stopped after several days, but the impact was what anthropologists call "culture shock"—a state of high anxiety and, in this case, paranoia, which made me fearful of eating almost anything or talking to people about anything but very mundane subjects. A week later I chanced to ask one of the name-calling kids whether he knew what the word "witch" means.

He said, "It's your nickname, right? I don't know the real meaning." I had a good laugh over this, but the effects of my culture shock took about a month to slowly fade.

However, by learning the terms used to talk about witchcraft and the contexts in which it is discussed as a matter of public concern, I was eventually more able to ask about it, but this would wait until I had lived in Amanalco for six months. I was only able to probe this subject in any real depth when I began to return consistently beginning in 1989. A decade later, when I started to use video in my research documentation, I saw that one of the positive impacts of this was helping stimulate group discussion of difficult topics and motivating people to come up with new examples that I had not heard before. Eventually I was able to learn the interesting details of not only tetlachiwes but also vampire-like *tlahuelpuches* and the *ahuake,* dwarf servants to Tlaloc, the Mexica rain god. These tiny spiritual beings were said to live in waterways, control lightening and hail, and could kill people by stealing their souls. It was not until 2010 that I learned about the mystery of *xocoleros*—twin births where one child grows up to commit sorcery and the other to cure it. One of the most interesting aspects of the long-term examination of such topics has been trying to figure out why, by the beginning of the twenty-first century, public witchcraft accusations had almost stopped. It had decreased from one or two a month to a similar number every one to two years. I analyze this dramatic change in Chapter 9, when I fit such beings as tetlachiwe and ahuake into the broader framework of religion and spiritual life.

Ethnography in a Hyper-Threaded World

The greater ease of global communication is something any anthropologist must now be aware of and assume that his or her work may be consumed and interrogated by research subjects. This issue is not all that new, as anthropologist Nancy Scheper-Hughes found out on her return in 1999 to an Irish village (2000). Its residents were the subject of her powerful 1981 book, *Saints, Scholars, and Schizophrenics,* which discussed the social disintegration of their community. Many residents had either read or heard about the book, and they not only bitterly complained about her revealing their cultural life, "warts and all," but also expelled her from the community. I was, therefore, a little apprehensive when a Mexican university press translated my PhD dissertation into Spanish in the late 1990s and I was finally able to fulfill a request from village members to provide copies in Spanish of this document. In 2000 I brought twenty copies to Amanalco and gave them to schools, the new community library, and the people who had been my key interlocutors. Fortunately I have never received any negative response from the community based on what is written in my dissertation, and some older adults tell me they often show it to their grandkids to validate things they told them were happening when they were young themselves.

Visualizing Anthropology: Digital Ethnography

In 1977 I tried taking some 8mm film of daily activities in Amanalco by using a borrowed university camera and was dissatisfied with the technical results. I also found that looking through the tiny viewfinder not only greatly narrowed my view of the culture before me but also impeded the immediacy and connection that face-to-face interaction afforded. In many ways an excessive focus on visual documentation can detract from the depth of inquiry made possible by other means of data gathering and potentially could lead to a self-deception that one is capturing a "real" and full reality. I did not think much about film or video again until the early part of 1998 when my compadres in Buena Vista called me in Florida and asked whether I could videotape the upcoming quinceañera of our goddaughter, Rosalba, in December of that year. I knew this would provide some challenges, as my wife and I were to be the main sponsors, or *padrinos,* of the event and would be intensely involved with the ritual itself. Fortunately, by the late 1990s the availability of small and modestly priced, high-quality video recording and editing technology made video production much more feasible to accomplish by a single researcher. Moreover, reductions in size and the addition of flip-out view screens, good low-light lenses, and shake-reduction technology helped overcome some of my hesitations about using video as a research tool. I settled on a semiprofessional camcorder that weighed just under two pounds. With long-life batteries it could fit in a large pouch secured around my waist and record for up to six hours before needing recharging. It allowed me to record while looking directly at a scene, often without a tripod or extra lighting, and sometimes when I was directly participating in the actions I was documenting. Fortunately one of my wife's former students was doing graduate work in Mexico City and was able to assist in recording some events during the quinceañera.

In both videotaping and editing these materials I attempt to represent the actual flow of events as they happened and let the cultural actors speak for themselves. But what viewers will see in the eighteen minutes of "Rosalba's Quinceañera" is distilled from almost fifteen hours of visual documentation, including the several hours of Rosalba practicing the dances or an equal amount of time viewing relatives caring for and then slaughtering animals that would feed three hundred people. As you watch the videos presented on the book website or the digital volume, try to think about what led up to the events viewed, what was left out, and what other kinds of knowledge could be learned from following up on the issues portrayed in the clips.

By 2010, with the steady drop in the cost of equipment and ease of simple editing on computers, a local mini-industry in Amanalco had emerged for doing videography and photography of life-cycle rituals. Now virtually all such events require a "compadre de video" who pays someone to take video and produce a DVD. Some of these enterprising individuals are involved with the group *Ollin Amanalco Pilhuame*, mentioned in Chapter 1, and have begun to post video of not only fiestas but also the restoration of the colonial church's historically important nineteenth-century organ. ◼◀

Digitally Engaging with the Community

Since 2000 community authorities have allowed me to use video extensively to document the changing nature of Amanalco's culture. Elders have urged me to record things that they see as being lost, especially orally transmitted stories and mythology. Each time I return I bring DVDs to deposit in the tiny community library, the local schools, and with families who are the subject of any such documentary work. In 2010 the accumulation of this visual documentation became useful in unexpected ways. The second day back at Buena Vista my comadre Anastacia asked me whether I had video from the harvesting of corn in 2003, carried out on the lands of another of their compadres. I pulled up some notes on my netbook and located the appropriate place on a video file. As we watched, sure enough, there we were picking the corn, documented with a time code embedded in the video. I was puzzled at their excitement, but Anastacia explained that the land in the video was owned by a man whose son had married her younger daughter. That man had died in 2009, and now his sister was claiming ownership of land in the video. The woman asserted that this property had not been used for more than twenty years and so should devolve to her rather than to the widow of the deceased. This visual documentation clearly settled the question in favor of the widow! Here you can link to part of this video as the deceased land owner was harvesting corn and telling me about his seventeen-year-old son. ◼◀ This young man was not working with us, as he had rejected campesino labor and instead was employed outside of the community driving a small intercity bus.

In certain situations I show my fieldwork videos in group settings so people can collectively comment and I can get varied feedback from questions. In 2010 I presented my edited video on the fiesta for Amanalco's patron saint to the local priest and the ritual stewards from the community who were to be responsible for that year's celebrations. ▐◀ Some of the key questions asked were, "What were you thinking when you were taking part in this procession?" "How has this changed from the time of your grandparents?" "What is the most difficult part of being a ritual steward for a year?" (See Chapter 8 for a full discussion of this fiesta.)

In 2010 I met with the community leaders to ask their permission to write this book about Amanalco. I gave them DVD copies of the latest videos and images I recorded in 2006 and committed to share a portion of any publication profits for a project benefiting all community members but especially school children. I told them about the wonder of YouTube, where I had already posted some visual materials from the community. I assured them that there were privacy protections built in and that I would block personal testimony until I received permission from the community member involved. Some already knew about YouTube and that people in Amanalco were posting recordings of festivals and music bands. At the same time, they were disturbed that some kids were posting stupid stuff like "the drunk in front of my house" or "my friends fighting."

The Delight and Dilemma of YouTube

After my return to the United States in 2010 I posted to YouTube some of the new video related to this book, and I began to get responses from residents. Typically these were from youth, who themselves had posted to that site, most often to promote a music group. Many of the comments offered a simple thank you or let me know that the writer was a nephew of someone in the video and encouraged me to post others. In one case I received a long nostalgic response from a young man who now lives in the United States. His grandmother grew up in Amanalco but had later moved to Mexico City where he spent much of his youth. When he was a child she would take him back to the community to visit relatives during fiestas. I also received a few comments from people outside of Mexico thanking me for letting them hear Nahuatl and, in one case, from a third-generation Mexican American teenager who was taking language lessons in Nahuatl from a recent migrant from Puebla, Mexico.[1]

YouTube postings have also connected me with a young adult man from Amanalco who is doing university study in linguistics and researching the contemporary uses of Nahuatl. I have been able to post for him much of the video I have with this indigenous language, and he has been keeping me up to date on the progress of his research and what has been happening in the village since 2010. In the concluding chapter I will discuss some of the information obtained from such sources since I was last in Amanalco.

For the most part YouTube comments by community members have been very positive. However, in one case, a video of an elder recalling a myth about the founding of the community sparked a virulent comment from a resident, essentially saying, "How dare I promote the words of a lying, enemy of the community!" I was initially shocked and taken back, as prior to this I only received very positive comments related to this video. Although the message disturbed me, it also reminded me that in any community anthropologists might study there will always be conflicts. Finding out how they are understood, handled, and sometimes submerged is an important part of understanding the real dynamics of any culture. As I read over this harsh comment I thought back to another surprising flash of hostility, brought on by what I had deemed a very simple visual document. In 2000 I was making the rounds of households and was waiting for an elder couple so I could give them some pictures I had taken previously. Sitting with their daughter-in-law before they arrived, she asked to see the pile of pictures of her relatives. She happily commented on people and places and gave me some interesting perspectives on environmental changes. However, included in this set of images was a picture of an elder from the other side of Amanalco. Upon seeing it, she froze in anger, and I thought she was going to physically attack the picture. Its subject was a man who was then in his early nineties and someone I had known for three decades as a kindly individual always eager to be helpful. "What's wrong?" I asked. At first the woman shook her head unable to speak. Then, with tears in her eyes, she recalled that many years ago in the 1950s when *that* man was a delegado, her uncle was accused of stealing cattle. After he was tried in the community and found guilty, she claimed that the man in the photo carried out the sentence of death with a shotgun blast.

Certainly in the emerging area of digital and visual anthropology there are powerful issues of representation and the quite difficult challenge of being an honest broker of cultural information (Underberg and Zorn 2013). Beginning with the early use of both still images and film in ethnographic documentation, during the 1898 Torres Straits expedition in Melanesia,[2] two concerns have remained central: Does this form of data really capture reality? If so, who has the authority to interpret its meaning? Visual documentation and representation are becoming increasingly complicated as digital images are shared more easily and now accessible across the globe. In thinking about this, keep in mind that "documentaries always speak about and never speak for a subject and that films never allow us to see the world through the eyes of the native, unless the native is behind the camera" (Ruby 1991, 62). The last three decades have witnessed a real explosion of interest in visual anthropology, including indigenous image production, especially in the Oaxaca and Chiapas areas of Mexico (Worthham 2013).

As I tell my research methods class, good twenty-first-century ethnography is like working on a globally collaborative but incomplete, three-dimensional jigsaw puzzle. Some of the pieces are always missing, some of the readily available pieces shape-shift over time, and, for some of the missing pieces, one must wait to inquire what they look like. I found this especially true in trying to comprehend the transformation of the campesino life course, as I discuss in the next chapter.

CHAPTER FIVE

"Never More Campesinos": The Life Course in Twenty-First-Century Perspective

Cultural Scripts, Cultural Spaces, and the Life Course

> **Field notes, May 25, 1973**: It is pouring rain, and I am trudging through the mud, semiprotected by my large umbrella. I spot Juan E., an elder man with a cane struggling toward his house. I go over and help him to the entrance. He invites me in, and as we enter I see Juan's young grandson, who is about ten years old. He had been playing in the house with a stick and laughing but rapidly changes to a somber demeanor and carefully approaches Juan. He bends to kiss his hand and whispers *nokulkn* (my grandfather). The boy helps Juan to a small wooden chair and then proceeds, with some struggle, to pull off his grandfather's muddy boots.

> **Field notes, June 15, 2003**: At one of the largest extended households in the community. I am talking to Don Edwardo, age seventy-eight, and his wife, Isabela, age seventy-four, who are working in their butcher shop attached to their house and facing the street. They look up at the noisy approach of a group of young teens. I recognize one of their grandsons, age thirteen, who greets me with a handshake. Then smiling and bobbing in a casual way, he skips to his grandmother, first casually kissing her hand and following this with a gentle affectionate kiss on her cheek. ▇

These two field notes separated by three decades reflect both continuity and dramatic changes in adaptation to the globalized world. Although today a strong majority of children grow up in an extended family, multigenerational house compound and have daily contact with elder kin, the cultural scripts for the life course of child and elder has been dramatically altered. Changes in the socially important, hand-kissing ritual of greeting and respect reflect profound changes in the cultural spaces in which the life course is now enacted. This chapter explores the nature of the life course in Amanalco, and how it is changing in relation to the important domestic and public cultural spaces in which it is situated.

Indigenous Mexico Engages the 21st Century, by Jay Sokolovsky, 79–102. © 2015 Left Coast Press, Inc. All rights reserved.

Over the forty years since my first fieldwork stay, indelible change has clearly occurred in the cultural script for the life course and the generational dynamics that provide a key cultural space in which it is enacted. In observing hand-kissing *respeto* greetings in 2010, the biggest difference from what I observed in 1972–1973 happens between elders and children or teenagers. In looking at the short video of two respeto greetings from 1998 and 2003 and in thinking about my notes beginning this chapter, the obvious difference in the second example is the casual kiss given to the grandparent. This reflects the changing nature of multigenerational domestic units and a significant shift toward more economic and social equality between generations. Most notable has been the reduced direct control by senior kin over the actions of junior relatives, especially in the passing down of resources with which to secure a viable campesino lifestyle. Although the boy in the video and most of his age mates live in house compounds with grandparents or great-grandparents, their economic future is no longer directly tied to land inheritance and agricultural production. This has created more emotional space for open affection and love and reflects the growing equality between generations as elder roles have diminished in the public spaces of ritual and civic power.

In the early 1970s the emotional structure of family systems was quite authoritarian, dominated by the elder couple, especially the male. Following Mexica legal tradition, parents could take disobedient children to the community judges for punishment in the form of labor for the community or a fine.[1] I witnessed several such cases during 1973. However, in 2010 this is an exceedingly rare event, and the current delegado could not recall the last such case. As will be noted later in this chapter, dramatic changes are also beginning in gender relations and a substantial expansion of opportunities for women to contribute in new ways within both domestic and public cultural spaces. 🔼

On a more subtle level, during my earliest research in Amanalco I found that the physical gesture of respeto masked an underlying tension and fear that embraced the realm of kinship. A system whereby a man's access to adult roles and community status was largely predicated on inherited lands engenders not only filial conflict but also tension among brothers and certain male cousins (the sons of a father's brother). The total acceptance of respeto behavior is thought to help avoid angry emotions and envy among relatives. It is such feelings that are believed to invite sorcery, with its subsequent misfortune.

The Campesino and Postcampesino Life Course

As children grow they quickly learn that their early world is centered around their *tochantlaca,* or house compound. This term also applies to the core relatives connected to both parents. Most important, however, are the surrounding homesteads of the father's brothers that form the boundaries of what anthropologists call a patrilineage—that is, a locally generated kin network tied together by brothers, male cousins, uncles, and grandparents. The social boundaries of these lineages are known by the last name of the father, such as Duran, Juarez, or Diaz. During the first decade of life a child is encouraged to primarily socialize with the children of the father's brothers. These playmates are referred to as *nuknewe(he)*, the Nahuatl term for sibling.[2] Today, unlike in 1973, in casual conversation most kids now mention these relatives as *primos*, the Spanish word for cousin. However, virtually all the children I interacted with in 2010 still understood the implications of the term nuknewe(he) and that the nearby cousins on the father's side of the family were to be treated as siblings. This included the stern admonition that any sexual interaction within this group of relatives was a horrible act of incest and must be avoided at all costs.

Figure 5.1 shows Nahuatl terms that adults use to think about the life course. [P] Even though in 2010 the majority of young children do not use Nahuatl in normal conversation, virtually all kids know these terms. By the time of shifting from being considered a *conetl* (infant, birth to two years) to an *ichpopocanton/pipiltonton* (two to twelve years) they are expected to develop a working understanding of these words and the appropriate behaviors at each level. Traditionally children under the age of ten were expected to play with their siblings and lineage cousins and would also go with grandparents to the fields and up in the mountains to tend animals or help gather forest resources (see Figures 5.2a and b).

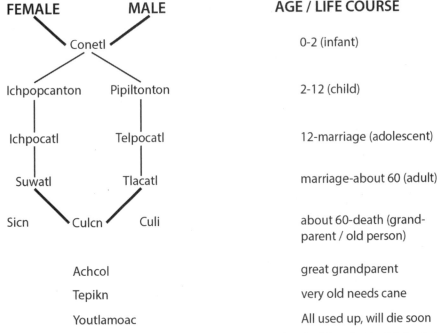

Figure 5.1   *Traditional campesino life course stages in Nahuatl. (Photo by Jay Sokolovsky)*

81

Figure 5.2a   An elder woman takes two of her resident grandchildren to graze cows and gather herbs in the high mountain pastures, 1978. (Photo by Jay Sokolovsky)

*Figure 5.2b   Elder **campesinos** try to train their young grandsons in tasks such as tending sheep, 2010.* ◼▶ *(Photo by Jay Sokolovsky)*

One can begin to understand the dramatic shifts in cultural spaces within the very youthful part of the life course by looking at the image from the 1970s in Figure 5.3. At that time young girls and boys were commonly observed playing at adult subsistence production activities. A web link provides a visual sequence from the 1970s through 2010. ᴘ The pictures show a shift from children in the 1970s being prepared to take on the campesino/a mantle in young adulthood to a growing engagement with a technologically mediated and culturally diverse world outside community borders.

Two images from 2010 are very striking. The first is a teen walking home with his custom-painted skateboard after a practice session with high school friends from another community. The other is a twelve-year-old sitting at her family computer doing homework as her father looks on. The dad is a successful studio musician and works with bands in Mexico City. He also was the head delegado from 2000–2003, and in the next chapter a video shows him pushing for the preservation of Amanalco's archaeological heritage and the building of a Nahuatl Heritage Center at the entrance to the community.

Adolescents (*ichpocatl/telpocatl*), in addition to attending secondary school, are expected to take on more responsibility in domestic chores. A greater stress

is placed on females, who up to this point would on occasion be expected to carry around young siblings, although grandmas were usually there to handle much of this work. During this part of the life course boys have much greater freedom of action than young females. Whereas neighborhood boys roam around in groups unmonitored, girls are very carefully watched and scolded if they are seen talking to boys who are not their kin. The biggest change in cultural space for teens has been the construction of a local secondary and high school in the late 1970s and 1980s. In many ways this has accelerated a

Figure 5.3   A four-year-old girl playing at making tortillas with a toy tortilla maker, 1978. (Photo by Jay Sokolovsky)

distancing in everyday experience from a campesino and Indio identity. Although, especially for boys, there is a very high dropout rate in the high school, this is a key site for exposure to Mexican national culture, teachers, and other students from nonindigenous communities, including the city of Texcoco. In 2010 60 percent of high school students who attended the school were from outside Amanalco, a fact that some elders linked to the increase in troubling habits and attitudes among their young kin.

As youth, especially males, began to work in the towns and cities during the 1980s, they became less absorbed into the campesino cultural script and more drawn to the style of urban neighborhood peer groups. In some ways this mimicked the urban gangs seen on TV or encountered in their city jobs. At first, during the early 1980s, there were small informal collectives of young males, such as the group "Los Quesos" (the Cheeses), who belonged to geographically adjacent lineages. Larger localized groups, like *Los Kiss* and its successor, *Los Yacson* (the Jacksons), began forming later in that decade with an attachment to these pop icons. This latter group could often be found hanging together to practice break dancing to the music of their musical idol, Michael Jackson.

Over the following decades, as documented in a master's thesis on Amanalco's youth by Guillermo Torres, ten named youth groups formed, covering every major residential zone (2008). Part of their identity is tied to hair style, clothes, and, especially, the bands and music they like. In the 2000s they began arranging *tardeas*—rave-like late-night music parties in vacant buildings or on their relatives' lands.

Of the ten named groups identified in 2010, only *Los Padrotes* (the Pimps) are viewed as functioning as a "real" urban-style gang, standing out for their ruthlessness and disrespect for proper behavior. In his research Guillermo Torres found that residents accounted for this difference by saying that the boys grew up in an area of Amanalco that had an unusually high number of male parents born outside the region, in other towns or cities. Many people claimed that these boys were not brought up to respect or participate in key community traditions (Torres 2008). With names like *Niños Pobres* (Poor Boys), *Quinto Infierno* (Fifth Hell), *SKA* (after the music style—see Figure 5.4a), or the notorious *Los Padrotes*, they marked their territory with graffiti tags (see Figure 5.4b) and, when necessary, their fists and knives. In many ways, however, most of these groups were mimicking the social organization of adulthood, focusing on building social and even religious solidarity within and among localized lineages. For example, in the center of the territory of the Niños Pobres the group constructed a small wood and glass icon station to the baby Jesus around which are held an annual minifiesta and dances. Such acts reinforce a key ideological principle passed down from their grandparents: be humble in front of God, but aggressively protect your own interests and that of the community.

Gang-oriented youth are a minority in each of their neighborhoods but have evoked a great deal of concern and anger. The community nickname for the worst of these groups came to be *los buitres*, or vultures. When I talked to adult

Figure 5.4a   Ska territory indicating their association with the music of The Two Tone Club and The Rude Girls, 2010. (Photo by Jay Sokolovsky)

residents about these kids they were angrily described as lazy and as drinkers and drug users who fight among themselves and with other groups. In the link here Alex Juarez speaks to me about los buitres. ◼️📹   In the concluding chapter I discuss what is happening to these youth as they mature and become absorbed into the more responsible adult world of the community. Most essentially the creation and evolution of these groups represents a shift from their parents' and grandparents' focus on kin connections to a developing focus on broader social worlds. For youth in Amanalco today lineage affiliation competes with networks

Figure 5.4b   Gang tag on the wall of Amanalco's cemetery signifying two groups, Los Pa-drotes and B/B-Bario Bajos, 2010. (Photo by Jay Sokolovsky)

of friends aligned by sports, globalized popular culture, schooling, and new work options, such as rock music bands.

Despite the concern over the teen gangs, I found the vast majority of youth to be exceptionally hard working and focused on bettering the life of their tochantlaca. By age twelve they are expected to have learned to contribute to the diverse tasks of the households, and by their midteens many have dropped out of high school to earn money working at urban jobs. Increasingly, boys have joined local soccer teams, and some have become serious bicycle and skateboard enthusiasts now that the nearby roads are mostly paved. Some have also been drawn to a relatively new rodeo club, which takes advantage of some of their learned campesino skills. Amidst these shifts in cultural scripts there remains a strong interest in religious celebrations. For Catholics of both genders there is great prestige in being selected to perform in the public fiesta dance troops that are the cultural highlight of these events. Youth are also attracted to a cycle of pilgrimages made in lineage groups or youth collectives, sometimes done on bicycles, horses, or on foot.

Life Course and Catholic Sacraments

For the 80 percent of Amanalco's residents who are Catholic, there is also a cultural script of religious maturity built into the sequential rituals of baptism,

First Communion, Confirmation, and marriage. Some girls also celebrate the quinceañera (fifteenth birthday). Importantly, from a social point of connection, at each stage along these ritual passages the maturing person acquires a set of godparents (*padrinos*) who sponsor the event.

As the video link to "Rosalba's Quinceañera" illustrates, this ritual embeds the godchild in a powerful social triangle. ◀ It not only connects Rosalba to her padrinos but also links her parents to compadres (coparents), the couple who accepts sponsorship responsibility. Unlike in North America, where the relationship of youth and their parents to a child's godparents can be relatively weak, in Amanalco and much of Mexico one's padrinos and especially one's compadres are among the most important and enduring social relationships in a person's life (see invitation, Figure 5.5.)

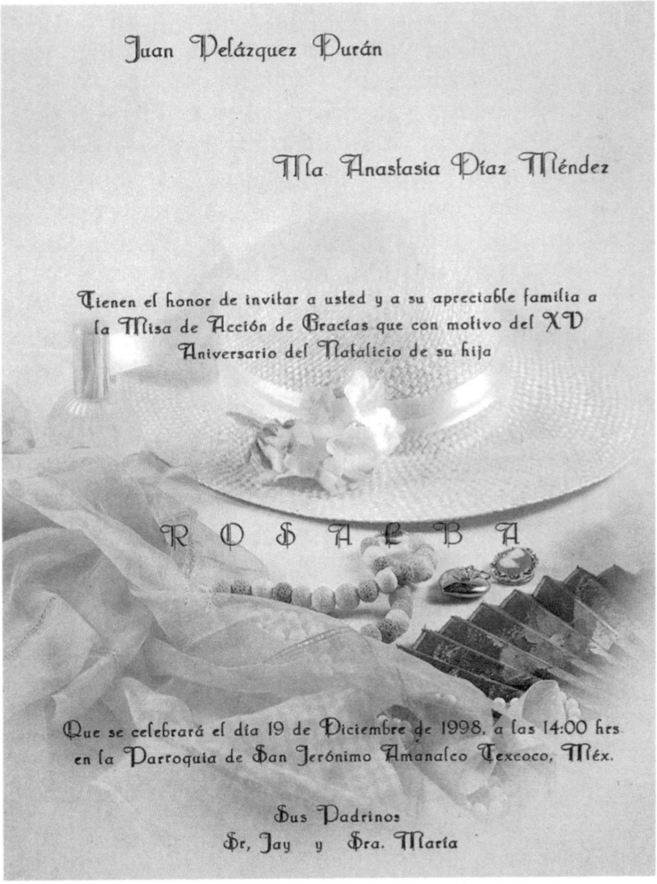

Juan Velázquez Durán

Ma. Anastasia Díaz Méndez

Tienen el honor de invitar a usted y a su apreciable familia a la Misa de Acción de Gracias que con motivo del XV Aniversario del Natalicio de su hija

R O S A L B A

Que se celebrará el día 19 de Diciembre de 1998, a las 14:00 hrs. en la Parroquia de San Jerónimo Amanalco Texcoco, Méx.

Sus Padrinos:
Sr. Jay y Sra. María

Figure 5.5   The formal invitation links you to Rosalba's Quinceañera. ◀ *(Photo by Jay Sokolovsky)*

Quinceañera celebrations are widely practiced in Spanish-speaking Catholic areas of Latin America, with distinct variations in countries such as Puerto Rico, Columbia, Cuba, and Mexico (Stavans 2010). Such celebrations are increasingly being carried out in North America within Latino heritage communities and are sometimes merged with the traditions of a "Sweet Sixteen" party. In Amanalco this ritual is not considered part of "traditional" culture; it began in the late 1970s among a few economically better-off families as an expression of being "modern" and more connected to the outside, urban world. Although a new tradition, it is organized around the pattern of long-existing forms of major life-cycle ritual, such as Rosalba's wedding ritual, discussed in Chapter 7. In the main quinceañera dance performances at night, she is accompanied by six male *chamblanes* (chamberlains) who are cousins she has chosen from within her father's lineage.

My wife and I sponsored a quinceañera for Rosalba in 1998, and as padrinos of the event, we led Rosalba through a sequence of activities that included a special Thanksgiving Mass, a huge Saturday night house party with live music, and, finally, a Sunday breakfast with close relatives, ending with the opening of gifts. Our expenses included the Mass, Rosalba's fancy dress, other clothes for her dances, the special hairdo she selected, and helping with costs of the refreshments.

The video on the quinceañera includes a section where a woman and her father who live near Buena Vista are discussing the ritual. The father suggests that this event is just an excuse to announce that a daughter is available for marriage. His daughter insists that this is really not the case. She goes on to assert that this celebration is still far from common and some even say that it is "bad" and "not normal." In the next chapter we again encounter this narrative of contention as the community attempts to negotiate the meaning of its indigenous heritage.

This coming-of-age ritual, symbolized by the gift of a last doll, focuses on the end of childhood and the beginning of social and religious maturity for the young girl. Although quinceañeras should ideally celebrate a fifteenth birthday, in Amanalco there is some leeway in the timing. For example, Rosalba's was held after her sixteenth birthday, as her paternal grandfather had died shortly before she turned fifteen. In such cases families must not hold major rituals until a year of mourning is complete. The success of a quinceañeras requires the involvement of the father's extended lineage, other kin of the girl's mother and grandmother, and also other godparents who will take secondary roles of support as compadres of the elaborate cake, music, and photography/video.

Demographic Imperatives, Gender, and the World of Work and Education

Early twenty-first-century Mexico, like many other globalizing nations, is still demographically young, with 6 percent of its populace aged sixty-five or older. In comparison, the US figure is 13 percent, and just over 21 percent for Japan and Italy. In Mexico this is changing radically, however. The patterns of the twentieth century are reversing; between 1997 and 2010 the population growth in young children (ages birth to five) was actually in decline by -0.4 percent, whereas the elder part of the population grew by 2.5 percent. The major factor here was that the nation, along with improved health care, witnessed a rapid drop in its fertility rate from 6.8 babies born per woman in 1970 to just 2.3 in 2010. In that same year Mexico's average life expectancy had risen to seventy-five years, just three and a half years less than the United States (WHO 2011).

When I began my research in the early 1970s Mexico was undergoing economic expansion, and Amanalco, like many other rural regions, witnessed a population explosion resulting from an extremely high rate of live births, averaging 9.39 per family (Millard 1985). This was counterbalanced by an extraordinarily high child mortality rate (ages birth to five) of 30 percent in 1970; that is, on average one out of three children could not be expected to live past age five. Largely because the community acquired clean piped household water and a medical clinic in the 1980s, by the next decade child mortality had plummeted to about 5 percent (Mindek 1994).

In Amanalco fertility rates also began to drop in the 1980s, facilitated by growing educational opportunities for females and the work of a local woman, Hipólita Duran. Despite strong parental opposition, she got support from an aunt and left the village to attend nursing school. Returning with a nursing degree, Hipólita eventually became Amanalco's first permanent public health nurse. She worked in collaboration with a doctor in the new village medical clinic, and together they initiated the first effective family planning program. This was accomplished despite strong initial resistance from husbands and mothers-in-law. She told me that in the beginning she would visit young women in their homes and, after an exam and quiet discussion with them, managed to dispense birth control pills under the gaze of mothers-in-law. The nurse would simply say that the pills were a candy reward for having the exam.

In 1973, when I would ask young men and women what the ideal family size was, the standard response was "only God knows." At that time most couples sought to have as many children as they could, and it was not unusual to record genealogies involving the eventual birth of ten to fourteen children. By the 1990s attitudes had changed dramatically. Almost like a Greek chorus, adults in their twenties would repeat the maxim, "*Dos hijos es mejor, pero cuatro es el maximo!*"— Two kids is ideal, but the maximum is four. Of the women who were practicing some form of birth control, the majority would only begin after they had given birth to three or four children, and this is still the case today. By the 1990s, when I asked about the changed desire for a limited number of children, young parents noted the great reduction in child mortality but also cited the rapidly rising costs of supporting children, especially in the area of education. Although by 2010 the average completed fertility for women had been reduced to about 3.2 children, the equally dramatic increased child survival and limited permanent migration meant that the population had soared to over seven thousand residents.

Other significant changes were occurring in the work and education patterns of young women. Up to the 1980s the only typical wage labor teenage girls sought was to work as live-in servants and nannies for middle- and upper-class families in Mexico City or Texcoco. Although this involved wage exploitation and difficult working conditions, some women spoke positively about how this experience provided access to new experiences. For example, my comadre Anastasia, aged forty-four in 2010, emphasized that, as a young teen, she was well treated when she worked in a restaurant and then as a nanny in Mexico City, caring for the child of a female doctor. She even got to ride in a plane for the first time, something almost no one in Amanalco has yet ever done. You can learn about her experience working as a nanny and in a restaurant by linking to this video icon.

Through the last two decades of the twentieth-century employment opportunities for young women began to slowly expand. For example, in the 1980s the town of Chiconcuac on the outskirts of Texcoco began to abandon its traditional small-scale manufacturing of wool products for large-scale production of inexpensive synthetic fiber clothing. For the prior one hundred years Amanalco's families had provided much of the wool for Chiconcuac's once-famous serapes and sweaters. Many a morning in 1973 I was awoken at 6 a.m. when a male from that town shouted a loud call, asking to buy wool. A decade later Amanalco's teenage daughters and sons began to work in Chiconcuac to produce, from synthetic fabrics, inexpensive dresses, shirts, and other clothes for markets throughout Mexico and even the United States.

By 2000 about two hundred villagers, including my goddaughter, Rosalba, still worked in Chiconcuac. However, early in that decade increasing global competition began to force these factories to drastically downsize. At that time about twenty families in Amanalco decided to use their children's accumulated skills and wages to invest in sewing and weaving machines and create clothing in their own homes for sale in regional markets. By 2010 this pattern was becoming very popular, with about 150 households engaged in the production of clothing.

For young couples like Rosalba and her Amanalco-born husband, who had also worked in Chiconcuac, home-based textile manufacture had become an attractive employment option. It allows them to work side-by-side while living in extended families and contributing monies to household coffers on a weekly basis. This home-based work also permits couples to remain most of the time in Amanalco, where they can contribute when necessary to agrarian tasks and keep an eye on their children. For the vast majority of households producing textiles, as was the case with crate making in the 1970s, this work stabilizes multigenerational households. Indeed, as the final chapter indicates, some elders are short-circuiting their late-life campesino script to support and help manage textile production in an extended family context.

A smaller core of young women also took advantage of growing educational opportunities, completing high school in the new local facility built in the early 1980s or a technical school completed in 1995. Some went on to outside technical schools, junior college, and even to university in Mexico City. A small core of these women became hair stylists, secretaries, nurses, and teachers in both regular grade schools and bilingual schools opening in the region. One such twenty-one-year-old female, a computer science major at Texcoco's junior college, opened Amanalco's first Internet café in 2003. In a video interview she proudly told me that this was something the community really needed and that it was made possible by the financial backing of her parents and other relatives. Here she can be seen talking about the development of this business.

Educated women as a group tend to remain in the village and are among the most vocal supporters of traditional indigenous culture, especially the retention of the Nahuatl language. About a dozen have found employment as bilingual, Nahuatl/Spanish teachers in bilingual schools in Amanalco as well as in more recently established programs in the region's other indigenous communities.

More dramatic and even radical was the election in 2009 of two middle-aged women to important civic posts in local government. Selected as third delegada was Berta Diaz Rojas, aged forty-four, who two years prior had become a widow. She was a respected teacher in the local elementary school and, along with her husband, had previously undertaken one of the most important religious sponsorship roles. The other woman, Maria Trinidad Espinoza, aged fifty-nine, was elected as *presidenta* of the important committee that oversees work on the community's infrastructure. In this role she commands the two men serving in that group. Before retiring with a pension at age fifty, Maria had been employed for more than twenty years as a secretary at the National Agricultural School in Chapingo, just south of Texcoco.

In 2010 I interviewed the delegada about the election and the biggest changes for women's lives since I first met her as a little girl (Figure 5.6).

Jay: There have been many changes since forty years ago, since I first saw you as a girl in your grandfather's house. . . . For women what have been the most important ones?

Delegada: Here recently . . . the most important changes in regards to women have been that she goes off to work. . . . This is for necessity, to help the family economically, and also simply to feel useful as a human being! . . . But also what I have been learning, it is a big social change, where they no longer allow submission, they no longer allow male chauvinism in any way, and that helps women to have work.

Jay: When someone nominated you for delegado, why do you think people chose you?

Delegada: First, I think I commented something about being a teacher, when I became a teacher in the community here, people would go to the principle and say, "You know what? She's a mother, she has a household, she has a husband, she has a car . . . what else does she want? She can't be a teacher."

*Figure 5.6   Interviewing the new 3rd **delegado**, 2010. (Photo by Jay Sokolovsky)*

Then, well, respect is something you earn. After a couple of years people began to know me. Now they all know me as the teacher.

Then, at the meeting someone said, "I nominate the teacher."

The final chapter includes more from the delegada and other women who have challenged gender-based expectations in ways that were unthinkable a decade ago.

Campesinos and Adulthood

When I first set foot in Amanalco in 1972 the cultural script for just about everyone's life course centered around subsistence corn farming and animal husbandry combined with occasional wage labor, playing music in traditional fiesta bands, and the sale of decorative flowers and wooden crates in Texcoco or Mexico City. When men were asked their occupation they invariably replied, "*Soy campesino*"—I am a farmer. A woman might have also stated, "*Soy campesina*" or sometimes just tell me in Nahuatl that she was a *suwat* (wife), a proud partner to her *tlacatl* in the domestic economy and the public ritual and civic life of the household. Even when men worked outside the community it was viewed as a supplemental activity that would be easily interrupted for either work in their fields or ritual and civil duties in the village. In 2010 it was mostly men over fifty who still identified themselves as campesinos, seldom getting consistent support in this endeavor from young adult children. As a slowly developing counter to this reduced agrarian support from sons, since 2000 I have seen a growing number of plastic greenhouses, usually about thirty by one hundred feet in size, being worked by men in their sixties and early seventies. Here they proudly employ their horticultural skills to grow specialty crops such as delicate lettuces and other vegetables for sale in urban markets or directly to restaurants.

To be sure, there were people in 1973 who told me they were also *comerciantes* (tradespeople), *curanderos* (healers), and *parteras* (midwives) and a few who were trying to make a living from playing music for fiesta or military bands. Yet the center of life's script was gaining sustenance from the land and domestic animals. Today people under fifty increasingly identify as taxi and bus drivers, textile/ clothes producers, teachers, nurses, bus drivers, police officers, hairdressers, engineers, store owners, videographers, and even one professional photo journalist who covers the Texcoco region for a national newspaper.

In a 2003 sample drawn from 156 fourth and fifth graders in the primary school, almost none of the children (2 percent) identify their fathers as campesinos, with the most commonly cited work being "other" (any commercial activities), merchant of some kind, clothes maker, bus or taxi driver, and musician (Ochoa Riviera 2011). P For mothers, just over two-thirds were said to be home-makers, with almost a fifth working in textiles and 10 percent selling flowers or other things for money. Interestingly, one mom was listed as working as a cook in Mexico City and another as a police woman in the capital. In fact, work histories for men over time show that many of these occupations are combined and, for a majority of men, also overlap with some kind of agricultural production in the community. A related survey with middle school children in 2006 found that only 17 percent of the students said their parents did no planting at all.

Clearly, over the past decades adults have been drawn to a much wider range of economic options than they had in previous generations. This has included drivers of small buses and vans that addressed the interurban transportation needs stimulated by a regional population explosion. For example, when I returned to Buena Vista in 1993 my compadre Encarnación and his eldest son had each turned full time to this trade, with the father driving a leased *Micro* (a small bus) and the son a *Mini* (large van), connecting Texcoco to surrounding communities. Some men were becoming cab drivers in Texcoco, and more recently three cab stands were established in Amanalco, staffed by young men in their twenties and thirties from the community. Although this brings in a regular but modest week's pay, it takes men away from their families for long stretches of time. Encarnación would typically do three- to five-day work stints, sleeping nights near the city bus terminal in cheap lodgings with other transportation workers from Amanalco. By the mid-1990s enough men were working this trade that a transportation cooperative society of rural transport workers was formed to build solidarity against the bus terminal owners who controlled the cost of vehicle leases and fees for particular routes. This group also enhanced its local prestige by sponsoring mariachi music performances during Amanalco's largest fiesta and organizing to win a difficult and violent labor dispute with the owner of Texcoco's major bus terminal.

Becoming a Full Adult

The full attainment of adult status, recognition as a *tlacatl* (man) or *suwatl* (women) comes through marriage. A majority of couples initially live together following a ritual called *"robo de esposa"* (robbing of the wife), in which the young woman secretly moves into her boyfriend's family's house and then his uncles appear with ritual gifts to inform the girl's family of this event. If her parents accept this, it immediately establishes a special ritual bond of compadres between the couple's parents and sets in motion a yearlong series of highly formal visits between the households.[3]

For the first few years the young couple will usually live under the roof and command of the boyfriend's parents and any living grandparents. This provides entree into a variety of responsibilities that link the couple to broader community responsibilities. Typically a couple will formally marry within three to five years after having "robbed" the wife and often after the birth of one or more children. One of the married sons will typically remain in the house of his parents, and as his male siblings marry, they will construct their own homes adjacent or nearby. As pointed out in Chapter 4, tensions can often flare within the house compound, especially after the father dies and the eldest son attempts to assert a senior prerogative over his younger brothers.

There is still a high level of village endogamy with most marriages involving persons who grew up in Amanalco—about 70 percent in 2010 (90 percent in 1973). One impact of this is an intense geographic density to the social networks of both younger and older adults. This is especially so for men, who typically remain in or near their natal house compound and are surrounded by many other male-linked kin. Due to this patrilocal pattern, a female's kin group is more geographically dispersed from her abode than a male's. Yet this does not imply that females are more isolated as they move throughout adulthood into late life. In fact, women past age sixty-five typically will maintain reciprocal support networks with more people and have greater frequency of exchange than their male age peers.

Music, Not Stones

As I was writing this chapter I received a Facebook message from a Mexican ethnomusicologist who had been writing a dissertation on the "classic" music bands in Amanalco. We had been in communication about the ethnographic details of her research, and she was letting me know about the first "Festival of Symphonic Bands," which was held in the center of Amanalco on March 24, 2012. This event highlighted for me the growing cultural and economic importance of music for

Amanalco and also how this occupation connects residents beyond the household and across generations. Although my 1972–1973 dissertation research indicated that sixty-nine individuals were working in fiesta bands, by 2010 the head delegado, himself a salaried musician in the National Naval Band, estimated that there were at least five hundred people in Amanalco who made money playing music.

By the middle of the last century various bands that focused on playing during traditional religious festivals had formed in Amanalco as well as in other Sierra communities. Since the 1950s these brass bands came to be called *bandas clási-cas*. They included ten to twenty members playing trumpets, flutes, tubas, and drums. Band leaders initially traveled to Texcoco or the town of Chiconcuac to find instructors who could teach them to play and read music. Brass bands were named after the leaders, and membership was largely recruited through male kin links that would sometimes initiate young adolescent boys into the culture of lo-cal music. In a video interview you can hear a musician talk about how his father taught him to play—literally by placing an instrument in his hands and forcing him to follow what was musically happening in the larger band.

It is only in the past few years that girls have been encouraged in this direction, and a few are now playing in these groups. In this way the growth of music bands, like flower and fruit box production in the 1970s, has fortified the economic viability of many multigenerational households as agriculture declined as the core sustenance for families. Music also strengthens the connection to religion and the power of saints for whom the bands are performing, either in the sacred areas around the church or in processions spiritually marking the community's boundaries.

Over the past several decades, as music became a popular adjunct to campesino life, several young men, at great personal sacrifice, sought formal training at the top music schools in Mexico City and Texcoco. A few have been successful enough to play in the national symphony and even teach at the National Conservatory of Music. One example is the tuba player Jose Lopez Juarez, who studied music in Mexico City and has gained fame with the brass quintet Metales M5, regarded as the best such group in Mexico. Another inspirational example is Lidio Durán, who teaches French horn at the National Conservatory of Music, where he stud-ied. He also founded the Children's Band of Amanalco, which played at the 2012 festival. A newspaper article about music in Amanalco noted that every Saturday twenty-five kids between the ages six and sixteen rehearse in his living room, and although the children sing in Nahuatl, when practicing music for "*Cielito Lindo*" (beautiful little sky), they prefer to play the Beatles. Mr. Duran commented in the same article that "when politicians arrive we always receive them with music, in the past we might have received them with rocks" (El Universal 2011).

Since the late 1980s young musicians who also played in their fathers' or uncles' fiesta band started forming their own groups with names like "*Unicornio*" or "*Realidad*" and played popular styles of music such as rock, two-step, and music *tropical*. Some made enough money to purchase large old trucks that they converted into mobile instrument transport systems and stages. These vehicles could be driven right up to a cornfield facing the house compound where an event needed music. In the video on Rosalba's quinceañera one can see such a band providing the dance music. Some of these groups, including Vientos del Cerro (Mountain Winds), highlighted in the first chapter, are getting regional and even national attention.

The Shift to Maturity

One of the most powerful frameworks for understanding the changing life course in Amanalco and elsewhere in Mexico is the dramatic and even startling fertility-linked demographic change mentioned earlier in this chapter. By 2005 Amanalco's community's age structure still had the classic pyramidal, youth-dominated shape, [P] although the reduction in childbirths was beginning to be seen at the youngest end of the lifespan. With just 3.4 percent over age sixty-five, this was still a young community, especially compared to other towns closer to Texcoco, where higher migration and earlier limitations on fertility typically doubled or even tripled this measure of agedness. [↑]

As people in Amanalco approach late life, individuals attempt to retain the image of fully functioning adults as long as possible. However, it is recognized that sometime during the sixth or seventh decade of life men and women will gradually give up total executive control of field and hearth to one of their married sons and his wife. People will begin to refer to such persons as old by generically using the term *culkn* (grandparent) or *culi* (old man) and *sicn* (old woman). They will begin to be seriously talked about as culi/sicn when several grandchildren have survived into childhood.

However, the culi/sicn label is not consistently applied to a person until changes in strength and vitality reduce work capacity in some way. Once persons are accepted as culi/sicn they will be excused from communal work groups and most public ritual sponsorship. Being defined as really old occurs when steep declines in functional abilities set in, with the most obvious sign of real old age being the need to walk with a cane. If this mobility shift is accompanied by other dramatic declines that might forecast an impending demise, people use a term I learned about in a somewhat alarming way during one of my return visits in the 1990s.

Who Are You Calling Used Up?

As my research in the community shifted toward an interest in the anthropology of the life course and late adulthood, probing cultural definitions of elderhood revealed a wider range of Nahuatl words about aging than I had encountered before. The experience also bruised my ego. On my second day back in 1993 I went to visit a neighbor, Juan Duran, who, at age fifty-eight, was in exceedingly good health and vigor; he was frequently mentioned as someone who was aging well. We had not seen each other since 1989 and now, my once deep black beard

96

was showing a good deal of gray. When he saw me he immediately looked quite concerned and said, *"Pues Don Che, que paso, parece yotla moak."* I was shocked when I translated in my head this greeting by my old friend to mean, "Well, Jay, what has happened? You look all used up!" Although I thought I was in fine shape for my age (then forty-six), having recently lost weight in preparation for playing a tennis tournament, to Juan my thinned face and torso combined with rapidly graying beard portrayed a very ancient personage who was "all used up" and at death's door. I quickly realized that I should have understood Juan's comments as both an expression of concern and a typical form of joking behavior. Before I could think of a witty comeback comment we were immediately joined in conversation by Juan's father, Manuel, aged eighty-three. Only in the last few years had he become quite hard of hearing, started to wear thick glasses, and sometimes walked slightly bent over with a cane. When I asked him about the phrase *yotla moak,* he gave a nervous laugh, patted himself on the chest, implying but not saying that this described himself. Immediately he excused himself and said he had some wooden fence posts to cut.

Over the following week I visited Manuel's house every day, and he made it a point to tell me each activity he was about to do such as cutting wood or walking halfway up the mountain to gather sap from his maguey plant to make fresh *pulque* (cactus beer). When we looked at old pictures I had taken of him working with his son in their cornfield in 1972 he thought back to how strong he had been then, in his midsixties, and readily said that now he was a culi. Reluctantly he admitted that most would call him in Nahuatl *tepikn,* meaning so old he needs a cane. He would never admit to being yotla moak, although many people were beginning to say this when he was not around.

Gendered Aging

For menopausal and older women there is a noticeable lessening of social constraints on behavior, and they are allowed greater latitude in social interaction, especially with male age peers. By the time a woman is sixty she may be seen on occasion casually chatting with a group of men or guzzling a beer at a public festival, things culturally taboo for younger females. Similar to Yewoubdar Beyene's findings in a study of older Mayan women in southern Mexico (1989), midlife females in Amanalco do not report the kinds of hot flashes or painful symptoms mentioned by many females in North America (see also Obermeyer and Sievert 2007; Sievert 2006). The local explanation of older women in Amanalco was that, unlike urban women, they are brought up not to complain, and anyway, females have no time for such symptoms or even illness—they just bear it.

Beginning in midlife and through their forties and fifties women may cultivate skills in nondomestic arenas. One of these is midwifery and/or some other traditional folk-healing specialty such as *tepatike* (general healer), *tlamemelawa* (massage), or *tlapupua* (herbal medicine). Of the six most active midwives in

97

2006, four were in their midforties, one was fifty-five, and the other two were in their midseventies. Each of these women practiced at least one of the other healing traditions in addition to assisting with childbirth. However, since 2006 midwives have almost been put out of the home-birthing business by a new regulation that requires that to get a government-issued birth certificate, which is the key to a child receiving any benefits from the state, birthing must now be done at a hospital or clinic. Despite this, many kinds of traditional healers, primarily women, are still functioning in Amanalco.

As is common in the life cycle of agrarian folk elsewhere, late-life females in Amanalco show a greater continuity in the roles they play than do men (Bledsoe 2002; Cool and McCabe 1987). Almost to the time of their deaths most elderly women continue a familiar domestic regimen centering on food preparation, weaving, nurturance of children, and the care of small livestock. Continuing this work pattern keeps old women deeply embedded in a network of both age peers and younger women drawn from four to six house compounds who must cooperate to produce the huge quantities of food consumed on ritual occasions. This can be seen in Rosalba's Quinceañera, and the pattern appears again in the video on her wedding (Chapter 7).

Men, even after relinquishing control of their farms, will continue to undertake arduous work alongside their sons until their mid- to late sixties. After this point, when they can no longer easily plow or plant, they switch to more sedentary tasks such as preparing cactus beer, repairing tools, or collecting wild vegetables from nearby cornfields. By 2010, however, with so many men in the twenty-to-forty age bracket working outside the village on any given day, it was not unusual to see a male in his sixties or seventies planting a field by himself or with a couple of age peers. Their sons would typically help when they could but only if it did not interfere with a wage-producing job.

Nonetheless, elders are in constant contact with children, if not with a resident grandchild then with a wide range of very young kin and godchildren living within a few hundred yards from them. The child-minding aspect of grandparenting has, in fact, increased over the last decade, as in many households at least one of the parents is working in the city during the day. Relations of the very old with their grandchildren are especially important. In extended families I have observed young children sleeping in the same bed as a grandparent. This seldom seemed a matter of space but rather a case of mutual benefit. The children help to warm up old bones, and the grandparent provides emotional security at night when various spirits and demons are thought to travel through the village.

The Public Face and Space of Adulthood and Late life

As others have noted, for Nahuatl-heritage communities an important basis for esteem, and regard by fellow residents, is the work one does to maintain the civic

98

and spiritual foundations of public life (Berdan et al. 2008). As in surrounding communities, this involves accepting responsible roles in the cultural spaces of the delegación and the church—that is, undertaking the burdens of public administration and religious stewardship in being a *mayordomo*. This involves a hierarchy of ranked positions (cargos) occupied for short periods of time by specific households—three years for civic cargos and one year for religious ones. In Amanalco these roles are loosely ranked, with the higher ones generally requiring more money and/or time but yielding more prestige and authority. The positions of the delegación form the local government, while cargos of the church carry out costly Catholic folk ritual (fiestas). It is within these cultural spaces and those regulating kinship that the Nahuatl concepts of *tequitl* (working together) and *nechpalewiko* (mutual exchange of labor) define the actions of a worthy individual (Chick 2002; Magazine 2012; Taggart 2008). It is an adult's essential responsibility to model this behavior for their children to enable them to be *mam papaka* (respected persons). Learning to display the appropriate respect behavior toward kin and giving of the self to the community when called upon marks a person as *mimati* (one who is clean) and not like a pig.

At the center of local political authority and administration is the first *delegado* (commissioner), who serves for three years as the combined community leader and head judge (see Figure 5.7). The second commissioner serves as his chief assistant by recording necessary documents, while the third is treasurer in charge of collecting fines and community taxes. The first delegado, referred to in Nahuatl as *altepetatli* (community father), is expected to oversee the community paternally, settle most levels of internal disputes, and protect local interests from any outside forces. He leads all village meetings and must solicit opinions from all present until a general consensus is reached. Other personnel in the political hierarchy distribute irrigation waters, protect community boundaries, and organize the traditional system of unremunerated collective labor (*faena*) that carries out public works projects. Since the late 1960s this civil wing of community service has initiated and carried out the series of modernizing infrastructure projects of which Amanalco is so proud. By the time most males reach age sixty they will have shouldered at least some local political or religious responsibility.

The annual religious cycle of fiestas is carried out by an annually elected group, led by two *fiscals* (overseers), a set of twenty ritual sponsors or *mayordomos* (stewards), and two bell ringers. These individuals work with the resident priest to carry out a single year of ritual.[4] The fiscal is the most prestigious religious position, with election to this post usually predicated on prior service in at least one other major religious cargo. Since 1988 the community has served as the center of a parish for the other Nahuatl villages in the area and has had its own priest living in the community since then. Over this time the number of fiestas has been reduced, and the financial burden has been spread more evenly within the community.

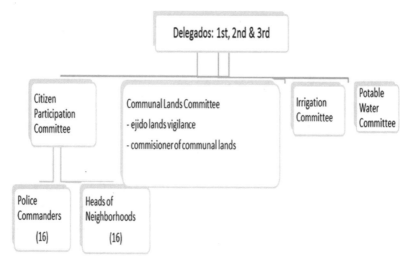

Figure 5.7   Civil-Political cargos of San Jerónimo Amanalco. (Adapted from Ochoa 2006: 55.)

From Leaders to Audience

In the case of Amanalco the decline in campesino identity and its associated work patterns has fostered the functional importance of elders and multigenerational links in domestic spaces, although this has not been the case in public cultural spaces of the delegación and the church. In the civil side of the cargo system there has been a reduction in roles for elders in favor of younger and better educated leaders. Prior to 1950 it was unheard of for a man to be considered for first delegado or senior fiscal before the age of fifty, and persons chosen were often at least sixty. For the last four decades first delegados, holders of the most potent political position, have been forty-one years of age or younger; the youngest was thirty-one. This change was partly compensated for by selecting the older men, aged fifty-five to sixty-five, as third delegado. I was told that this facilitated working with other elders who serve as informal judicial go-betweens in difficult cases where parties initially refused to abide by legal decisions. Since 2003 all delegados have been under forty years of age. This is related to a need for leaders to have better education and Spanish-language skills to successfully interact with the Mexican nation-state at its various political levels.

Similarly, in the religious realm, prior to 2000 one of the two fiscals was designated as "senior" and typically was in his midfifties or older. Since then the senior title has been dropped, and community leaders of the religious hierarchy are likely to be under fifty years of age. A broader change was occurring at this time for older men and, to a lesser extent, women, who could volunteer to take roles as dance leaders, instructors, special musicians, or simply as participants. Such activities proclaimed not only moral uprightness and continuing prestige but also that one is still actively involved in the life of the community. A fuller discussion of the fiesta system in Chapter 8 indicates that although the new millennium has brought greater engagement by women in these activities, elder males have been largely pushed from being active participants to being in the audience, from center to periphery of this key cultural space.

Indicative of this was the coming in 2006 of an urban institution for elders, the *Casa de la Tercera Edad* (House of the Third Age). Started as a political initiative by the PRD political party, social workers from Mexico City and Texcoco came to initially organize the group, which is housed in a small public building a couple of blocks down the street from the central plaza. A local elder couple was elected president and vice president; there is also a secretary, treasurer, and two assistants. In monthly meetings, such as the one I attended in 2010, there might be distribution of inexpensive food staples and talks on various topics; in this case it was a discussion of the health issues involved with diabetes and some assistance in getting glasses from a visiting optometrist who works in Texcoco (Figure 5.8).

Figure 5.8   A meeting at the House of the Third Age discussing eye health and diabetes with an optometrist from Texcoco, 2010. (Photo by Jay Sokolovsky)

In 1983 Mexico instituted an official "Day of the Elderly" on August 28. Since 2000, state and municipal governments have become more aware more aware that extended families in rural areas are not always capable of caring for the needs of the elderly (Sokolovsky forthcoming). For example, in August 2014 Amanalco's elder club took part in a large, municipal-supported elder-day celebration in Texcoco where wheelchairs, walkers, and blankets were distributed (El Observador en el Estado de Mexico 2014).

Although most seniors expressed appreciation for even the limited material support provided through this new organization, in talking to participants, they were acutely conscious of the social and cultural losses that were occurring in the central public cultural spaces. Some regarded this club as a pale substitute for what was lost and equated it with the withering of Nahuatl as the centerpiece of an Indio, campesino-centered identity that was quickly fading. Yet others viewed the club as a positive indication of Amanalco entering the twenty-first century and, along with younger adults, contested their traditional ethnoscape and the very need for an indigenous identity.

CHAPTER SIX

Who Are You Calling Indio?

Ethnoscapes and the False Faces of Tradition and Modernity

Figure 6.1   In a small store minutes before the interaction described below took place, June 15, 1977. (Photo by Jay Sokolovsky)

June 15, 1977. It is Monday afternoon, and I am sitting in the local store off the plaza with a group of men who carried out the weekly community labor called *faena.* I helped out as much as I could, and we are now resting, laughing, and enjoying some beers. In walks a villager in his midforties. He is in a foul mood and cursing under his breath in a combination of Nahuatl and Spanish. I ask why he is so angry. He pauses, looks at the other men, and begins to leave but catches himself and sits down next to me:

I just came back from Texcoco, and on the main square I met my elderly uncle from the village, and so of course I respectfully took off my hat, bent to kiss his hand, and said the proper words in Mexicano. I could hear the laughs and the whispered "Look, there are some dirty Indios." I know I have often dealt with this, but it really bothered me, and I felt embarrassed for my uncle. Perhaps it is time we think about giving up our language.

The men of the village sat silently, as they had all heard similar things and likely felt the same way at some point in their lives. I chimed in, saying, "Look, you speak two languages, and that means you are more sophisticated than those ignorant people—Mexicano is a beautiful language that I am proud to be learning." This brash statement by an outsider was again met by silence as people moved to change the subject.

June 18, 2010, Video interview with a young man who was listening to me discuss this book with the delegados.

Yes, I know stories you can use. One day I found my father and mother talking in Nahuatl, and I understood what they were saying.
This is about Nezahualcóyotl.
And there was a man and woman, and they could not have children.
And they were collecting wood in the forest.
And that is where they found an egg.
And she said in Nahuatl, "Those eggs have yolks."
And the woman says, "I wish a baby could be born there in the yolk."
Then they took the egg and, unexpectedly, was born a child.
And he is to become Nezahualcóyotl.
Well, I am not sure . . . or becomes the father of Nezahualcóyotl.
And from then the history starts. . .
Nezahualcóyotl never received baptism.
And then the Spanish hounded him, but he goes through the hills of Mount Tetzcotzingo and leaves through Mount Tlaloc.
When the Spanish were in one place, he was in another . . . and for that reason they never caught him.
This is the reason why I am sometimes considering myself from the original race of Nezahualcóyotl. Because this is something we have inside [touches chest], very deep in this town and that we cannot find this heritage as deep in other towns.
I work in Texcoco, and sometimes I find people and ask them, "Tell me about Texcoco—can you talk to me in Nahuatl?—and no I can't speak [they say]". . .
This happens to others, and I realize that there are not many who are able to speak Nahuatl like in my town.
And then I conclude that it is here where people speak more Nahuatl.
This is the reason why I consider that my regrettable conclusion is that we are an original race that speaks Nahuatl and preserves it always.
Not like other people who cannot speak it.

Indigenous Identity in Twenty-First-Century Mexico

Given what you have read so far you might suspect that the years I recorded the observations listed above seem oddly out of place. However, one of the important things about fieldwork is the need to understand such data in the full community context. No matter how compelling, it is critical to not have information from one individual stand for the complex dynamics of any cultural system.

The first incident represents a common experience of marginalized minorities in which the term that identifies them may resonate in certain social circles outside their communities as fashionable and be seen by the nonindigenous middle class as a link to a reconstructed, glorious past. Yet the people who are taunted as "the other"—the dirty Indian—experience this glorification as an assault on their very being, a mocking of the marginality and vulnerability they frequently encounter. This is a commonly expressed perception of Native Americans in the United States when they encounter Indian sports mascots said to praise their past or when they view antiquated natural history museum dioramas depicting indigenous ancestors next to nonhuman wild life. This highlights the complexity of the ethnoscape of indigenous Mexicans, such as the people of Amanalco, and involves not only the cultural elements connecting them to a deep past but also the fluid enterprise of political nation building.

The second field note comes from a thirty-year-old-man who in 2010 held one of the minor civic cargos in the group politically ruling the community at that time. I had just concluded a discussion with these leaders on the scope of the book I was hoping to write and mentioned my interest in understanding the change in local ethnic identity. As a group we had also looked at a short video I had made in 2006 of an elder reciting, in Nahuatl, a variant of the mythical tale about the naming of the village (see Chapter 9). Most of the people there lamented the rapid decline of Mexicano language skills, and they were not sure whether further loss could be stopped. But the man telling me the myth about the birth of Nezahualcóyotl wanted to provide a more hopeful conclusion to the discussion and reassert the power of their indigenous identity. In Chapter 9 we will explore in other myths the complex meanings of the conflict between the culture hero Nezahualcóyotl and the devil, Tamilo.

Globalized Indigenous Ethnicity and Ethnoscapes

Both of these field recordings establish a starting point for understanding the complex and changing markers of ethnic culture that people in Amanalco have lived within for the past four decades. As some clear indicators of Indio cultural behavior such as Nahuatl language and the use of sweat baths have faded over the past several decades, indigenous identity has been affected by national cultural and educational institutions as well as the entertainment and tourist industry. This chapter will look at the very rapidly changing ethnoscape in Amanalco and the ongoing efforts to establish an indigenous identity shielded from the denigration of the past.

Ethnicity is commonly understood as social differentiation derived from cultural criteria such as a shared history, a common place of origin, language, dress, food preferences, and values that engender a sense of exclusiveness and self-awareness of membership in a distinct social group. The expression of ethnic identity and the performance of ethnically rooted behaviors invariably take place under new conditions and in different locales from where the traditions geographically or historically originated. Ethnicity is essentially a creative act. It nests ancestral "native" patterns within social and political constraints, and is increasingly influenced by globally transmitted media. Recall the influence on Amanalco's youth of American pop and rock music mentioned in the last chapter. In 2010, when I interviewed a high school teacher about what influenced her students the most, she lamented that it was violent movies about *Cholos,* the slang word for Mexican-American street gang members who terrorize neighborhoods in Los Angeles and the American southwest.

The creative aspect of ethnicity and its increasingly globalized context is the reason I chose to explore this topic through the concept of ethnoscape introduced in Chapter 2. This term stresses the fluidity of ethnicity as it is influenced by forces and players from outside local communities. As Marison de la Cadena and Orin Starn remark, those claiming the indigenous mantle have the problem of "being categorized by others, and seeking to define themselves within and against indigeneity's dense web of symbols, fantasies, and meanings" (2007, 2). To see this, readers can review video of Yanni's concert in Acapulco with children singers from Amanalco. 📤 Notice how it is staged, with a background video of ancient monuments, the children dressed as simple rural folk, and many of the backup musicians costumed as versions of imagined pre-Hispanic performers (See also Berdan et al. 2008).[1]

Another curious example comes from the southern Mexican state of Oaxaca, where Rhonda Brulotte documents both national and international inputs into the construct of indigenous identity in a region known for handicraft production (2009). She focuses on Arrazola, a small pottery-making village in southern Mexico, only established in the twentieth century but situated almost adjacent to a top international tourist site, the two-thousand-year-old pyramids of Monte Alban. This area's heritage and its local handicrafts are intensely marketed by private business and the state for its association with Zapotec and Mixtec ethnic communities and the ancient Olmec civilization. The crafts people of Arrazola only speak Spanish and have no direct connection to indigenous identity rooted in their cultural or historical heritage. Yet they sell replicas of pre-Hispanic artifacts in front of a major archaeological site to North American and European tourists who hope they are buying goods from "Indians." These artisans are developing a proxy sense of indigenous identity, although its nature is highly contested in Arrazola. This is just one aspect of the complex construction of the idea of *indigenismo* in Mexico (see also Stephen 1996).

The Public Face of Indigenismo

As I was driving for the first time from the US border to Mexico City, all along the way I tried to listen to as many radio stations as possible to get a feel for popular music and local news. I frankly do not remember much of the song titles played in 1972, but one thing stuck in my mind: as I picked up the first station from Mexico City it was near the end of a show, and as the last song finished, the DJ signed off by saying "*Hasta mustla.*" Although I was yet to learn the basics of speaking Nahuatl in the year ahead, I remember writing down and memorizing some of the basic vocabulary such as *mustla* (tomorrow) and translated the sign off, in mixed Spanish and Nahuatl, as "see you tomorrow." It was curious that the show was not connected to any indigenous programming, and this was the only reference to Nahuatl I ever heard on the station.

This was a classic example of what has come to be called indigenismo, a "discourse about indigenous peoples by largely non-indigenous government officials, policymakers, and educators associated with the post-Revolutionary Mexican State" (Brulotte 2009). Its counterpoint is *mestizaje,* the biological and social intermixing of Indian people with those of European heritage to produce a unitary *mestizo* nation. Throughout much of Latin America, as noted by Rebecca Earle in *The Return of the Native* (2007), nineteenth-century elites, in the process of postcolonial nation building, made extensive use of preconquest symbolism and mythology (see also Giraudo and Lewis 2012). At the same time, they were displaying disdain for contemporary indigenous populations.

In Mexico, following the twentieth-century revolution against these elites, there began a national project of assimilating Indians into the Mexican modern economy and society. Roger Magazine suggests that this brought two contradictory forces into play. On the one hand, in an effort to secure indigenous people as appropriate subjects of the nation and global capitalism, "the state has attempted to transform indigenous people into Mexicans or 'mestizos' ("mixed people") in local terms, since nationalist myth has it that Mexicans are a mix between Spanish and indigenous culture and blood. On the other hand, a national myth that values the country's indigenous past as what makes it unique encourages efforts to protect and display contemporary indigenous culture as a vestige of that past" (2012, 100). (To further understand the public spaces of Mexica grandeur and its connection to indigenismo, access the following added value resource.) 🔼

One of the early promoters of this process was Mexican anthropologist Manuel Gamio, who received graduate training in the United States. His focus was to push indigenous populations into the larger embrace of a mestizo culture and, in this process, move the supposedly tradition-bound Indians toward modernity (Gamio 1979). Gamio was convinced that indigenous people had little chance of modernizing and becoming part of a modern Mexican nation because of their culture, especially their folk religious traditions and their weak command of Spanish. As is demonstrated in the example of Amanalco, it was not their culture but rather the lack of access to modern infrastructure such as roads, transport, electricity, and communication technology that hampered them from taking advantage of being "modern." It was indeed their traditional organizational structure for collaborative work, morally set in the fiesta system, that enabled them to begin modernizing once the state sought to provide a modicum of support. In turn, it enabled and promoted a rapid movement of young adults to urban jobs whose income helped sustain extended family households. Although the cultural space within households is flexibly adapting to more generational equity, it is the cultural rules defining family and community relations that allow citizens to engage a "modern" life (see Brading 1988). In the broader sense, as will be emphasized in Chapter 8, as globalization overlapped with the transformation of a campesino economy, the community adapted its fiesta organization to accommodate the changed world its citizens were coming to live in.

What Are You Doing Here with Us Indios?

In the 1970s, during the first months of fieldwork, people would regularly confront me by asking, "What are you doing here with us Indios?" or "You must know by now that we are Indio, so what is a person like you doing here with us?" This frequent taunting was partly a test, partly a form of joking behavior. It also established a boundary between people such as themselves and socially superior others who were perceived to be in control of society. It took about four months of residence in the community and serious struggles with learning Nahuatl and participating in everyday life before this type of questioning ceased. A real turning point that enhanced my comprehension of the way an Indio label bounded the community occurred shortly after this time, when a contingent of state and municipal officials were to be in Amanalco as part of a tour of the high mountain communities. The delegados had asked me to meet these visitors, but on the day of their short visit I was very sick with a high fever and sent word that I could not participate. Nevertheless, an elder I knew was sent to convince me to come, and when I arrived in my bedraggled condition, the head delegado made an impassioned speech about how, although the Mexican state might not care about the Nahuatl language, America had sent an important scientist to stay with them and learn to speak their language so it could be taught to other Americans. I was asked to speak a few words in Nahuatl to the assembled visitors, and it was clear to me that I was asked to perform as a general counter to the generic denigration of their native language and, by proxy, themselves.

What slowly emerged in my understanding of their indigenous identity was that the very utterance of the word "Indio," although connected to elements of pride, also came packaged with the potential feelings of inferiority. This caused most individuals to shield such an identity from outsiders who were associated in their minds with the urban and rural mestizos who would exercise control over their lives if given a chance. It quickly became apparent that as proudly as people proclaimed *"somos Indios"* in words or cultural behaviors, outsiders perceived persons with this identity as inferior, ignorant, and as carriers of a shameful personhood. In the book's opening chapter we encountered this attitude in a rural mestizo village when Monolitón tried to talk me out of moving into Amanalco.

The Changing Landscape of Indio Identity

As already noted, in the early 1970s residents of Amanalco were thought to be the most ardent followers of Indigenous traditions in their region. At this time their distinct ethnic identification was localized both in the broad sense of being distinctly different from urban dwellers in Texcoco or the mestizo, agrarian communities closer to that city as well as more narrowly to the microvariation of Nahuatl dialect and local customs seen in three other nearby Indio communities. To people in nearby cities like Texcoco, the Indio signified those who were poor, culturally ignorant, and lower-class citizens.[2]

In my first contact with Amanalco many houses still contained a *cuexcómatl*, circular adobe grain storage bins of pre-Hispanic origin, and virtually all residences had a Mexica-style sweat bath (*temazcal*) used primarily by women in many of their healing regimens but especially following childbirth. Most people were bilingual in Spanish, and the classic form of the main language of the Aztec empire, Nahuatl, and they usually talked about it as speaking Mexicano, meaning the true Mexican idiom. Although there were only a few dozen monolingual native speakers, this language was the first most children learned, often while being carried around, wrapped in the long shawl of their resident grandmother or older sister. The Nahuatl language set the cognitive framework for everyday constructs of kin, land, space, and health.

Elders used Mexicano to transmit local history and mythology such as how the village got its name, why the church tower is painted red, and how King Nezahualcóyotl was miraculously birthed from a bird egg (see Chapters 8 and 9). Although Amanalco's residents were then almost exclusively Roman Catholic, public religious festivals, called fiestas, were largely of Roman Catholic derivation overlaying foreshortened cycles of pre-Hispanic ritual. The populace also kept in their spiritual pantheon some types of sorcerers, called tetlachiwes and tlawelpuchis, as well as the tiny deity, called ahuake, who controlled lightening and hail. Besides a variety of traditional healers, there were also a select set of ritual specialists called *tesukteros* (alternately known as *graniceros*) who were thought capable of communicating with the ahuakes. The tesukteros were instrumental in both magically staving off destructive weather sent by the ahuakes and healing people bewitched by these dangerous magical gnomes (see Chapter 9 for further discussion of this topic).

An important way the Amanalcanos regarded themselves as Indio was the manner in which they celebrated the cycle of public fiesta and life-cycle rituals within households. The touchstones of this belief ranged from the processions of the saints, the art of colorful church front decorations, called *portadas* ⎡P⎤ created for each fiesta, and the greeting ritual for kin and compadres with a flower, lit candle, and leafy head wreath. It is important to keep in mind that some of these cultural features, especially those connected to saint-focused fiestas, were fusions of Spanish colonial ritual with pre-Hispanic patterns. What was most important, however, in defining these customs as Indio was their connection to Nahuatl-heritage patterns of collaborative work exchange at the lineage and community levels that underlay these rituals.

In the early 1970s perhaps the most powerful way most people thought about an us/them boundary and that sustained them in an Indio cultural space was their administration of local justice relying on pre-Hispanic oral legal traditions as well as their distinctive hand-kissing greeting. As noted in the opening of Chapter 5, the enactment of ritual greetings of certain relatives was learned in early childhood and was a profound respect gesture that marked the most important kin boundaries and generational relations in a person's life.

Language, Schooling, and the Indigena Ethnoscape

Mexico is a quite diverse nation, the result of biological and cultural conjoining between the Spanish conquerors, indigenous populations, imported African slaves, and immigrants from around the world. Besides Spanish, there are sixty-eight recognized indigenous languages, spoken by over 6 million people. Although less than 10 percent of its 101 million residents spoke a native language in 2010, the country remains one of the most linguistically diverse in the world in terms of the number of languages spoken, behind Papua New Guinea, Indonesia, and India. Nahuatl, with just over 1.5 million speakers, is the most commonly spoken indigenous language, although it is in the southern Mexican states of Oaxaca, Yucatan, and Chiapas where is found the highest local concentration of those speaking varied native languages such as Zapotec, Yucatecan Maya, or Tzotzil. P

The 1948 law creating the National Indigenist Institute (INI[3]) facilitated an assimilationist national policy, and over the next several decades a strong effort was made to bring basic "modern" education into indigenous communities to speed up the replacement of native languages with Spanish. In Amanalco the first functional elementary school was opened in 1963, and, as noted in Chapter 3, students received physical punishment for responding in Nahuatl during school.[4] However, even in the early 1970s, when the second wave of children were graduating from this school, many parents saw this as a long-overdue resource for their children and were already anticipating that many youth would need better and less accented Spanish if they were to compete for urban jobs.

Nothing But Gringos Here Now

During the last three decades of the twentieth century Amanalco's downward shift in Nahuatl-language competency happened rapidly (as indicated in Figure

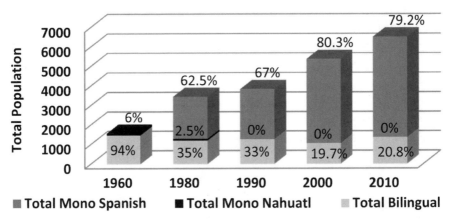

Figure 6.2 Rate of Monolingual and Bilingual Speakers, Amanalco,1960–2010. (Source: Data from INEGI: Cuadernos de Integracion Territorial 1960-2005 and from Manuel Moreno 2010.) P

6.2 and the linked Power Point). P   According to Mexican federal data, the 94 percent of bilingual speakers in 1960 dropped, two decades later, to only a little over a third of the population speaking both Spanish and Nahuatl. Although the number of monolingual Nahuatl speakers had made a negligible drop during this period, by 1990 only a handful were left. Since that time the rate of native language loss has slowed, but the cultural space in which language is used in daily life has been profoundly altered.

When I returned to Amanalco in 1989 to begin a serious restudy of the community, one of the most powerful things I began to experience was that the use of Nahuatl in daily interaction between youth and older generations had been dramatically reduced. The changing cultural script of an Indigenous campesino/a was being altered by the increasingly rapid loss of native language fluency by persons under age forty. Whereas in the early 1970s children knew Nahuatl better than Spanish, by the end of the 1990s this had totally reversed. Although 80 percent of the residents have retained some understanding of their indigenous language, a 2006 survey among fifth and sixth grade students indicated only 21 percent had conversational mastery of Nahuatl (Ochoa Riviera 2011).

Especially since 2000 I began to hear complaints from elders about this linguistic rift. Typical is this discussion, in 2000, with Anna, an eighty-five-year-old woman, along with her forty-three-year-old daughter and forty-five-year-old son-in-law, both of whom spoke the native language well.

Anna: [speaking in Nahuatl] I tell you my grandchildren are all gringos now!"

Jay: Why do you call the grandchildren gringos?

Anna: They don't speak anymore. . .

Granddaughter: Yes, she likes to call my kids "gringos" now that they really don't like to speak the language anymore, even though my husband and I taught it to them. They understand, but ... she calls them that because they prefer speaking Spanish ... to her they are all "gringos."

Jay: Which of your children actively speak Mexicano?

Anna: Only three of the five who survived, such as my daughter here, who speaks the language.

Son-in-law: Well, I also speak it.

Anna: I seldom hear you use it.

Son-in-law. Yes, but it's just that I often work in Texcoco, and I don't have many chances there to speak ... that's why I mostly speak Spanish now, but I do speak Mexicano!

Jay: Overall, how do you feel about the grandchildren not speaking Mexicano?

Anna: I get annoyed and even angry that they can't really understand what I say to them in Nahuatl. I get angry mostly because they don't want to learn.

The Battle Over Bilingual Schools

As you could tell from this chapter's introduction, the issue of Nahuatl-language retention was a subject of contention even in the early 1970s. Yet it really got heated in the next decade when a head delegado from the Serrano side of Amanalco pushed for bilingual schools to be built. A social and political battle ensued in the community over this central issue of indigenous identity. At that time a majority of young adults were working outside of the community, and some were thinking of seeking higher education in Mexico City. Many on both sides of the community understood the ease at which discrimination flowed from city folks hearing not only spoken Nahuatl but also a person's simplistic and highly accented mountain Spanish. The most basic dividing line emerged between those in Amanalco who argued for the retention of their cultural heritage through Mexicano and others who saw this as a step backward, away from progress. The public school teachers got into the fray by telling parents that bilingual schools would harm their children's education and chance of getting ahead. Community opponents even mounted demonstrations in the plaza denouncing bilingual education and calling for the resignation of the delegados.[5]

Despite the great conflict and division this argument caused, in the early 1990s, after classes were initially held in people's houses, with the help of federal funds, both a preschool and elementary school were eventually built on the Serrano side, well away from the central plaza. Initially the schools developed a bad reputation of having few resources, being dirty, and providing a poor education. However, since 2000 this situation has gradually changed as more resources were put into the school from federal funds and people began to realize that they might provide a reasonable alternative to the overcrowded elementary school in the center of town.

The essential debate over the value of these schools and the way indigenous identity should be understood has been an interesting and evolving issue. In contrast to the interview above with Anna was a conversation with Federico, age sixty-eight, who lived in the Caliente zone, the side of Amanalco that had opposed the bilingual schools. In 2003 he served as third delegado, and I knew him to be a proud and fluent speaker of Nahuatl and still carried out a very active campesino lifestyle. At that time, when I asked for his thoughts about the bilingual schools, he replied,

> Jay, you know me for a long time and that as a delegado I always work to defend the traditions of this place . . . but I thought it was a bad idea. Look, when my grandsons go to Texcoco or Mexico City to look for a good job, what advantage would speaking Mexicano give them? Instead, it would have been better to build a school where they could learn English along with Spanish. This would really give them an advantage.

If You Want To Find an Indian, Go to India!

This kind of controversy and rapid language loss was also happening in other areas of Mexico throughout the last two decades of the twentieth century. The question of indigenous cultural survival was becoming a national issue and also reverberating throughout Central America and other developing regions.[6] In the 1990s there developed an unprecedented focus on the plight of indigenous communities. The 1992 Nobel Prize was awarded to a Guatemalan Mayan woman, Rigoberta Menchú, during the five hundredth anniversary year of Columbus's conquests. This was followed in 1994 by the successful Zapatista revolt in Chiapas, Mexico, and the UN's International Decade of the World's Indigenous People (1994–2004). In 2003 the Mexican government created a new bureaucratic entity, the National Commission for the Development of Indigenous Communities (CDI), which instituted a new General Law of Indigenous Peoples' Linguistic Rights and developed indigenous language maintenance programs. The legislation gives native languages equal status with Spanish and, at least by law, seeks to promote and preserve these idioms. 🔼 To date, these bilingual education programs, as I observed in Amanalco, are under-resourced and relatively weak in developing serious competence in native languages (Yoshioka 2010).

Interestingly, in Amanalco, as native language and material indicators of Indio traditions such as weaving cactus fiber were dying out, on a broader level identity as a people with history and value was being amplified. In 2000 I visited the bilingual elementary school to observe some classes and interview some of the teachers and children. The brightly painted entrance with pyramids in a rustic setting is set off by the legend: *"Xi Ualmikakan Nikan Kaltlamachtiloyan"*—Come here to learn. The standard public school curriculum is taught in Spanish, with

113

Figure 6.3   A visit to the bilingual School, including some interaction with students, 2003.
◼️ *(Photo by Jay Sokolovsky)*

lessons in Nahuatl typically one day a week. The focus is learning the very basics of grammar, words for numbers (*se*—one), colors (*ixtac*—white), common nouns (*chi chi*—dog) or simple phrases such as (*Se sojuatl tlaxkaloa*—a woman makes tortillas). As seen in the video link below, Nahuatl lessons often will use poems or simple songs to assist in learning.

In my interaction with one of the male teachers at a bilingual school (see the video link associated with Figure 6.3) you can see how what I thought was a simple question provoked a strong response.

I had known this teacher since he was a boy, and his father had proudly told me many things about Indio identity. I casually asked his now grown son,

Jay: So tell me, are there also bilingual schools in the other Indio villages like Santa Catarina or Santa Maria?

Teacher: [Angry] Look, we are not Indians, none of us. You have to go to India to find Indians! We are in the state of Mexico, so take care in calling us Indians!

It soon became clear that virtually everyone now objected to be called an Indio. Instead, many embraced an ethnoscape linked to the term *indigena*—"person of indigenous origin." Over the past decade, while parts of the community still totally rejected and hid from any hint of indigenous identity, efforts were being made to amplify this connection from various directions.

Can Indigenas Be Modern?

During one of my early visits to Amanalco, in 1972, I was taken to the archaeo-logical zone of the Aztec-era village and photographed many clay artifacts lying on the ground, especially those lying around a fifteen-foot-tall structure that was likely an Aztec religious temple. Here I spotted not only shards of pottery utensils but also some broken fertility figurines and an amulet likely belonging to the resident priest of the temple (see Figures 6.4a/b). P️ Wearing this object gave him the right to ritually sacrifice a small breed of barkless dog called *Techichi*; these dogs were typically sacrificed in association with the death ritual to assist the departed in crossing rivers and managing hazards in their transit to the other world. Scattered about were parts of grinding stones for processing corn and ceramic household items for preparing chili peppers or spinning fiber. Such objects in their modern form were in most people's houses.

At that time, when I asked what the villagers thought about this area, people mostly shrugged and said the land there was largely barren and of little use except for limited grazing of livestock. Throughout my first year in the village I detected little interest in this heritage area. However, since 2000 a core group of citizens has come to recognize the importance of these ancient material remains and is trying to help preserve the area and incorporate its meaning into a new sense of indigenous ethnic identity.

 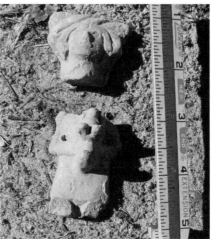

Figure 6.4a   Aztec-era clay fertility figurine usually buried under household hearths to ensure fertility of the women who cooked at that fire and the fields associated with the household. (Photo by Jay Sokolovsky)

Figure 6.4b   Clay amulet likely worn by a priest who had the right to sacrifice dogs in death rituals. (Photo by Jay Sokolovsky)

This became apparent to me in 2003 after I introduced myself to the head delegado, Vicente Hidalgo, aged thirty-seven. He was a professional musician who spent a good deal of time recording songs in Mexico City. To my surprise, almost immediately he asked whether I had been to the archaeological area of his ancestors. I told him that I had been there a few times in past years, but people seemed to have no interest in this part of their heritage. He replied that for some this has changed, and he was eager for me to videotape the area.

In the resulting video (Figure 6.5) ◼️ we see the objects he has collected, including pieces of pots, corn grinding stones, spindle whorls for weaving, figurines, and a six-inch-high stone head of a warrior. He also took me to the houses of two people who had found two major cultural items—a dual-headed depiction of life and death and a large zoomorphic stone figure. In the tour of part of the archeological zone we looked at the landscape and the kinds of remains visible on the ground. Off camera he lamented that when he was a boy and sent to graze goats in that area, he thoughtlessly picked up these objects and smashed them to bits, thinking it was fun. He was now ashamed of this and realized that it was a terrible insult to the valuable heritage of his ancestors. Eventually he tells me of a plan his administration initiated with the National Polytechnic Institute and the *municipio* of Texcoco to develop a Cultural Center, to be formally called the Casa de la Cultura Comunitaria Nahuatl (House of Nahuatl Community Culture). This center was planned to be situated at the entrance

Figure 6.5   One of the pre-Hispanic objects found by a community member in the mountain area of Amanalco. (Photo by Jay Sokolovsky)

to Amanalco, and the project was part of broader governmental efforts to develop regional heritage sites.

As was the case with bilingual schools, the idea of such a center and the potential for tourists coming to Amanalco was very controversial. There was a strong and vocal minority who thought resources should be spent for other economic activities and that this cultural center would result in too many outsiders coming into the community. At one of the early public meetings to discuss the project, although most seemed to think it was a worthwhile effort to pursue, one of the dissenters, a middle-aged woman, not only shouted her objections but also walked up to the delegado, Vicente Hidalgo, and slapped him hard in the face.

Nevertheless he persisted, and Amanalco purchased land at the entrance of the community for a future center and began to discuss with the Polytechnic how they could help design the building. As of 2014, although very professional plans had been drawn up for an *impressive center,* [↑] no state action had been taken to fund the project, and I was told that money had been diverted to other related activities elsewhere in the state. Despite this setback, other related efforts were being pushed to both intensify connections to regional Nahuatl communities and to connect the idea of an indigena identity to also being a modern person.

In the first instance, in 2000, there was formed in Mexico state a Council of Nahuatl Communities, and some of Amanalco's bilingual teachers became active in that organization. One of these individuals, Delfino Guillermo Duran, served as president of that council in 2003, but that organization began to flounder later in the decade. Undaunted, he, along with four other bilingual educators, including his wife, Lydia, developed in 2009 a proposal to enhance the learning of Nahuatl in the Sierra communities where it was still spoken.[7] One of their projects has been to develop better learning resources for the bilingual schools such as a storyboard project that Lydia was developing. Through a video linked to Figure 6.6 you can see Lydia demonstrate a portion of this project that would encourage kids to draw out their life story and talk about it in their native language. ◼ As will dramatically be shown in Chapter 10, the community is actively taking heritage preservation into its own hands.

Figure 6.6   A page from the draft version of a "Story Book Project" for learning Nahuatl. (Photo by Jay Sokolovsky)

Importantly, those pushing hardest to retain an indigenous identity are often residents with the most education. As noted in Chapter 1, this includes a collective of students and graduates ages fifteen to twenty-five who in 2007 formed a group called Ollin Amanalco Pilhuame (sons of Amanalco Moving Ahead). They are seeking to honor local history and, as their name implies, are working to remove the idea of backwardness from the identity of an "indigenous person." Their first concrete action was to successfully raise money to restore the 1889 organ in Amanalco's church that had not worked for forty years. They also organized a substantial cultural festival in 2008 celebrating Amanalco's traditions, and they

117

invited participation from regional artists, musicians, and dancers and even hosted a small conference discussing indigenous traditions.

Such efforts to smash the false contradictions between indigenous tradition and modernity must face the reality of the adults' community life, which is well observed in the daily acts of living within the framework of family, kin networks, and making a living. This is what we turn to next, beginning with the wedding of my goddaughter, Rosalba.

CHAPTER SEVEN

Why Rosalba Fainted at Her Wedding, and Other Tales of Family, Work, and Globalization

Figure 7.1   Rosalba and Herardo wait in front of Buena Vista with his kin and godparents, 2010. They are about to be ritually greeted by Rosalba's kin and godparents waiting inside the house. (Photo by Jay Sokolovsky)

Friday, February 26, 2006, 7:45 p.m.

The lovely mild weather that greeted our arrival back in the village two days earlier was taking a foreboding turn for the worse. Preparing the initial stage of a marriage ceremony, the Buena Vista household was anxiously making preparations for the first of several *bendiciones*, blessings of the couple by close kin and assembled godparents in front of a household altar.

Both Herardo and Rosalba met as teens while making clothes in the commercial textile town of Chiconcuac. As is custom in Amanalco, three years ago Rosalba, at age nineteen, had begun a premarriage process called in Nahuatl *Nikichitikitu*, or *robo de esposa* in Spanish (robbing of the bride). This involved secretly moving into the household of her twenty-year-old boyfriend, Herardo, and his parents. The arrangement only became permanent after Rosalba's mother and father had accepted a ritual basket of food, rum, sweets, and cigars from the boy's uncles, who pleaded with her parents that night to accept the situation. Garnering financial support for the actual marriage ritual typically takes several years, and the ceremony itself ranges over three days, involving a large pre-Mass breakfast, the church ceremony, processions through the community, and two huge nighttime celebrations in the parental households of the bride and groom. This is all made possible through the collaborative efforts of the parents' extended kin links and a network of godparents who agreed to foster Rosalba and Herardo through key points of their respective life courses. The pair would be led through the entire wedding process by the *padrinos de velación* (godparents of the wedding), a married couple who will also serve as the baptismal godparents for Rosalba's children.

As we waited in Buena Vista a fierce wind blew from over the high eastern mountains, and the temperature plummeted into the 30-degree range. Rosalba's even-tempered father, Juan, appeared on edge. He was anticipating the arrival of the couple, Herardo's kin, and godparents, and he wondered why they were more than two hours late. A small musical band in the patio sporadically tuned their instruments while awaiting the group's arrival. Suddenly some young neighborhood children danced into our courtyard, shouting of the bride's appearance. From inside the doorway I saw the group at the entrance to the house compound, waiting to be formally greeted and led into the house. My wife and I, having served as padrinos for Rosalba's quinceañera celebration, each put leafy coronas on our heads, grabbed a single white carnation in one hand, and a lit candle in the other. This was the ancient greeting of respect marking every major family ritual—the corona a sign of status and respect, the flower opens the sense of smell, and a candle to light the path to understanding. With the band playing we were led out by the eldest couple in Rosalba's lineage while a great-aunt swung copal incense to spiritually purify the entourage. Together we marched to the visitors, placed our coronas on their heads, gave them the flowers and candles, and escorted them to the family altar.

Even in the fading light, with my first sight of Rosalba, I knew something was wrong. Her face was ashen, and it seemed as if she had recently been crying. As our groups commingled, Rosalba quickly steeled herself and put on a braver face for the coming solemn ceremony.

Inside, kneeling before the family altar, the couple stoically accepted the advice and blessings that the assembled relatives and godparents gave in turn.

Figure 7.2   A similar scene of greeting ritual painted in the mid-16th century. From the Florentine Codex. 🌐   *(© Wikipedia Creative Commons)*

The bendiciones preceded smoothly, with my wife and I each giving simple blessings, calling for a long and happy life. However, at her father's turn Rosalba broke down sobbing, clinging fiercely to him as he tenderly whispered, "It will be okay, it will be okay."

From hushed conversations I learned that although Rosalba had resided in the household of Herardo's parents for the past three years and had given birth to her son while living there, conflict had flared with the mother-in-law during the past month, and she refused to help Rosalba prepare for this major event in her life. It was said that shortly after the procession to Buena Vista began, Rosalba fainted and had to be brought back to the house before restarting the procession. However, now back at her parent's home, the bride-to-be gradually regained her composure by the end of the blessings and began to relax as festivities moved outside for a meal and music. My wife and I were pleased to see that over the next couple of days Rosalba joyously threw herself into the festivities, especially a performance of role reversal, with the couple dancing as the opposite gender. 🎥

Weddings in rural Mexican communities like Amanalco are very elaborate and costly events typically lasting three days, but for some wealthy families it could extend over five nights. Rosalba's wedding ran over three days, with the first household bendiciones on Friday evening, followed on Saturday by a formal breakfast with all the godparents of the couple. This was immediately followed by the church wedding and a music-filled procession of the wedding party to the padrinos' house for more blessings and food. That night a huge party was held at Rosalba's parents' house with about three hundred guests and copious amounts of food and alcohol. Three bands, including a Mariachi group, provided the music. The provisions included one hundred chickens; four large pigs, five large turkeys; 300 liters of soda, 150 liters of rum; ten cartons of beer; ten cartons of large tequila bottles; and a huge multitiered cake. On Sunday an equally large party was held at the house of the groom's parents. Resources for such celebrations take anywhere from three to five years to secure and involve the contributions from all the godparents of the couple, especially the padrinos of the wedding, who take center stage at all rituals along with the eldest members of each lineage linked to the couple.[1] My goal here is to look at how marriage activates the social space inhabited by adulthood and intersects with broader social realms of kinship, the globalizing world of work, and godparenthood obligations.

It All Starts with *El Robo*

My visit to Buena Vista in 2000 provided a surprise. Following Rosalba's quinceañera in 1998 I asked her younger sister Elizabeth whether she also wanted a big fifteenth birthday party. She immediately replied, "Oh no, I would much rather come to visit you and my godmother Maria in Florida." Upon my return to the village in 2000 I was prepared to process the complicated documents to get a travel visa for Elizabeth. However, at my arrival to Buena Vista, when I asked her parents whether I could speak with Elizabeth, there was a very awkward silence and a quick change of subject. I persisted and quickly found out that one evening two months prior she did not come home at the usual time. Later that night two uncles of her boyfriend arrived at Buena Vista with a large basket filled with ritual foods. They announced that Elizabeth was well and had been "robbed" into the residence of their seventeen-year-old nephew Cirillo and his parents. She now lived in the house called Tlametonton on the other side of the village. That evening, along with the rest of the family in Buena Vista, we paid a surprise visit to Elizabeth and her boyfriend. After Elizabeth nervously served us food she had helped prepare with her boyfriend's mother, a lighter mood prevailed, and we sensed that she was adapting well to her new extended family household. When I next returned in 2003 the young couple seemed to be quite happy. By 2010 they had three children who were often looked after by Cirillo's mother as he and Elizabeth worked together sewing clothes for sale in regional markets.

A majority of marriages are preceded by robo de esposa, although on occasion parents demand their daughter back. I was told that even when there were strong objections to the match, few families reject this situation, as to do so would be the ultimate insult to the family of the young man. If this arrangement is accepted, it initiates a formal series of visits and gift giving between both sets of parents and their closest relatives, and it sets the stage for a lifetime of frequent contact between the families. Robo de esposa also allows young women to adapt to their new residential setting and to the other persons making up that household.

The protective gaze of their parents and siblings is facilitated by the persistence of a high rate of what anthropologists would classify as community *endogamy*, meaning that in 2010 just over 70 percent of marriage partners were found in Amanalco. Yet the degree of *exogamy*, taking marriage partners outside Amanalco, has increased since the early 1970s, when nine of ten residents found spouses within their own community. As I discuss below and in the final chapter, the consequences of that shift have interesting implications for the patterns of change I observed in 2010.

The Tochantlaca as a Key Cultural Space

As was noted in Chapter 2, the Nahuatl word *tochantlaca* (people of my place) evokes a fluid cultural space that connects a person, in the first instance, to the people within the house compound where they were born and to several surrounding households where their father's brothers have established their own families. Anthropologists call this broader kin network a patrilineage, in this case a relatively small configuration that interconnects households of adult brothers and their older and younger male family members often living on contiguous lands. A given surname name group such as Duran, Arias, and Velazquez tends to have many of its households in the same area on one side of the community's dual division, although they can be found on both sides. Each individual has two surnames—the first and most important from the father's lineage group, and the second is the first surname of the mother (e.g., Anna Arias Duran). There is a general prohibition against marrying someone with the same patronym (father's surname); however, in the larger name groups, such as Duran, a man may find a mate considered a distant enough relative to marry.

The word tochantlaca also encompasses the network of relatives in the mother's natal household and that of one's own spouse when a person marries. Despite the dominance of patrilineal descent, key kinship ties generated through one's mother are also acknowledged by respeto behavior and have great practical importance. Maternal relatives have increasingly come to comprise a significant portion of a household's total personal network of support. It is through the exchange of labor, tangible goods, and money with both male and female kin links that families are able to carry out costly and time-consuming public ritual. For example, during Rosalba's wedding almost 40 percent of the labor was provided by people linked to the tochantlacas where her mother and grandmother were born.

Tochantlaca, Families, and Generation

Family systems in all societies go through a developmental cycle shaped by cultural ideas of how families should be formed and generations linked. In Amanalco the norm for adults is to live in multigenerational, multifamily households at some time during their life. My archival research showed that the percent of older adults living in extended family households has remained at about 60 percent or higher over the past eighty years. However, from the 1920s to the twenty-first century several major shifts have occurred. One change has involved the significant reduction of very large extended households, where two or more married sons stayed in the parent's household to work with and eventually care for them. Such "joint" patrilineal households, containing twelve to twenty-five persons, were enclosed within 120-by-70-foot long compounds protected by 15-foot-high adobe walls and at least two dogs. By the early 1980s reductions in per capita land holdings and the rise of new money-making activities outside the village had stimulated a shift from "joint" to "stem" patrilineal households, where almost 90 percent of such kin groupings involved only one married son who would remain with the parents.

Of more recent vintage is the formation of extended households by incorporating an adult daughter's family into her parent's residence, either by themselves or along with a married son. In some of these cases the adult daughter has married someone from a poor family outside the village who had little to offer the young couple. As we saw in Chapter 5 in the discussion of gangs, people often attribute bad behavior of teens to growing up in these households. Such marriages are also more unstable than most, and in cases of marital dissolution, the daughter will remain in her parent's house, especially if she has any young children.

In the past decade better employment and educational options have increased the number of partners from diverse areas. This has been a source of some of the significant changes in the community. For example, in the case of the young woman Rosia, who started the first Internet store in 2003, her mother had grown up in Amanalco and met her Mexico City–born husband when they were both beginning teachers in another Sierra community. It was the father who had especially encouraged Rosia and her two sisters to seek college education.

Another shift has been in the expectation of who cares for parents as they age. In Amanalco extended-family organization is still the normative form of residence that older adults hope to generate over the long run. Ideally, as male offspring get married, at least one is expected to raise children in his parent's house and provide the core basis of support in old age. More often than not these days, resident married sons and their families live in a physically independent house set within a residential compound, a moment's walk from their parents' dwelling, such as just across a courtyard or down a dirt path. In the final chapter I evaluate recent claims by older adults that lately many elders have been abandoned.

The experience of aged individuals living by themselves is still extremely rare and usually happens following the death of a spouse, where the older couple had been living alone in one of the relatively isolated mountain neighborhoods. As elder parents get frail, they may be urged to move into a son's house, but as I witnessed in numerous cases, elders retain an extraordinary attachment to their old houses, even if they are alone and the dwelling might be collapsing around them. In most such instances there will be an attempt to send a teenage child to live with and help grandparents who otherwise would be living by themselves.

A poignant example was that of my elderly neighbor Manuel Duran (see Chapter 5 page 97). His son Juan built a nice new brick house a minute's walk from the large but ancient adobe structure where his father still lived. Manuel had been a widower for many years and took most of his meals at this new house but could not be convinced to move from the crumbling dwelling his own father had built. In 2000 Juan asked me to visit Manuel, then aged ninety, to see whether I could talk some sense into him. Nothing I could say swayed him, despite my pointing out the chickens that seemed to have made a permanent home (and mess) on his bed. Instead, it was eventually decided that the one son of Juan who was devoted to the campesino life would move in with his grandfather. This son, Raul, helped make the dwelling more livable and remained there after Manuel's death in 2003. He inherited the house and the associated cornfield that gave the house its name—*Hueyotenco* (big canal).

One of the most subtle but profound changes, also found in many other developing world regions, is the gradual social distancing of nuclear family units from the parental generation (Aboderin 2006). I am not talking about the dramatic privatization of living and social space that North American families expect; people in Amanalco, even though they now see such things on TV dramas and soap operas, remain puzzled and even repulsed by the idea that young children can have their own room with a door they can close! Most would consider this child abuse through isolation.

Over the past two decades there has developed a feeling that young couples require a more "companionate" social and emotional connection to each other while basing the strong respect still directed toward elder kin more on earned affection and less on unquestioned authority. This is reinforced by some new economic strategies such as household garment manufacture, where couples work as equal partners to form the core of family teams that produce clothing for market sale. In a majority of such cases it is typically the husband's parents who provide the capital for these endeavors. As noted in Chapter 5, this is also reflected in the shift of hand-kissing greetings of close elder kin. This behavior is now often punctuated with an affectionate kiss to the cheek and a smile, altering the totally somber respect gesture I observed in the 1970s.

In 2010, even as young adults recognized that their culture is still largely organized around male dominance and elder respect, they realize that the new options propelling them into full adulthood are rewriting the cultural scripts they witnessed in their parent's lives. For Rosalba's and Herardo's generation, as the campesino lifestyle quickly fades, it is affecting gender relations and altering how intergenerational ties are being renegotiated in a globalized age. In the next section I elaborate on these issues, using three examples of how family systems are adapting to new employment strategies.

Reluctant Campesinos, Eager Proletariats

We begin looking at these issues with the tochantlaca where Rosalba was born, Buena Vista. In 2010 this house compound contained two extended family units that have taken a different path in adapting to the modern world. The eldest member is the shy, widowed, Nahuatl-speaking Concha Duran Juarez, aged seventy-one, whose husband, Encarnación, died in 1997, at age sixty-four. Concha has four living children, including two adult sons, Juan and Angel, who live with their families in Buena Vista. One daughter, Ana, until 2005 had lived there with her own child following the breakup of a relationship with a man she met while working in Chiconcuac. Shortly before Rosalba's wedding Ana had moved in with a truck driver from the nearby town of Santa Inés, where they live with his parents. Concha's elder daughter, Leticia, wed within Amanalco and is a frequent visitor with her family.

Although Concha's husband had been fluent in Nahuatl and enjoyed participating in the traditional fiesta system, he had never liked farming and was deeply conflicted about the agrarian way of life. He would often intersperse tending his small fields with temporary factory jobs or making change on buses in Texcoco. Encarnación also made wooden crates for sale with his sons or bought and sold flowers with Concha in the shanty towns springing up around Mexico City.

Three of his four brothers remained in a typical lineage cluster of households. The youngest of these siblings rejected a campesino lifestyle and, shortly after he married, moved to Texcoco and worked in a small fertilizer factory. At one point in the late 1960s Encarnación also moved his wife and their young son to Texcoco, but Concha became distraught in this setting, and they moved back in less than a year. In 1984 their oldest son, Juan, "robbed" his village-born wife, Anastasia, into the house. Over a fifteen-year period they had four children, the oldest of whom is Rosalba. By the 1990s, with population and urban congestion booming in the Texcoco region, the government encouraged individuals to lease buses or vans to enhance the existing intercity public transport system. By 1994 Encarnación and his eldest son leased a large van and a small bus and would drive in long shifts that sometimes took them out of Amanalco for days at time.

Following Encarnación's death in 1997 the family gave up one of the buses, and by the late 1990s Concha's resident teenage granddaughter Rosalba had dropped

House called *Buena Vista* ("Wonderful View") 1998

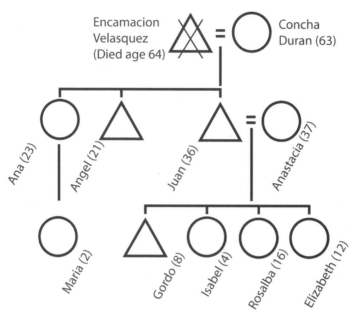

Figure 7.3   Kin Chart of the Buena Vista household, December, 1998. (Figure by Jay Sokolovsky)

out of school and was commuting daily to make sweaters in a small factory in the nearby town of Chiconcuac. (Figure 7.3 shows the kin chart of the extended multigenerational family living in Buena Vista during 1998.)

In 2010 the kin configuration in Buena Vista found two extended family clusters residing on either side of an enclosed courtyard (see Figure 7.4). Juan's younger brother, Angel, had "robbed" his longtime girlfriend, Anita, into Buena Vista, four years prior, and they now had a three-year-old son. Angel had just completed a new extension to the oldest building in the compound to provide for his young family and his mother, Concha. Bringing Anita into the household was a tricky business, as her father had invested in her education to be a school teacher, and Angel swore everyone—including me—to secrecy about his plans until she had graduated. Things had worked out, and while Concha cheerfully watched Anita's child, the younger woman traveled during the week to a teaching job an hour away in a town on the edge of Mexico City.

Concha, at age seventy-five, proudly maintains her campesina, indigenous identity. In the back of the house she maintains a garden of greens, chilies, and herbs and tends chickens and turkeys as well as a handful of pigs. She also raised an occasional small bull to be slaughtered for feasts or sold for extra money.

Concha, following the death of her husband, admitted she was now old and let her elder son's wife, Anastacia, know that she could take charge of the domestic scene. In fact, living in their household, one could scarcely determine who was in charge, as they just did things with and for each other with such unspoken ease that it appeared to occur via mental telepathy.

Angel, spending less time driving a bus, with the help of his older brother invested in sewing machines and had begun making clothing for sale. Eventually he gave that up and started selling flowers in urban markets, with the clothes machines being passed on to his brother's son, affectionately known to all as Gordo. He had completed a technical studies program in the local high school town and had become a highly skilled garment maker.

Gordo and his new bride, Maria (since December 2009), live with his parents and younger sister Isabel just across the courtyard from his grandmother and uncle's family. Several days a week Gordo works for a compadre of his parents who has a small family textile business on the same side of the community. The rest of the time he and his very pregnant wife made clothes together in Buena Vista.

In looking at Figure 7.4, and the 2nd slide of this power point, P we can note some other specifics for 2010: of the five households shown in any detail,

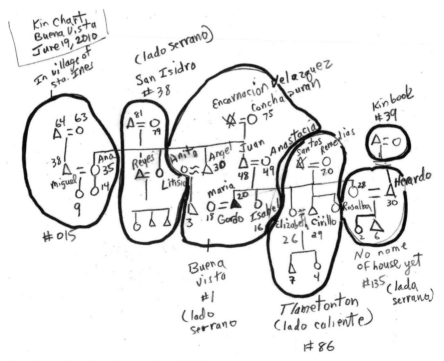

Figure 7.4   Kin Chart, Buena Vista, 2010.

four are multigenerational, extended households with a patrilocal residence pattern that involved movement of females into the male's parent's abode On the far right (#135) you see the small nuclear family household of Gordo's sister Rosalba, her husband, Herardo, and their young children. Their small house is on land given to them by Herardo's paternal uncle who lives next door to them and in which he has a small family shop making children's clothes. Since 2003 they had been living with Herardo's parents. It was their long-term plans of moving next to the uncle that sparked Rosalba's conflict with her mother-in-law, making the start of her wedding so stressful.

By 2010 peace had been restored, and both sides of the female generations had resumed the mutual support behavior each had been culturally trained to undertake. In Figure 7.5 Rosalba and Herardo are seen doing their textile production with their children playing around them. ■◀ Actually, they were working temporarily in Buena Vista at the time, as there was a problem with the electricity in their own house.

Such cases help us understand how family developmental cycles operate within dynamic domestic cultural space and reflect altering scripts for different parts of the life course. All of the couples in the 2010 Buena Vista kin chart (Figure 7.4), from the youngest to the oldest, began their long-term relationships when

Figure 7.5   Rosalba and Herardo at work together making clothes, 2010. (Photo by Jay Sokolovsky)

the women were voluntarily "robbed" into the households of their boyfriend's parents, with the expectation of formal marriage in future years. The big difference is that although all persons past age fifty in these households had a core identity focused on a campesino life course, *none* of their younger kin has this lifestyle orientation. This disjuncture is becoming pervasive in Amanalco and creating a profound challenge to the cultural adaptability that served them so well in the late twentieth century.

Despite the conflict between Rosalba and her mother-in-law, I have always been amazed at how seemingly easy young women worked their way into their boyfriend's household and fluidly seemed to know how to exist with the mother-in-law. Even in cultures where virtually everyone begins couplehood in this way, anthropological reports are replete with conflict in this relationship. This has been especially reported in parts of India, where incidents of abuse and death by bride burning over the issue of bride price have made global news. In Amanalco women in both older and younger generations realize that smooth integration into extended family life is not always possible but proudly stress that this is an important part of their culture that only meanness and bad personality could render broken.

In Amanalco the high levels of community endogamy combined with the expectation of frequent visiting and supportive interaction moderate the chances for serious domestic abuse. Circulating widely in Amanalco are cautionary tales about mistreatment flowing toward and from elders. Such narratives reinforce proper behavior but can also forecast what many see as a collapse of the system of respect and other the central tenets of their culture (see Chapter 10).

Campesinos, Elders, and College-Educated Youth

To me one of most interesting families is that connected to Alex Juarez. In Chapter 4 you were introduced to Alex, who lives in the large house compound called Tlaxomulco (next to the canal), halfway up the mountain road from the center of town. At age twenty-five in 2010, he was the youngest of seven siblings and often teased by them in Nahuatl as the *xocoyote*, the youngest son in a family. When I met him as an eighteen-year-old he was one of the few teens who were eager to speak in Nahuatl. Alex readily shared the knowledge passed down from his parents whom he lived with and his paternal grandparents who lived in an adjacent house compound. He also proudly talked about going to college, studying anthropology, and specializing in ecotourism. When he was not helping out at his married sister's small store downtown he would be assisting with agrarian tasks, especially up in mountain fields or grazing areas, places for which he expressed a particular love. Unlike Gordo's parents, in 2010 his were dedicated and highly competent campesinos nurturing a living from field, animals, and hearth and seemed to be a throwback to many adult couples I met in the 1970s.

As seen in Figure 7.6, Alex is one of three brothers. ⏄ The eldest, Salomé (aged forty-two), had gone to college in the state capital, Toluca, in a special

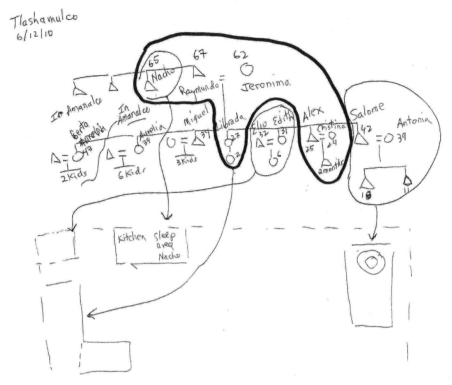

Figure 7.6   Kin chart for the house compound called Tlaxomulco, June 2010.

program for bilingual educators. It was there he met his wife, Antonia, also a student at the school. She had grown up in the eastern state of Veracruz in an area where many people also speak Nahuatl and now taught in a bilingual school in another nearby community. Salomé taught elementary school in Texcoco and was very involved with promoting bilingual education in the region. Pride in his indigenous heritage was shown in giving his two sons Nahuatl names after two famous Aztec rulers, Cuauhtémoc and Axayacatl.

In 2010, dropping down the dirt mountain road to Tlaxomulco, I always felt I was experiencing the last forty years of Amanalco's history compressed into one place, with a bit of the future thrown in. Toward the back of a large courtyard was a simple adobe and wood traditional kitchen and sleeping area. If Alex's mother, Jerónima, did not immediately come over to give a big hug to my wife and me, she would likely be at the stone hearth preparing tortillas and watching one or more grandchildren. Her husband, Raymundo, is likely to show up in campesino garb from work in his fields or feeding livestock. His younger brother, who everyone called "Nacho," had been single for all of his sixty-two years and lived simply in the back area of the kitchen. Nacho is likely to be found tending to the twenty or so sheep as he takes them out of their pen behind the kitchen and directs them up the mountain road to pasture.

My research assistant, Manuel, during his graduate fieldwork lived with Salomé and his family who reside in a very modern two-story brick, cement, and stone house complete with a hot shower, satellite TV, and wireless Internet. In 2010 many mornings I would sit talking with Salomé's oldest son, Cuauhtémoc, while we compared our netbooks, and he would tell me about his intention to go to university like his parents. He would use his netbook to do high school homework and swap e-mails with friends, while I sent my field notes from the previous day to a server at my university in Florida. This was a very busy household, with two boys (ages eighteen and eleven) and both parents working outside of Amanalco as teachers. Yet this tochantlaca provided a great deal of security with grandparents forty feet away and the families of great uncles just past a large garden plot behind the adobe kitchen.

Another building in Tlaxomulco is a one story L-shaped cement structure that houses in one leg living space for Raymundo and Jerónima as well as their twenty-seven-year-old daughter Librada, who has an infant daughter from a former relationship. The other end of the structure houses Alex and his new wife, Cristina, who is from another community. They were married during the prior year and now have a two-month-old baby boy. For the time being Alex's plans of being an anthropologist are on hold. A few years ago he was in a terrible car accident and was hospitalized for over a year. He eventually recovered, but he is now working in Texcoco in an appliance store. Finally, at this extended house compound is found a new small house built for Edith, one of Alex's sisters who is married to Elio, a man from Veracruz state. The couple had met in Mexico City, and when they got married and moved to Amanalco, it was he who began the new Veracruz-style seafood restaurant on the main road just before the center of town.

Music and Families

Guillermo Torres, whose research focused on teens in Amanalco, found that youth frequently talked about music in an idealized way as an occupational space they could imagine combining with some agrarian work (2008). Unlike bus drivers who are out of the community for much of the week and may stay out for two to three days at a stretch, musicians will practice with their groups a couple of times during the week in someone's house and try to have gigs during the weekends in the surrounding region. As noted in Chapter 5, some of the musicians have steady incomes from making or teaching music and might be employed playing in Mexico City in one of the varied military or police bands. A few have become well-known music teachers and even nationally known performers.

Successful musicians have gained substantial respect in the community, and two of the last three head delegados have supported their families in this occupation. One is a studio musician who was the first person in town to have an architect design his new house. The other, who was the community leader in 2010, plays in the National Navy Band. When I asked him how he learned to play, he said his father, who played in a fiesta band, took him to a performance when he was eight years old, gave him an instrument, and simply told him to play along.

Many of the performance groups such as Vientos del Cerro (Chapter 1) are formed from age peers in a local patrilineage and sometimes from siblings or close relatives. When band members start families the music in most cases must be combined with other economic pursuits such as agricultural work, making clothing, or having a small local store. Such was the case with the group Los Liberales, which you can see in this link from a performance from 2003 at a dance in the town of Chiconcuac. ▌◢

The core of this group is composed of four male siblings (ages twenty-seven to thirty-two) and a singer keyboard player who is the daughter of the eldest brother (see figure 7.7). ⌐P⌐ Their lone sister married into an extended family household on the same side of the community. Over time they have added other performers who are either cousins or neighborhood friends. When I met them in 2003 they lived in adjacent cement houses, all bearing the name *Tlalchichilpa* (red earth), while their mother and father lived by themselves in an adobe structure

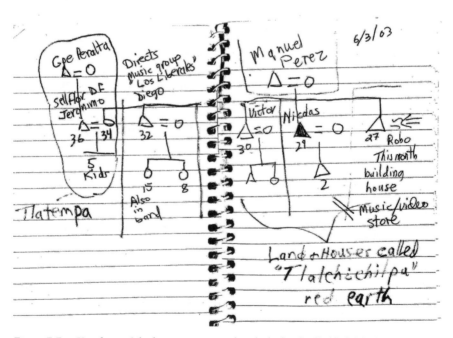

Figure 7.7   Kin chart of the lineage associated with the land called "Tlalchichilpa" (red earth), June 2003.

across the road. The brothers, although they seem to cherish their independence as adults, recognize that one of the children will eventually bring the parents into their household if they become infirm or if one becomes widowed.

The parents were self-identified campesinos in their mid-fifties who planted a modest amount of corn and, with sporadic help from their sons, also made money by making tables and other wood products from forest trees. The father in his younger years had also been part of a traditional fiesta band. His eldest son, Diego, the leader of Los Liberales, stressed that, unlike those of the older generation, his band played *musica de hoy*, (music of today): mambo, cha-cha, and, especially, *cumbia* dance music, which was their specialty.

All of the brothers were economically independent from the parents but shared the profits from their music and had cooperatively purchased a large truck to be able to perform widely in the region. One of the brothers and his wife run a small music CD and video DVD shop attached to his house. He is also trying to establish a videography business not only for documenting ritual events in Amanalco but also for taking video of the bands in the area. His other siblings earned extra money making clothes at home or selling flowers in urban markets. Three of the brothers were already married and had some children, and the youngest of the group was about to "rob" his girlfriend into a new house being built on the edge of their tochantlaca lands.

Marriage as a Nodal Point

Marriage and the expanded social connections it creates provide a window into the intertwining fabric of community life by which people order their adulthoods. It provides a central nodal point by which others fully recognize you as an adult in Amanalco's changing culture script. This is especially important for full participation in public religious life, which includes being asked *as a couple* to sponsor life course events of a child from another family. In this regard it is also interesting to learn that in the act of robo de esposa, at the moment Rosalba's parents accepted the basket from the boyfriend's uncles they also created a spiritual bond of kinship with the boy's parents. This meant that they would mutually be considered compadres.

The Special Nature of Mexican Godparenthood

Many people reading this book will have some sense of the idea of a godparent and likely have one themselves. However, unless you are of Hispanic heritage, it might be hard to fully comprehend the powerful system of godparenthood, referred to by scholars as *compadrazgo*, which is ubiquitous throughout Mexico and most of Latin America. Following the conquest of the Mexica early in the sixteenth-century, Spanish Franciscan friars, in the process of enforcing Christianity as the official religion of the land, imposed their idea of godparents upon an already existing indigenous system of ceremonial sponsorship. In addition to a child's baptism, the core of the European godparenthood system, they also introduced a set of other ritual relationships that marked Christian life-cycle rituals, including first Communion, Confirmation, marriage, and the blessing of the dead. Over time the Mexican compadrazgo system adapted to some of the cataclysmic changes following conquest. These included a radical loss in population and the banning of the large formal system of clans, called *calpulli*, that, through kin ties, had dominated the social, religious, and political life in Mexica communities. David Robichaux notes that in many areas of Mexico a common response was the devolution of large corporate kin institutions into systems of "attenuated descent," which often involved small localized patrilineal clusters of several contiguous domestic groups (2005). As such, the shift of godparent relations to the coparents (compadres) sought to add a bulwark of social capital to local kin systems that had been decimated in numbers and structure. This is especially seen in rural areas of Mexico where "fictive" kin, compadre relationships, are sought outside the network of those considered "regular" kin.

Michael Schnegg and Douglas White have suggested that in Mexico the godparenthood system became distinguished from its European roots in other essential ways (2008). First, the key focus on the child-godparent dyad in Catholic doctrine shifted more toward an emphasis on the compadre relationship—that is, between the parents and the godparents. Second, compadrazgo links were no longer dependent on ties engendered by the blessing of a child but could be also applied to other religious and secular events and even to objects, such as the building of a house or bridge. Although the individual or object that is the focus of this kind of sponsorship is essential for establishing the relationship, once the responsibility is accepted it is the compadre relationship itself that becomes most powerful in the long run.

In Amanalco the compadrazco system serves as one of the most important social mechanisms binding people together. In many ways it can be as strong and more compelling than some "real" kin ties, especially in garnering material support for a household. It is expected that padrino and compadre relationships are publicly recognized with the same hand-kissing gestures as regular kin and have the added strength of having been generated by religious vows.

As mentioned in Chapter 4, in accepting the role of padrinos, the main ritual sponsors of Rosalba's quinceañera, my wife and I were forever tied to all the other compadres connected to her parent's primary kin group and would have roles in future rituals for her. For example, at Rosalba's wedding we were given yet another ritual sponsorship, this time paying for the huge tent and electric generator needed during the Saturday night outdoor party. As quinceañeras and weddings have gradually become more elaborate and costly, in addition to the main sponsors of the event there will be added compadres of the cake, photography, video, and music.

Another significant aspect of individual adaptive responses to the pressure of a changing world has been in the selection of compadres. Prior to the mid-1950s compadres were sought almost exclusively from within Amanalco or occasionally from nearby villages in the mountain zone and lower piedmont region. Gradually people in the community began to seek such relationships with families in the urban areas, first in Chiconcuac or Texcoco and, more recently, in Mexico City. This has been especially true of men who wish to work extensively outside of the village and/or have political ambitions. In seeking compadres outside of the community one hopes to find a wealthy person, a store owner, the owner of a factory, or, better yet, a lawyer. In other words, this is someone who might be of some help in obtaining a loan, finding a job, or otherwise interacting with the world outside of Amanalco. In the 1970s about 10 percent of compadres were chosen from outside of Amanalco, and by 2010 this had doubled to about 20 percent of such relationships.

If anything, since my first stay in Amanalco it appears that the compadrazco system, especially in association with life-course ritual, has increased in importance. This has aided families as they cope with the shift away from a campesino lifestyle and the adoption of a multitude of ways to support a household. In this way, along with the concept of tochantlaca, it has been one of the adaptive kin-based responses to the globalizing economy. Godparenthood in many ways facilitates a synthesis of social function and religious meaning, which, along with marriage, propels people more fully into the cultural space of religion, which is the subject of the next chapter.

CHAPTER EIGHT

Ritual Drama, Religion, and Spiritual Spaces in Between

Figure 8.1   Performing the dance of the pastorelas, July 19, 1973. (Photo by Jay Sokolovsky)

July 19, 1973, 2 p.m.: I had just come from watching community leaders firing rockets in the air. These were directed at some dark clouds coming from the high mountains to the east. I asked an elder male standing next to me about this, and he said it was to drive away the ahuake, dwarf-like beings who reside in high mountain waterways and control hail and lightening. Now, standing in the cool doorway of this ancient church dedicated in 1609, I watch and photograph the picturesque "dance of the *pastorelas* [shepherds]," led by an elder male who lives in my neighborhood. Over the prior weeks I had been allowed to observe the practice sessions at his house, where a group ranging in age from five to about sixty practiced the music and dance steps of this passion play passed on by Catholic Franciscan missionaries in the mid-sixteenth century. Next to me is a visiting priest who has come from the parish center of another village to perform Mass. He is here because Amanalco does not yet have its own cleric. The priest has a disgusted look on his face as he whispers to me, "I don't know if we will ever get rid of these heathen practices."

Indigenous Mexico Engages the 21st Century, by Jay Sokolovsky, 137–148. © 2015 Left Coast Press, Inc. All rights reserved.

September 30, 2000, 5:30 a.m.: I was exhausted from the past four days of continuous fieldwork and dealing with back spasms from hauling around my video equipment. Somehow I slept through the midnight start of Amanalco's most important religious procession with its patron saint, San Jerónimo Doctor. This begins the most important day of the community's biggest fiesta, orchestrated by the lay spiritual stewards called *mayordomos* who are elected to carry on the cycle of Catholic sacred celebration for a particular year. The procession slowly carries the image of the patron saint from the church on paths winding throughout the high mountain reaches of the community and eventually returning to the starting point. Jolted awake by the loud music at 4 a.m., I quickly dressed, grabbed my video camera, and ran in the muddy ground to join the procession. The passage of several hundred people is syncopated with traditional marching music from a local band and prayers to the saint, stopping at the houses of each of the twenty-four fiesta mayordomos. The pace picks up in the final surge back toward the church in the predawn haze. After almost thirty years of connection to Amanalco, it is in such events that I really inch closer to understanding the full emotional experience of people's lives and the communal spiritual passion of fiestas. Nearing the plaza, we pass the carnival rides and site of an upcoming rodeo, new additions to the otherwise sacred activities. Later that day there is to be a High Mass led by Amanalco's resident priest and the bishop of Texcoco, who is here to rededicate the ancient church and celebrate the Catholic Jubilee year of 2000. ▇◢

Figure 8.2   Entrance to the 1609 church in preparation for the most important religious festival of the year, September 30, 2000. (Photo by Jay Sokolovsky)

Spiritual Ideas in Their Varied Layers

In these two sets of fieldnotes from 1973 and 2000 I try to present the multilay-ered nature of the public and more individual aspects of religious life and spiritual beliefs held by Amanalco's residents. At the ecclesiastical level involving priests and the world religion of Catholicism there is a clear devotion to the sacraments of the Church that sits uneasily with communal fiesta performances held outside of its walls. There is also the mention of the ahuakes, mysterious dwarf-sized magical beings who reside in mountain waterways. These beings are said not only to control hail and lightening but can also cause a powerful soul loss illness that is thought to kill people. One of the things that was significantly changing between 1973 the 2000s was a public downplaying of such magical beings and even the claim that they have lost their powers. Fuller discussion of the ahuake and other entities related to sorcery will be found in the next chapter.

The Folk Catholic Tradition in Mexico

My note above from 1973 captures a very perplexing time for me in trying to understand the religious life and spiritual spaces people in Amanalco experience. I had already heard some fabulous stories of the tiny ahuake, helpers of the Mexica water god Tlaloc. They were described as tiny handsome people who lived in water, dressed in elaborate, colorful clothing, and had awesome powers that they unleashed when they were angered. As the rockets were being shot skyward to ward off these beings, the community was also carrying out the elemental rituals of Catholicism, although it was in conjunction with the communal performance of the *pastorela* dance. I remember being initially shocked by the visiting priest's disdain, although it made sense to me based on outsiders' general prejudice di-rected toward Indios. Instead of responding, I remember thinking, *How much more traditionally Catholic can you get than a sixteenth-century passion play performance?*

Religious Pluralism

In some Mexican communities connected to Nahua heritage, such as in the northern Veracruz coast area, there have been very substantial conversions to Protestant evangelical religions over the past several decades (Dow and Sand-strom 2001). For example, in the Mexican community of Amatlán, by the 1990s, almost one-half of the population converted to several forms of Pentecostalism, creating serious internal conflict (Sandstrom and Sandstrom 2010). In Amanalco the abandonment of Catholicism has been less dramatic. When I arrived in 1972 the village had just ended a five-year period of intense internal conflict sparked by the conversion of ten families to Protestantism. According to oral histories with some of the Protestant families, the conversions began with a herbalist who in the late 1920s sold his wares in Mexico City and was converted there. Years later, in the early 1960s, a man from the textile-making town of Chiconcuac came to the village to help raise money to build a temple for the slowly growing group of Protestants in the area. This was really the spark that gave others encouragement to profess their divergent beliefs. The big problem was that Protestantism rejects the need for elaborate and costly fiesta rituals, and at first these families refused to pay the annual contribution all families were expected to pay toward these events. The delegados took a strong stand and threatened to cut off water rights and deny access to the cemetery to those who refused to contribute to the fiestas. This battle raged for a few years, but finally an agreement was reached whereby the Protestant households regained water rights. These families, though they refused to undertake any responsibilities as mayordomos, would pay the contributions that Catholic households paid for the fiestas. In 1973 the Protestant temple was under construction, and this aspect of religious pluralism was still a raw, delicate subject to discuss. However, by the end of that decade, when I asked Catholics about Amanalco's Protestant families, a typical reply was, "*Pues, todo está bien. Llaman a su Cristo de otra manera. Cada quien tiene derecho a su religion*"—Well, all is well. They are called to their Christ in their own way. Everyone has a right to their own religion.

Although in 2010 a new Jehovah's Witnesses temple opened along Amanalco's main road, over 80 percent of Amanalco's residents still follow their folk version of Roman Catholicism introduced by cadres of priests in the aftermath of the Spanish conquest in 1521.[1] As happened elsewhere in the course of colonial conquest, there emerged an almost seamless blending, what anthropologists call a syncretism, of varied traditions into a new set of sacred beliefs and practices. ◼️◀ The contemporary religious worlds that rural Mexican Catholics inhabit is a fused ceremonial landscape solidified in the second half of the sixteenth century (Stresser-Péan 2009). As noted in *Adoring the Saints* (Lastra, Sherzer, and Sherzer 2009), as early as 1585 images of saints and voluntary groups celebrating their power were part of the religious ritual throughout villages in Mexico. The emergent pattern of fiesta celebrations incorporated indigenous, pre-Hispanic traditions. These included the cleansing and perfuming of religious icons with copal incense (the incense of gods); music and singing; the eating of traditional foods such as maize, beans, squash and chili; and the construction of flower-adorned panels seen in the video about Amanalco's fiesta. Interestingly there was much indigenous overlap with colonial Spanish celebration of saints. For example, in the 1550s the Church hierarchy mandated that music, processions, and emblematic banners be part of the religious formula that were to motivate the local people to participate in the new religion being imposed on them.

In Amanalco the ritual cycle that exists today has some correspondence with pre-Hispanic patterns. Annual selection of the religious position holders for a given year begins on February 2, the starting date of the Mexica solar calendar. At this time the new religious cargo holders are nominated, and after election by a majority vote of Catholic residents, they begin their term of office. The new *fiscales* who will manage that year's ceremonial cycle receive from their predecessors symbols of this transition: each receives a candle, and one is passed a staff and the other the church keys. When I began fieldwork in 1972 this event was preceded on January 30 by the largest fiesta of the year celebrating Amanalco's patron saint, San Jerónimo. It was only after Amanalco gained the status of a parish center in 1988 and acquired its own priest that he pushed the community to shift the date to the standard Catholic celebration of Jerónimo's birth on September 30. The prior time of his celebration in January is now a period for a smaller feast of St. Joseph, with a special focus on blessing the harvest.

The procession viewed in Amanalco's fiesta video would feel familiar to people who have witnessed the ethnic Italian Feast of San Gennaro, held each year in older American cities like Boston and New York as a tribute to the patron saint of Naples, Italy. In this feast, like in Mexico, a local group of citizens responsible for the celebration joyously carries a large image of the saint around the boundaries of the community, led by local musicians. This is combined with a formal Mass in the parish church and public celebrations involving food and entertainment. 🔼

As other scholars have noted about Mexican religious festivals focused on saints, this kind of event is typically the strongest cultural element unifying rural campesino communities (Magazine 2012; Lastra, Sherzer, and Sherzer 2009). Although the idea of indigenous identity is very much a point of serious local contention in Amanalco, the enactment of such ritual and the varied activities associated with it are an almost universal source of pride and a positive emblem of community membership. As noted in the video mentioned above, the high point of the annual cycle of such celebrations is focused on the community's patron saint, and throughout rural Mexico this *fiesta patronal* "is the prime moment for recreating and reasserting communal identity" (Gross 2009, 9). The nature of fiestas is a critical aspect of Amanalco's ethnic identity and a powerful part of its ethnoscape.

Celebrating a Patron Saint

This largest of Amanalco's fiestas begins its final day with the procession of the figure of the saint Jerónimo. ▰ It includes ritual stops at the houses of the mayordomos for that year before the saint is returned back to the church just before dawn. As an outdoor breakfast is served to the faithful, a Mexico City–based mariachi band plays, having been paid by the Amanalco's new Association of Transport Workers. Later that morning there begins the first of two dance groups, the *Arrieros* (the mule drivers/handlers), dressed in white outfits with embroidered religious symbols, especially of the Virgin of Guadalupe. This female saint evokes a special meaning and dedication in Amanalco, as people claim that early in the twentieth century a miraculous image of the virgin appeared to a villager in a wooden box.

141

Slow and meticulous in their steps and music, this group of residents perform during the day in the sacred space closest to the church itself, and its members include people ranging from small children to adults in their sixth decade. The Arrieros' performance has remained one of the only fiesta dances in which there is still a high degree of multigenerational participation and elder males take on the role of performance teachers and participants. Today the dance of the pastorelas, depicted in the image at the top of this chapter, is no longer held. I was told that after the elder dance master died no one seemed interested in taking his place.

A second performance group seen in the patron saint fiesta video is the *Sembradores* (the seed planters). This dance group begins in front of the church after a Mass and moves to a more secular public space in the heart of the plaza where their music and dance dominate the night. The prior day the group visited about twenty houses around the community where they danced, gave the families fruit, and received soda in return. Just prior to their nighttime performance (but not seen in the video) there was a formal petition to Saint Isidro for a good harvest and a benediction by the priest. The loud, boisterous Sembradores' performance is the comedic drama of the masked *Huey, Huey,* the ancient overseer of colonial-era hacienda workers, and *Tia Maria* (Aunt Maria), the mistress of the owner of that land. When I played back the video of that drama for a group of women they all agreed that Maria, who is always played by a man, is depicted as the crazy "other women" of the hacienda owner, who, along with her cohort of young girls, seduces Huey, Huey just because she could.

Unlike the Arrieros dance, which is all about slow, meticulous dedication to work and sacred devotion, this second performance is more focused on entertainment. In the guise of signifying campesino labor, made visible through the rustic clothing some wear and the plastic oxen and plow, this dance is about comic relief and bringing enjoyment to a hard and sometimes boring agrarian existence. There is another element to note here: such performances developed during the colonial period as a way to subversively mock the Spanish overlords who came to have so much control over the native peoples' lives (Najera-Ramirez 1997).

You may also notice in the video that one of the lead sembradores dancers carries an attaché case in his hand. I was told that this had been recently added at the suggestion of performers who worked in the town of Chiconcuac and had spotted a similar effect in a fiesta there. In fact, the use of this symbolic object, juxtaposed within a quintessential celebration of campesino heritage, had become popular in other nearby rural communities. When I persisted—and probably annoyed people by asking for "the real" meaning of this performance—one elder said, "Yes, this is a grand comedy, it keeps the traditions alive, but it is not really to teach specific things to the children."

Quite evident in the fiesta video is the intense interplay of sacred activities with varied commercial and secular undertakings. You see my goddaughter, Rosalba, come back into Amanalco with a group of forty other youth who jointly were completing a two-day pilgrimage by truck and foot to northern Mexico City.

They had traveled to the Basilica of Our Lady of Guadalupe (the Virgin Mary) to show their devotion and to have an image of Saint Jerome blessed at this sacred national shrine. Adjacent to the church there are dozens of booths selling food and drink, making this an important money-making activity for residents and a few outsiders who, for example, rent space to sell rotisserie chicken. There is also a major rodeo just beyond the plaza, put on by Amanalco's rodeo club. This organization was begun in 1995 by a fifty-year-old male resident who saw this as a way to encourage youth to retain interest in at least some aspects of campesino life.

Besides carnival rides for children there is a dance starting around midnight for teens while adults carefully monitor the scene for fights breaking out between members of rival gangs. All those gaining entrance had a full-body search for weapons, especially knives. Fiestas blend times of joy, celebration, and the search for romance with an enhanced chance of physical conflict. Nighttime is especially a time of relative abandon and excessive alcohol consumption. Individuals who might be rivals or have long-simmering feuds might take the opportunity to settle a score. When I was talking to people about this issue while videotaping the night dance I was warned to be careful and told of a famous knife fight that had taken place the prior year between two older teens. One was killed, and his assailant fled the community and was thought to be hiding somewhere in the United States.

Sacred Performance, Public Recognition, and Reproducing a Transforming Community

As you recall from Chapter 5, a key part of the cultural script expected of adults adhering to the Catholic faith involves accepting a religious position (*cargo*). This supports the annual cycle of ritual and brings with it public recognition for individuals and their households. Of these roles, the lowest prestige is for two church bell ringers (*campaneros*) who take charge of the church's keys for opening and closing the building every day. As their title implies, their main task is ringing the steeple bell, alerting the community to religious services or special community meetings in the plaza. Next in esteem are four-person sets of stewards (*mayordomos*) focusing on carrying out fiestas and other church activities. The stewards and their families are also responsible for cleaning the churchyard and streets around it, maintaining fresh flowers in the church and for funerals, monitoring alms, and, most importantly, organizing religious festivals throughout the year. Their biggest expenses are for the fiestas, in paying and feeding the musicians and purchasing fireworks and candles.[2] The four-person sets of mayordomos are responsible for a specific fiesta and share the expenses. However, each week they collect small contributions from all households, called in Nahuatl *huentl* (party payment), which might come to an annual equivalent of $50 (see Table 8.1).[3]

In terms of authority and prestige, at the top of the local religious hierarchy are two managers (*fiscales*) of the religious cycle who also serve as assistants to the resident priest. Along with the priest, these managers coordinate the work of

143

Table 8.1   The Religious Hierarchy of *Cargos* in San Jerónimo Amanalco.

Administrative Areas of Amanalco	
San Francisco (Serrano)	Santo Domingo (Caliente)
Fiscal (1)—Manager	Fiscal (1)—Manager
Mayordomos (14)—Ritual Stewards	Mayordomos (14)—Ritual Stewards
Campanero (1)—Bell Ringer	Campanero (1)—Bell Ringer

the other community religious personnel in carrying out every Church-related celebration. The family of the fiscales, typically his wife and daughters, must also keep washed and ironed the priest's clothes and the linens used in Church ritual. There are other minor expenses related to the provision of food, but the big cost is time, in that most days the fiscales must be at the church for long periods.

As Roger Magazine argues in his recent analysis of fiestas, taking on support positions for sustaining this system is not a simple matter of "prestige" (2012). He suggests that it involves a process of transforming the socially marked status of different roles into a cultural form of social "recognition." Among men in Amanalco there can be a certain degree of competition for performing well in the higher-ranked cargos. For example, when I asked a man who had rejected a campesino lifestyle early in his adult life what religious cargos he would like, he declared, "I don't like the small ones like that of bell ringer. I don't like it. I like to have one of the major mayordomas or to become fiscal. I can have an expense for the community, where the band will play at my house, to invite all my friends to come and eat there. They will give me preference. The neighbors ask, Who has taken it? [The big cargos], let's go to his house. But who will say, Let's go the house of the bell ringer?"

There are several important things to notice here:

1. All of the types of religious positions are equally divided between the two administrative halves of Amanalco, San Francisco (Serrano) and Santo Domingo (Caliente); that is, each side has one fiscal; fourteen mayordomos, and one campanero (see this link for the parish organization).[4] P

2. Two of the mayordomo positions, sponsoring the September 30 patron saint fiesta and that of March 19 for San Jose, have more prestige and require somewhat greater outlay of expense to properly carry out the responsibilities of the role. This latter celebration focuses on the beginning of the agricultural cycle and involves the blessing of the corn that will be used in that year's planting.

3. There remains a close connection between the civil cargos and those that carry out public ritual. As we saw in the opening note, it was the delegados who organized the firing of rockets to discourage the ahuakes from sending down hail to disrupt the event. It is the head delegado who, in his three-year rule as *altepetatl* (father of the community), backs up the efforts of the

community's religious office holders to make sure people cooperate with the complex and costly ceremonial cycle.

4. Religious connection to saints is never just about fiestas but also involves pilgrimages to sacred places. The idea of pilgrimage travel to sacred sites in Mexico is very popular and attractive to many teens and young adults, and this is another form of group-based religious activity. Individual devotion groups or households travel by foot, bicycle, horse, family car, or bus caravan to such places as San Miguel del Milagro in Tlaxcala, Cholula in Puebla, or the Basilica of the Virgin Mary in Mexico City. These are all pre-Hispanic sacred areas upon which Catholic shrines had been constructed.

The Fiesta as a Mirror to Globalization

Since the 1990s the local religious cargo system has adapted to being a parish center with a permanent priest and competition from a variety of Protestant denominations. It has also been confronted by the dramatic economic changes that have involved a substantial number of residents, including women, working full time outside the community. Prior to this time the emphasis was on individual mayordomos and their immediate families taking on the sacred sponsorships, but now the costs are much more balanced, with contributions from the community.

This last point is crucial, as it has permitted the cultural rules of household and community ceremonial support to continue to function at a high level. What is not seen in the video are the behind-the-scenes activities that happened in the many dozens of houses of families and compadres connected to the persons who have taken on the sacred responsibility of religious cargos for the year. Here they are operating the exchange mechanisms of *nechpaleweco* (calculated reciprocal exchange labor) and *tequitl* (interdependent exchange of labor for the betterment of others). It is this second type of exchange that, when done properly, is not seen as acting individually, no matter how worthy the effort, but instead as leading groups of people to accomplish common goals that give recognition to individuals and merit to the community.

One of the things I examined in my earliest work in Amanalco was the relation of economic stratification to participation in the fiesta complex. At that time, in the early 1970s, most economic differentiation was made on the basis of agricultural holdings. Then, 40 percent of households had enough land to feed their families, and 56 percent lacked that amount; 4 percent were considered wealthy, and, of those households lacking sufficient land, 10 percent were considered very poor with little or no land. This was a time when mayordomos and their family networks undertook most of the ritual costs. I found that the community generally selected the households with the most resources to take the more expensive cargos and that in a few cases people had to borrow money to complete the cargo well. I was told that although some men had lost land and

Since 1995, with the changes in
financing fiestas, the economic burden for putting them on has become much
more dispersed among Catholic households. Moreover, since that time, with
the significant increase in population, there might be a two-decade gap between
when a household undertakes a major cargo.

In his book *Mary, Michael, and Lucifer: Folk Catholicism in Central Mexico*,
John Ingham sees the vital cultural role of the fiestas "as a folk elaboration of the
universal spiritual family" (1986, 5). He suggests that carrying out these communal rituals takes the broad model of "spiritual kinship" embedded in Mexican
godparenthood, and extends this notion to the community. Importantly for thinking of how such systems respond to globalization, Ingham rejects the view of the
fiesta system as necessarily being an impediment to change and development in
Indian communities; rather, he argues that economic investment opportunities
were severely restricted for such communities until the 1960s. This was certainly
the case for Amanalco, where even by the early 1970s transportation and communication infrastructure and local educational options were extremely limited.
As detailed in Chapters 2 and 3, it is the model of the moral religious landscape
that has enforced the collective work ethic that moved the community forward
in the past three decades. My fieldwork suggests that if a cultural institution like
the fiesta system does not become exploitive of the population and its resources,
it can be a vital tool for accomplishing common community goals. When this
is the case, fiesta systems can adapt to many aspects of globalization and make
a strong contribution in motivating people for the economic viability of communities (see especially Magazine 2012).

It is the spiritually tinged basis of community cooperation central to the fiesta
system that not only carries out basic infrastructure tasks but also accelerates the
early modernization changes in road, school, and health clinic construction, all
of which puts Amanalco squarely in the bull's eye of globalization. The spirit of
tequitl is certainly in effect for civic leadership roles and the community tasks of
regular communal labor. In the political realm, especially at the top level of first
delegado, enforcing the ideals of acting for others are very strongly felt but are
harder to accomplish as a consistent reality. Periodically I would hear of delegados
using their position to enrich themselves, especially by making side deals to sell
water. More recently there have been some administrations, especially in the last
ten years, who have simply not done the work they were elected to do and let the
community fend for itself. This was the explanation for the sad state of the public
square in 2010 so vividly contrasted against the enhanced appearance of the
church courtyard. I was told that the delegación building was almost constantly
closed during parts of 2008 and 2009 and that nothing got done. Fortunately
this had changed with the election of the new political leaders taking office in
2010, which included for the first time two very serious, hardworking women
who were determined to help Amanalco move forward.

146

It is important to note that women have also made inroads into the male-dominated realm of fiesta. It is the male who is elected mayordomo, is most publically visible in this role, and is recognized as the leader of the household that carries out the ritual for the community. However, his wife is referred to as the *mayordorma* (female steward), and besides doing much of the physical labor of the cargo, key decisions are made as a couple. Since 2002, however, there have been a small number of single women elected to minor religious cargos, and in 2008, at the major fiesta for San Jose on March 19, gender boundaries were further unsettled. At this event, for the first time an all-woman dance group burst onto the plaza performance area and upended this cultural space within which it was previously viewed as unseemly for women to dance by themselves in this public space and context.

Underlying the expressed enthusiasm for taking religious cargos and performing well is also a fear of harm by the saints if one does not meet their obligations *con gusto*—with heartfelt enthusiasm. I was told many times that people sought to act well with this responsibility so as to avoid sickness and maintain the health of their family. Manuel Moreno, during his recent research in Amanalco, was told that in the mid-2000s the residents thought the stewards of the Patron Saint fiesta were not acting with any indication of "gusto" in their duties (2010). The residents took this as a reason why one of the massive fireworks displays would not light and that a man involved with the installation of the pyrotechnics had died that day. It was said that this happened because the stewards did not work with "gusto."

Power of the Saints

In most houses you will see a family altar adorned with pictures of saints who serve as the intermediary between humans and god. Many such images have been purchased during one of the various pilgrimages people make throughout the year to sacred sites. Saints are thought to protect the faithful and help people with a wide range of problems. In 1998, when I was visiting an elderly neighbor in Amanalco, he and his adult daughter were showing me some of the images of saints adorning their altar and telling me about the last miracle one performed for the daughter's husband, whose horse had run off.

Jay: Yes, which ones are these on the altar?

Father: The Virgin of Guadalupe, Jesus's Sacred Heart, Saint Michael, St. Jose, St. Atocha...

Daughter: This is St. Anthony. This is St. Anthony, see.... This is the virgin of the altar. This is the holy child. Yes, yes. There are people, for example, some people say that the saints help them. Here, we have these saints because we consider that they all help us, watch over us, take care of the family.

Father: My daughter lost, I think... and one of these saints performed a small miracle...

147

Daughter: San Antonio. It was San Antonio.

Jay: And what happened?

Daughter: Last year we lost a black horse that Paco [daughter's husband] rides. That horse was lost. He was lost about fifteen days. And St. Antonio, we put him on his head. They tied him where the horse is tied. They tied the saint there and placed him on his head. Well, the horse was found all the way in the state of Puebla. But the horse appeared. And when they found him, they found the saint standing upright. They left the saint tied upside down and he righted himself! He turned on his own!

Magical powers of saints, especially those celebrated through fiestas, hold a special place in the spiritual beliefs and oral mythology traditions of Amanalco's residents. In the late 1990s, when I returned to the community, many elders were becoming leery of the rapid changes in their community and getting concerned that the younger generations were ignoring their knowledge about the world and that it would soon be lost. One such story involves the current name of the community and its religious patron, Saint Jerónimo, a canonized fourth-century priest from eastern Europe.

You have to record this well! There was a man who was clearing land along with his donkeys. Then his donkeys wandered off away from him. So he dropped his gathered wood to find them so he could carry his cargo to sell. Well, they never appeared. And an old man found them, he was our patron, Saint Jerónimo. The saint came upon him. And he asked him, "What are you looking for, good man?" And the man replied, "I'm looking for my donkeys. Have you seen them?" He said, "Yes. They're over there. They're eating well. I'm taking care of them. But I'm going to ask a favor of you. Go home and don't worry about the donkeys. Go to your house and bring a candle. When you get here, your donkeys will be fine." So this man left. He brought the candle and returned. When he arrived he found the donkeys at the clearing. That's where they were pasturing. So then he lit the candle, and the saint was standing on a rock, a very high rock. You can still see it, the one on which he stood. Then he told him, "Sir, here is what you asked of me." And he replied, "That's good. Thank you very much. Now, go and tell your townspeople that they should come for me. I want to go and live in your village. It doesn't have a name, does it?" He answered, "Yes, it does. The name is Amanalco." The saint replied, "All right, then. Don't worry. My name is Jerónimo. And if I go there to live, the town can be named San Jerónimo." And that's how it was. A lot of people from the town went, leaders and everything. And they brought him back. And that's when it became San Jerónimo Amanalco. Yes, and until now it's stayed that way, San Jerónimo Amanalco. That's how it went.

Although in many ways the campesino traditions of Amanalco imbue people with a down-to-earth sense of how to easily accomplish many practical things, the spiritual and magical aspects of such tales of lost animals reveals another level of Amanalco's culture. In the next chapter I explore this through discussion of mythology, magical beings, and indigenous health beliefs.

Chapter Nine

Magical Cosmology
Myth, Witches, Vampires, and Water Dwarfs

Figure 9.1   Interviewing Maria Juarez and receiving a newly made tortilla, 2010. (© Maria Vesperi)

June 18, 2010, 10 a.m.: I am in the house called Tlaxomulco, having just finished an interview with the elder Don Isidro regarding a shape-shifting witch, people call *tlahuelpuche*, and the belief about *xocoleros,* or Nahuatl for "twins." Xocoleros are thought to have opposite propensities: one will be a sorcerer who can magically give people boils on the skin, and the other will have the gift of healing the evil their sibling sends. I begin talking with Isidro's sister-in-law Jerónima Juarez, aged sixty-six, who was listening to the discussion. After first saying, "Well, some people say they don't believe in these things anymore," Maria assures me such things are very real and proceeds to remind me in a brief summary of her experience with water dwarfs known as the ahuake:

> When I was a young woman I was up in the mountains by a stream at about noon, and since it was hot, I washed my face in the water. A short time after that I became very weak, had a hard time seeing, and was very confused. I was grabbed by the ahuakes. Apparently a special healer, a *tesuktero,* was hired, who cleansed me and pleaded for the return of my soul from the little ones. Somehow I survived, but many die from this kind of bewitchment, even today.

As was learned in the last chapter, devotion to a saint is thought to offer the possibility of help for oneself and one's family, but failure to properly perform rituals in their honor with "gusto" can result in disaster, especially in unexpected accidents or unexplained health problems. This belief is universally and openly expressed in Amanalco not only from elder campesinos but also from university-educated teachers born in the community. Although centered in the world religion of Catholicism, ideas about the power of saints are a key part of a local cosmology, a set of beliefs that help people interpret and understand their known world.

The opening notes from 2010 address another aspect of that cosmology; it takes one into the realm of evil and culturally recognized beings who not only have the power of transformation but can also cause harm to individuals. Such ideas are part of a spiritual landscape that entails mythological stories involving magical powers, beliefs about transformation into animal familiars, and a notion that one's soul can be dislocated from the physical body, instigating various kinds of illnesses. The cultural space controlled by such beings as the ahuakes is centered in the mountain forest, a place of key resources, mystery, and danger. It is a zone where culture and nature are in a constant battle. As Jerónima reminded me, the everyday discussion of such beings has greatly diminished since my first days in Amanalco, but it is still part of how people think about the world. Powerful myths reinforce this state of affairs. Here we will first look at such myths as a link to pervasive notions of spiritual power, shape-shifting, and the realm of health.

Myth and the Transformed Indigenous Spiritual World

Some of the myths discussed here were not revealed to me until the 1990s, as people became more confident in my commitment to working with them to preserve their heritage. Also, over the past decade there has emerged a real fear among elders that the younger parental generation would not have the interest in passing this knowledge on. This has strongly motivated many community members to ask me to visually record and make accessible such knowledge for everyone in the community.

Alongside the public practice of Catholicism or Protestantism resides a trans-formed realm of indigenously inspired myth and a set of spiritual ideas connected to the action of cultural heroes, malevolent beings, and folk health beliefs. In the opening of Chapter 4 we learned about a myth detailing the magical birth from a bird egg, of the culture hero Nezahualcóyotl. With maturity he also assumes magical powers of impossible strength and rapid movement over space and time. He uses that ability to elude the Spanish conquerors trying to baptize him. Nezahualcóyotl was a real ruler of the kingdom centered in Texcoco. He died in 1472 and was likely involved with the establishment of Amanalco in the middle of that century. His reputation as a philosopher, architect, and poet come to us largely through the writings of his descendants Fernando de Alva Ixtlixóchitl and Juan Bautista Pomar, who both, after the Spanish conquest, became well-regarded bilingual writers and historians in sixteenth-century Mexico. Nezahualcóyotl is known as a historical figure throughout the nation, with his face on a 100 peso bill and a postage stamp (Ixtlixóchitl 1965; Pomar 1941). ⊕ However, for the people of the Texcoco region he is a central cultural icon of their heritage. In Amanalco his personage becomes a man-god whose exploits define their community's existence, strength, and resistance to outside forces.

To anthropologists myths are sacred narratives that reveal how things came into being and help people make sense of the world around them. These stories can involve tales of origin or explain specific historical events, cultural ideals, or behaviors. Mythology often involves supernatural happenings such as the transformation of one life form into another, factually incorrect compressions of historical periods, or plot elements of reprehensible behavior that involve violations of culturally normal behavior. It is important to realize that myths are typically handed down orally and that there will always be slightly different versions floating around in people's minds. For example, in the myth introduced at the beginning of Chapter 4 about the miraculous birth of Nezahualcóyotl, the narrator says that the Spanish wanted to baptize him, and he eluded them by supernatural movement around the landscape. In another version I was told that the parents wanted to baptize their miraculous boy, but just as the godparents came to the house, Nezahualcóyotl changed into a vulture and flew away and forever refused to be baptized. This particular myth is part of a larger origin tale for the community of Amanalco and linked to an indigenous ethnic identity. Recall, in the telling of the myth beginning Chapter 4, the speaker concludes, "This is the reason why I am sometimes considering myself from the original race of Nezahualcóyotl." The broader myth entails the origins of *AmanalKotla: ka,* or "Amanalcos people."

One version published by Valentín Peralta Ramirez, an Amanalco resident who gained a university degree in anthropology, recalls how it was told by his grandfather (1995). It recounts a series of competitions between beings known as *Achikoli* (Nezahualcóyotl) and *Temilo* (the devil), who fought to establish the known world and the people who would populate it. Achikoli prevailed in the first competition, which involved the movement of mountains on their backs. The devil moved Tetzcotzingo Mountain just a bit, and that is why today it is tilted (see Figure 9.2). The pair accepted a final bet to see who could most quickly build a cathedral and establish the cultural center for their people. Temilo began his work in the Mexican state of Puebla, and Achicoli asked his mother, the eagle, for advice. Told to roll on a hill, he turned into a snake and raised up to spy the perfect place in the lake sitting in the valley of Mexico. As the competition intensifies, Achikoli went up to mount Tlaloc and, from there, hurled giant stones to quickly build his temple. In the version from Peralta's grandfather, the myth concludes,

It was in the valley of Mexico where bells chimed. And thus the Achikoli won the world, and the Temilo did not believe it. He came to look and saw that he had lost. Why is the cathedral of Puebla incomplete? Because the devil built it, he who was

151

Figure 9.2   A view from Amanalco of the tilted sacred mountain of Tetzcotzingo with a remnant of the lake of Texcoco in the background, 2010. (Photo by Jay Sokolovsky)

the Temilo. And since Mexico first heard chiming of the bells, we are here, because the Achikoli won: he is our grandfather. And they say that the Achikoli was Nezahualcóyotl. (1995, 344)

Here we see a classic battle of good and evil, the transformation of life forms (Nezahualcóyotl to snake), super-human powers (ability to move mountains and hurl huge boulders), and the connection to sacred places (mount Tlaloc and Tetzcotzingo). Today residents point to visible signs of this myth in an area of immense stones on Tlaloc Mountain called "The footsteps of Nezahualcóyotl." Valentín Peralta, in his analysis of the myth, takes it both to represent the traditional notion of duality built into Mexica religious sensibility and to signify that for his community there are two nations that its residents are connected to: the political entity of the Mexican state and the realm of the *Nahauatlaca,* the Nahua peoples created in the mytho-historic past.

As found in many myths around the world, there is also some confounding of historic time. Nezahualcóyotl died almost a half-century before the Spanish entered central Mexico, yet the myth talks about the building of cathedrals. A glaring cultural contradiction also manifests itself. This revered culture hero refused to get baptized, a Christian sacrament that today in Amanalco is an essential act, beginning the passage into personhood. However, because this is a myth, its telling allows people to process contradictory ideas: while refusing to be a Catholic, Nezahualcóyotl is a miraculously created and transforming survivor providing a link to a heroic past.

As noted above, myths often have elements of transformation and can detail horrific happenings. These might violate a culture's central ideals but tell listeners something important about their existence. One such tale, "Pedro, Pedro, Petsintowian," tells a story of fratricide. It involves two young brothers, one about six or seven and the other a small toddler. The older brother began building a church with stone as his younger brother crawled nearby. They were left by themselves as their parents went to do some work. The older boy looked around, saw the red roof of the village church, and wondered, *How can I paint mine?* Finding a knife, he cut the sibling's throat and adorned his little church with the blood. The parents returned and were aghast at the scene. They could not kill their own son directly, so the father asked the child to accompany him with the family donkey up to the deep mountains. The son was told to wait for him and he will return. The father never came. As night closed in, the boy became scared and started calling, "Father, father!" It was intended that the coyotes would eat him for what he had done. The father never came but,

> Like we say here, "God helped him." The coyotes had started to arrive along with other animals of the mountain. They all wanted to eat him. In that moment the boy became . . . he transformed into a bird. He flew up atop a tree where the animals could not catch him. . . . So he became a bird. . . . That little bird that goes around singing, "Pedro, Pedro, petsintowian" [Pedro, Pedro, where have you gone?]. That little bird wanders around, but he always wanders alone. . . . It's like he's talking; "Ti, ti," then he starts to sing, "Pedro, Pedro, petsintowian," That is what the little bird says. That is the boy whose father left him in the middle of the forest, and I don't know how he became a little bird. God didn't want the other animals to eat him, so he became a bird. That is the story. (Interview with Juan Duran, Amanalco, 2003)

Clearly this myth is about transformation and shape-shifting after an evil act, brought on by the neglect of parents. Because the child is very young and still innocent, it was not God's plan that he be consumed by the forest animals. Yet the evil son is perpetually wandering as a small bird and singing to seek forgiveness from his father, calling, "Pedro, Pedro, where have you gone?" This myth is also about the inherent conflict between male siblings, as discussed in Chapter 4, and perhaps represents a never-to-be-fulfilled wish of totally controlling the life of the younger brother. The potential antipathy between older and younger brothers is very real in family dynamics and a source of unspoken tension in many of the households with which I am familiar.

In another way certain kinds of siblings are connected to another potential evil, sorcery. It is said that when twins are born one of them will be a minor sorcerer, called a *xoxolero*, who causes boils (*xoxol*) to erupt on the skin, whereas the other will be able to cure it. It is said that the affliction of xoxol is connected to extreme jealousy, and, as we will see, varied perceptions of sorcery are strongly connected to undo envy.

Shape-Shifting, Soul Loss, and Things That Once Glowed Bright in the Night

Mention of xoxoleros brings one into the realm of sorcery, harmful magic, and spiritually caused illness. I eventually learned the need to be very circumspect in any inquiry about sorcery and types of beings that practice witchcraft. Sorcery, witchcraft, and magic have been common subjects of anthropology. In the most general sense these terms involve ideas that are used to account for misfortune within a community. As Caple (2012) notes in talking about the continuity of such beliefs in Haiti, they refer to persons who channel potent occult forces to cause harm to others but sometimes also work to counter such actions or to determine whether misfortune is tied to supernatural activities.

During the first year in Amanalco I acquired some of the basic information distinguishing *naguals/tlahuelpueches* (blood-sucking vampires), *tetlachiwes* (witches), and ahuakes (water-controlling dwarfs). Deeper knowledge would only slowly be revealed. Throughout indigenous cultures of the Americas and many other regions there is a common belief that there are animal doubles or familiars in the environment, and under certain conditions humans can shape-shift, changing into their nonhuman animal form (Knab 2009). In many parts of Mexico the Nahuatl term *naguale* refers to this capability of magical body change into an animal form. It is also usually associated with humans who have very evil intent and are the cause of great fear. The first modern study of this phenomenon in Mexico was done by Daniel Brinton (1896) during his late-nineteenth-century research. ⊕ He noted the continuity with colonial sources, which, shortly after the sixteenth-century Spanish conquest, mention the *naualli*, a frightening person who sucks the blood of children at night. As in this early account, twentieth- and twenty-first-century ethnographies describe a wide variety of animal familiars such as owls, turkeys, cats, mountain lions, or dogs (Galinier 2004; Nutini and Roberts 1993). In Amanalco both the nagual/tlahuelpueche and the tetlachiwe are thought to be capable of shape-shifting their bodily forms to move through the landscape as turkeys, cats, or the feared *huey mistli*—the seldom-seen mountain lion.

Early on I was told to be concerned about *shushali*, the bite of the tetlachiwe that might be noticed when you awoke to see unusual welts on your arm or chest that could be the precursor of bad illness and even death. This unnerved me enough that whenever I was not feeling well I examined my skin with a special interest and concern. Yet I was told that the real problem with tetlachiwes was either their disease-causing breath (*ounechilpitz*) or their construction of small dolls. Like the more famous instance of "voodoo" dolls, using what anthropologists refer to as "contagious magic," in Amanalco they are made from the hair or old clothes of the victim.[1] These objects will be stuck through with cactus needles and metal nails and then buried in the cemetery. I was told that the victim will feel sharp inexplicable pains in their body, and if the doll is not found and removed from the cemetery, the person is expected to die.[2]

In Amanalco, of the two basic kinds of sorcerers, it is the vampire-like nagual/tlahuelpuche who traditionally evoked the most fear and concern. The following is an excerpt from an interview I did in 2006 with a father and his adult son listening and commenting as well:

Jay: Do you know about naguals?

Father: Yes, they suck blood. They're like vampires.

Jay: Can the naguals change into another shape?

Father: Yes. They can change into a cat, into a turkey, and into a crow.

Jay: What do the naguals do?

Father: They suck blood.

Jay: Where? What part of the body?]

Father: Here [shows me], on the neck.

Jay: What happens when they suck a person's blood?

Father: When one's strong, nothing happens, but if one's weak, then one gets sick. A bad, bad illness we call *Kokolistri* in Mexicano.

Jay: Are there still naguals here?

Father: Yes. But they're not seen like before. Because there's [electric] light and all this ... [pointing to his eldest son's modern house].

Jay: Is the tlahuelpuche the same as a nagual?

Son: [interjects to continue to discussion] They are very similar, but the nagual only sucks blood, while the tlahuelpuche can also bewitch you. Both of them are associated with evil. But their actions are particularly evil. They steal children. . . . See, they don't eat food like we do. They need blood or human flesh. They change their identities, and when they fly they light themselves on fire. They become fire balls and move from side to side as they transform. If one sees them, one is horrified.

It is interesting to note that these persons are among the very few Amanalcanos who would talk about the concept of the nagual. Everyone else either fearfully changed the subject or merged the idea of a blood-sucking vampire into the shape-shifting tlahuelpuche. These beings were most typically thought to be women who could turn themselves into another life form such as a cat or large type of turkey, enter a house quietly at night, and attack people, especially small children to suck their blood.[3] As documented in a variety of sources such as the book *Blood-Sucking Witchcraft* (Nutini and Roberts 1993), this is a widespread belief in central Mexico's indigenous communities (see also Galinier 2004).

Over the years I have been told a number of stories about the shape-shifting tlahuelpuche. One typical case involved a woman who saw a strange-looking cat enter her house late at night. She suspected the feline was a vampire creature in disguise and killed it. The next day she heard that a local woman who was suspected of being a tlahuelpuche had also died that very same night. In 2010 I heard a variant of a tale other anthropologists have described in both Nahua and Otomi ethnic communities elsewhere in Mexico. Such stories involve female tlahuelpuches who could detach their human legs, put on substitute turkey limbs, and transform into that animal. They would then magically fly through the night seeking the blood of young infants (Galinier 2004). The story I was told involved a married couple, where the husband woke up in the middle of the night to find his wife gone but her legs were there in the bed. He was so frightened that he threw her legs in the fire and went back to sleep. Later that night, when the wife returned on her turkey legs, she found that her now-charred human legs would no longer fit. Forever after she could be seen going around in a wooden box without her legs.[4]

The idea of shape-shifting being associated with spiritual power, healing, and sorcery is widely found in many parts of the world. In her study of contemporary Haiti following the devastation of the 2010 earthquake, Erica Caple found a continuing belief in the vampire-like *lougawou*. These beings are largely females who can transform into a disembodied force to eat and suck the souls and blood, especially of children (2012). Similarly, in West Africa, among the Igbo peoples of Nigeria, persons known as a certain kind of shape-shifter are represented by a mask called *Ochoko* depicted as a sleeping human visage below a figure of a bird in flight. ▆ When moving around in a shape-shifted form they might travel to another region to seek knowledge, acquire healing medicinals, or magically attack individuals. Interestingly, as I found in Amanalco, it is said that when such an Igbo shape-shifter travels as a bird they can sometimes be perceived as a ball of light (2012, personal communication, Oscar Mokeme).[5]

As with the local ideas about health, illness, and curing (discussed below) there has been a great deal written about the historical roots of such things in contemporary Mexico. Edgar del Campo, in an article titled "The Global Making of a Mexican Vampire" (2009), makes the point that European and African ideas about witchcraft and vampire-like creatures entered public discourse after the Spanish conquest and the importation of slaves into the New World; however, such beliefs intersected with similar ideas already powerfully present among indigenous populations. Like the *Chupacabra* phenomena in Puerto Rico, Campo also shows how highly globalized media in the late twentieth century have affected the public perception and representation of Mexican vampires (see Radford 2011 for discussion of Chupacabras).

Dangerous Dwarfs and the World of Water

Perhaps the most intriguing of the beings in Amanalco's cosmological universe are the *ahuakes*, who are also more recently talked about in Spanish as *duendes*, or "owners" of the water sources.[6] Some of the most specific descriptions about these entities and the healers who deal with them came from Alex Juarez and his parents. While he was a teenager, Alex told me,

> Here in San Jerónimo legends are told about some elves who take care of water. They are in charge of dividing water among all of the communities. But if someone interrupts them in the days when the ahuakes rest, they can punish them by grabbing

their soul. And until they receive a proper offering, they do not return that person's soul. It has been said that the person who commands them is the god Tlaloc. He is a prince of the water. And nearby here is the mountain called Tlaloc, where many people go there to leave offerings.

The ahuakes are reported in the pre-Hispanic literature as those killed under the command of the god Tlaloc, whose function not only was to provide rain but could also throw lightning and damage crops with destructive storms and hail (Lorente 2010). A classic description of being "grabbed by the ahuakes" was told to me in detail by Alex's mother, Jerónima Juarez, in 2003. She claimed it had happened in the late 1970s and, as in so many other cases, involved washing in a mountain stream and gathering buckets of water at midday. When she got home and walked to the front of the house to get firewood she felt something strange:

Jerónima: I got back here [to her house], and it seems that one of them grabbed me like this [makes turning motion with body]. I made a complete turn and I fell over there. I fell, and then I didn't know where I was. After I fell I'm told that I was doing many strange things [she wildly waves her hands]. I went crazy in an ugly way. After that was over I was left in a deep sleep. They had taken my heart above, I think, up there with my spirit. And I'm just lying there, only a body, and they had taken my spirit! When I awoke they had brought me back. They returned me. How well I saw it all!

Jay: What did the gnomes look like?

Jerónima: But they were so pretty! So little! Very small, but very shiny. They took me in their fruit orchard, and later a very pretty granny came. She was very small, and she hit me very hard like this [chopping hand motion]. That's why I fell down. And they . . . I could no longer see! I fell asleep. . . . When they woke me up I complained from the pain. My body is a ruin. Keep in mind I'm separated from my body. I'm no longer from here. And every time they take me for a ride. . . . Then they started to play music like this [mimics playing a violin] and to dance. In my deepest dream I saw them. . . . And when they take my heart I feel good because they take me traveling with them.

Jay: Are the gnomes both men and women?

Jerónima: Men and women. They're even pretty. . . . That's how they look. Women and men playing their tiny violins. Dancing too, very nicely. A knowledgeable man who was called Don Isidro healed me.

Jay: What did he do?

Jerónima: They cleansed me. They told me the gnomes had gotten me. That they had taken me on a trip but that he hadn't let them take me. If they had taken me, I wouldn't be here now. I would have died. He healed me with a lot of medicines, including turkey eggs. . . . And he said I was to buy some miniature dishes; because when I stepped into the water I broke the gnomes' plates that were set on their table as they were eating. It was one in the afternoon, and I ruined their meal. I had done mischief when I splashed the water washing my feet. . . . The man who healed me sent me some very shiny miniature dishes, which were to be left on the spot where the gnomes got me.

Jay: You are lucky, then, because some people die from this, right?

Jerónima: If they were to get me again, I would die, but they can no longer attack me. I dream about them traveling, but they can no longer attack me because I'm cured. It's no longer allowed for them to mess with me! Ha! Ha!

The Realm of the Ahuake and Its Consequences

According to their descriptions in Amanalco the ahuake are very small—about one or two feet high. When observed they are typically described in Spanish as *muy guapa* (very attractive) and are dressed in elaborate, colorful *charro* outfits, associated with rustic folkloric performances. As related in Jerónima's testimony, they are most often seen in dreams after one is spiritually "grabbed." Of the fifteen people I have interviewed who have claimed to have had some interaction with the ahuake, only three claimed to have seen them in a conscious state. When I challenged them, saying other people only viewed them in dreams, each of these persons was adamant in stating that they were not asleep when they saw these water dwarfs. People commonly talk about having seen the ahuake eating meals on tiny dishes, twirling lariats, playing the violin, and dancing. People say they have an entire home in the water, with furniture and other household items. Curiously, it is thought only possible to see them between the hours of noon and 2 p.m. If you disturb them or do not talk to them correctly, they can get mad and attack you, sending lightening or hail to show their displeasure and/or bewitch you.

In testimony about being attacked by the ahuake people report severe weakness, inability to stand, feeling very cold, and loss of consciousness for a short period, and then when people awake, they are not themselves. In half the cases I recorded, persons describe a strong dissociative state that might involve having severe short-term memory loss and even not knowing one's identity. As in the case of Jerónima, it is not uncommon to have a perception of being struck on the body. Males especially claim that such strikes can disfigure a person's face, moving the jaw permanently off-center. Ahuakes are thought capable of not only directing damaging hail and rain on specific fields but also sending lightning strikes against people who anger them. In an interview with a man about such an attack directed at his male cousin, he claimed that his relative stumbled to his house with charred clothing, briefly describing an encounter with the ahuake, and then collapsed after displaying singed hair and a circular burn on his stomach.

To counter the ahuakes there existed in the community a secretive group of healer/sorcerers known as *tesuewkteros* in Nahuatl, or *graniseros* in Spanish. Their reputed occult abilities were directed in two directions. One was to protect individuals or the community from harmful rain or hail storms, and the other was to attempt a cure of persons grabbed by the ahuake. I was told that these individuals had the ability to talk to the water dwarfs and learn what was required to restore the afflicted to normal health. As noted in Jerónima's interview, one of these healers ritually cleansed her and also placed a set of special small dishes in the waterway where she was grabbed. In other cases healers would have to trek five hours to the top of mount Tlaloc with such offerings in addition to special fruits and flowers. Here they would beseech the ahuakes to return the soul of the person they had grabbed. 🔼

Spiritual Illness, Soul Loss, and Its Cures

A great deal has been written about core "folk" illnesses, or what have been generally called "culture-bound syndromes" in Mexico and within Hispanic migrant communities to North America (Bayles and Katerndahl 2009; Rubel, O'Nell, and Collado-Ardon 1991). They are called "culture-bound" because the symptoms and health response are very specific to a cultural zone of the world. Today in Amanalco most people understand some basics about diseases such as diabetes or cancer, yet they find it hard to fully believe that such illnesses lie fully in the realm of Western "medicine" and are only to be treated in the local clinic or hospital by a doctor. There are also a set of maladies that people think of as "spiritual" and are *only* amenable to cure by a traditional healer.

Aigre and Susto: Evil Winds and Dislocating Shocks

As noted in the interview materials from Alex and his mother about being attacked by the ahuakes, such an affliction involves at its root a disturbance or even loss of one's spirit or soul essence. In Amanalco soul dislocation can be caused by a variety of causes. One is the perception that evil "winds" produce a disease called *aigre* (literally, air) in Spanish, and *iyeyecatl* in Nahuatl. The most commonly perceived causes of aigre are from the breath of a witch (*tetlachiwe*) or being captured by a water dwarf near the mountain springs. In the case of being afflicted by the ahuakes, this enables spirits of the dead that cling to a person causing extreme tiredness and disorientation. A particular kind of aigre can target young children via the gaze of an evil eye directed by powerful, envious individuals. Figure 9.3 depicts a typical kind of amulet worn by children, typically under two years old, to ward off this kind of attack. 🅿

The general symptoms of aigre include trouble eating, throwing up, and feeling very week and nauseated. The general cure for this is multiple spiritual cleansings with herbs such as a leaf from the Perul tree and a week's treatment with medicinal teas. The cleansings involve rubbing the leaves along the body to draw out the evil, and these herbs are then tied up and buried in a deep ravine.

The other major form of soul dislocation is caused by some kind of fright and in Spanish is called either *espanto* or *susto* and is known in Nahuatl as *moumo(w)*

159

Figure 9.3   Notice the amulet around the neck of the young child in the middle, Amanalco, 1993. It is worn by young children to ward off the evil eye. The use of these was much less common in 2010 than in the 1990s. (Photo by Jay Sokolovsky)

ti—literally "he is frightened." It can occur through a series of horrifying dreams or having seen or experienced a severe accident. It particularly afflicts children, and parents tell me that the symptoms involve great agitation in sleep with sudden sharp movement, unexplained crying, loss of appetite, and a depressed mood. Interesting enough, across a diverse span of human cultures some form of "fright" illness is locally defined, such as *kesambet* in Bali, *narahati* in Iran, or *ceeb* among the Hmong people of southeast Asia (Quinlan 2010).[7]

Within Mexico and among Mexican immigrants in North America, various studies of susto have shown an interaction with stress, depression, and other underlying clinical illness (Glazer et al. 2004; Weller et al. 2008). A long-term study across three Mexican communities examined a matched sample of one hundred individuals, with one-half locally diagnosed as having susto (Rubel and Moore 2001). Using a stress scale and medical exam data, the authors followed this cohort over seven years and found that the susto group not only had more stress and clinical signs of disease but also substantially higher mortality.

Although 17 percent of the susto sample had died at the end of seven years, all of the comparison group were still alive.

Healing, Health Practices, and the Persistence of Belief

In the local etiology of susto as an illness, it is the shock that dislocates the soul and opens up a space for the spirit of a dead person to move into the body and reduce one's vitality. As with aigre, the most typical healing begins with calming herbal teas and a ritual cleaning with herbs and, occasionally, whole eggs. If this is not successful, the family may take the victim to an individual spiritual healer or one of the four small spiritual healing temples, where a séance may reveal the spirit inhabiting the patient's body. ◼◀

There still exists a wide variety of traditional healers in Amanalco known generically in Nahuatl as *tepatike* (*curandero/a* in Spanish). Typically each practitioner is known for a variety of specialties, which might include herbal medicine, bone setting, massage, or spiritual healing. A majority of tepatike are also midwives, and besides delivering babies, virtually all of them also practice at least one other medical tradition just mentioned. ⬆ These females range in age from the mid-forties through the mid-seventies. Since 2000, however, their role in baby delivery has greatly diminished, as the national health system has expanded rural programs and encouraged woman to give birth either in the local clinic or in Texcoco's hospital. This has intensified since 2005, as it became very difficult to get a formal identity card for newborns birthed outside of formal medical settings.

The Witches Are Dead, Long Live Witchcraft

By the mid-1990s almost universally people would say to me that, compared to my first residence in Amanalco, the action of supernatural beings, be they tetlachiwes, tlahuelpuches, or ahuakes, had greatly diminished; some even claimed they no longer existed in the community. Certainly, from a public perspective, within the first few years of the twenty-first century the delegados were hearing only one to two cases every three years, versus five to ten cases a year in the 1970s. In 1973, while talking about witchcraft with one of my cultural interlocutors, he casually said, "You know, when we see a poor relative coming down the street we think, 'Here comes a witch.'" This perception fits well with classic studies of witchcraft and sorcery in anthropology suggesting that such actions "emerge from tensions between members of kin or closely related social groups—especially in conflicts over land, commodities, or other material resources" (Caple 2012, 50, see also Geschiere 2012).[8] We have seen that one of the notable things about the kinds of changes discussed throughout the book has been the explosion of economic diversity in the community and within large extended households. With the rapid abandonment of a campesino life course and supporting families through working the land, there has been a reduction in very direct competition between siblings and cousins over this resource. Suspicion and envy still persists at a significant level but are more directly tied to the acquiring and display of material resources.

In fact, there is still a profound persistence in beliefs about spiritual illness and the possibility of sorcery. This continues despite having a physician and medical clinic in the community since the 1980s and dramatic reductions in child and general mortality. In interviewing the physicians serving Amanalco over the years, they tell a consistent story of residents coming in to see them very late in the process of serious illness or only after visiting a traditional healer. During a 2006 interview with a doctor about his time working in Amanalco he told me,

> Belief in sorcery is hard to break. For example, one of my patients had testicular cancer, and half of his testicle was destroyed. His wife said that he'd been bewitched. But I told them, "This isn't an enchantment! This is either cancer . . ." I sent him to the general hospital in Mexico City, exactly where I'm working now. After a couple of months he died. The man never went to the hospital. Everyone agreed with the wife that he had been bewitched. Having compadres in Amanalco, I visit often and can tell you that these beliefs persist.

The Light of Globalization

As has been well documented in other parts Mexico, indigenous beliefs about magical illness causation can persist alongside access to Western medicine. For example, a multi-decade project in the state of Michoacán found that irrespective of the wide availability and use of biomedical clinics and economic shifts even more dramatic than in Amanalco, folk-medical knowledge and beliefs "remained largely unchanged with respect to its distribution and content. . . . It is the medical models of clinic personnel that stand out as odd within the community" (Ross, Timura, and Maupin 2012). In other words, there is no simple replacement of folk health beliefs with the exposure to Western biomedical practitioners and concepts, and this applies both to Mexican urban populations and to ethnic communities in the United States (Whiteford 1999).

In Amanalco persistence of belief about illnesses such as susto and aigre and their cures are centered around the perceived permeability between corporal and spiritual states of being. One of the most interesting connections of this idea to magical entities such as ahuake is the shared understanding that when they travel, they transform into balls of light. I was also told that one of the small hills on the northern edge of the village was nicknamed "Ahuake Mountain." It is here that the water dwarfs hang out at night and can be noticed by red lights they give off; this contrasts with the white lights emitted by tetlachiwe and the green lights associated with the Tlahuelpuche. In 2010, when I asked about the decline of such beings within the residential zone, the consistent answer I received was that in these more modern times, with electricity and house lights everywhere, those entities are scared away from these areas.

Yet as people told me this, their body language and facial expression would communicate the ambivalence that many have toward the dramatic changes experienced over the past forty years. As we move to the concluding chapter I will look at these transformations and how they are playing out since I was last in Amanalco.

CHAPTER TEN

Conclusions: The Varied Meanings of "Never More Campesinos"

With the Assistance of Manuel Moreno

Diary, May 15, 1989: On clear nights toward the end of the winter in 1973 I would sometimes sit on a flat rooftop with a small group of five to six older teen boys and watch from Amanalco the twinkling lights of Mexico City. They talked bravely about wanting to venture into the city to work in markets, sell the flowers and wooden boxes their families were producing, and perhaps taste the many pleasures of this exciting urban zone. In the next breath, however, they would lament that their life was meant to be the dull life of a campesino and firmly tied forever to the soil of their village. They knew their fathers and grandfathers had lethally defended their soil, forest, and water against anyone and were in the process of passing on this determination and fierceness to them. In those early months of my fieldwork and first residence in this community I had but a bare glimpse what the globalizing future held for these boys and their yet-to-be-born children who I was now getting to meet in this recent visit.

E-mail from a bilingual educator from Amanalco, June 12, 2011: Well, it does not seem that the Nahuatl cultural center will be funded soon, if ever, but heard that there will be improvements to the plaza and the road to the *colonia* [original in Spanish].

E-mail from a college student in Amanalco, June 18, 2011: Regarding the organization *Amanalco Pilhuame Ollin,* which I was part of as I went to school with most of the members. Unfortunately the group disintegrated this year from reasons of work, school, and other activities of community life [original in Spanish].

E-News item from the Texcoco Region. October 5, 2012: In a working trip to Texcoco, Municipal President Arturo Martinez Alfaro presided in the inauguration of a public plaza in the community of San Jerónimo Amanalco. It is part of the "Rescue Texcoco" program, which consists of the construction and renovation of public spaces in the different communities of the municipality.

Telephone notes from Mexican anthropologist Manuel Moreno, April 10, 2013: Manuel talked this week in Amanalco with Miguel Osorio. He was recently elected second delegado, although he had a very troubled youth involving

Figure 10.1   The new central plaza in Amanalco, March 10, 2013. (© Manuel Moreno)

addiction. He is twenty-seven years old and claims to be interested in both pre-serving heritage like weaving of *ixtle* as well as moving people ahead. Over the past three years he developed a new cultural group called *Miyotl* [Nahuatl for "rays of sun"]. The group has space in the delegación by the plaza, and somehow ten teachers without pay come here to give free classes in things like English, guitar, hair cutting, taekwondo, and exercising for the elders!

Even in the early 1970s the families of the teens mentioned in my 1989 diary entry were connected to the outside world. They had market and administrative interaction in urban areas like Texcoco and Mexico City and had strong trading relations with the textile town of Chiconcuac. Yet their economic and cultural existence was highly circumscribed by both the weak village infrastructure and the indigenous customs perniciously marking them to outsiders as Indios. Back then this outside interaction was used and viewed essentially as a means to sustain their local economic and cultural life and not as a means to a whole different way of life. Even before the end of the 1970s, while the various forms of what were then still called Indio behavior were outwardly holding strong, the rapid monetization of the economy had begun a transit to the globalized future described elsewhere in this book.

As noted in the shaded area above, I have been trying to keep up with what is happening in Amanalco via e-mail, reading Mexican web-based news, phone calls, and a visit to the community in 2013–2014 by anthropologist Manuel Moreno, who worked with me in 2010. These varied sources of information from Amanalco reflect my interest in exploring interrelated themes discussed throughout this book, which revolve around youth rejecting a dominant cultural script tying them to the land and the complex meaning of the phrase "Never more campesinos." In this brief concluding chapter I will draw upon my most recent encounters with Amanalco, both face-to-face and virtually, to reflect on (1) how the transformations of cultural scripts and spaces is producing a new narrative of generational abandonment expressed by the older generation, (2) the varied impact of globalization, and (3) the degree to which traditional culture and the community's ethnoscape can adapt to ongoing change. In the sections that follow I will explore how these issues connect to the varied meanings of "Never more campesinos."

"Never More Campesinos" Means Transformed Cultural Scripts, Generations, and Genders in Altered Cultural Spaces

A central part of this book has discussed the transforming cultural script of campesinos in new cultural spaces and the centrality of concept of tochantlaca, the core kin networks tying people to a set of named house compounds. In Chapter 5 I laid out the scope of the campesino life course and the cultural script it was ideally to follow in 1972. During succeeding decades, as substantial numbers of young adults began seeking full-time wage employment outside of Amanalco, this shift in both script and the cultural space of work transformed feelings about working the land and personal identity. From the twenty-first-century perspective of the young, especially males, campesino life is most commonly viewed as a recreational activity, including horse riding, rodeo activities, trips up the mountain, or part-time commercial activity when nothing else much is happening.

One aspect of this in Amanalco was the differing generational responses to the demise of the campesino life course. I would hear youth disparage elders as clinging to a lost world with little value and that the older generation did not appreciate how they, the young, were the ones who *really* understood the present. They would mockingly comment that elders say the young do not work and just take drugs. The youth would counter this by saying, "Well, here in the village there are two groups of older men, nicknamed 'squadrons of the dead,' who are drinking themselves into an early grave."

From the other side of the life course there was an even louder counternarrative. What began in whispered comments during the 1990s became a conversational shout into my ears in the twenty-first century. This was heard in bitter complaints by older adults:

"These young are really bad at working but really good at getting drunk." Interview with seventy-two-year-old male, September 30, 2000.

167

And, more reflectively: "Us elders had a different life, different work. Now the younger people with just a little bit of training or education, they say, 'Nah, the older people don't know how to do things and we know better.' And it's like they exaggerate. They say that old people aren't worth anything anymore. . . . The thing is, they say that what the older people say and think has no value anymore." Interview with sixty-six-year-old male, May 20, 2003.

"I get really angry when my son tells me directly to stop talking to him in Nahuatl. He says this is a thing of the past." Interview with sixty-year-old female, June 15, 2010.

"The youth have forgotten everything. They are all about graffiti, drugs, and robbing." Interview with seventy-year-old male, June 13, 2010.

What I encountered and observed "on the ground" was much more complex than these common expressions of generational angst that others have recorded under similar kinds of community transformations (Rosenberg 2009). Even the hardest-working youth and young adults will complain about the difficulty of their matching elders' agrarian lifestyle. Behind such statements is also the realization, by *both* generations, that to now support a family with the contemporary needs of children one must produce a constant flow of money. In a video clip 🎥 listen to the dialog between a father and his son, a young man who works making clothes in the household of his campesino father. Here the son laments the physical difficulty of working the fields, while the older man calmly notes the monetary benefit of his son's work compared to his own agrarian pursuits.

The Retired Campesino Mapping a New Cultural Script?

Some elders such as the one in this video have already seen the cultural handwriting on the wall and are radically altering the last phases of their campesino lifestyle and how they support and relate to their younger generations. When I first entered his house compound in 1972 I found that Santos Dias, although not well off, had just enough land to support his large family, economically supplemented by making wood crates and growing small amounts of flowers. Most people considered him one of the best farmers in the village and someone who managed to feed his large family through his skill and knowledge of the land.

By 2010 the cornfield was gone, replaced by two new dwellings, housing his son's young families, a textile workshop, and a small grazing area for the few horses, goats, and cows they had left. He proudly explained that he was *really* retired, and he would just watch the young do the work—words I had never heard uttered by a healthy, vigorous man in his early sixties. This was not the only dramatic change

168

in his life. Several years earlier his wife had succumbed to diabetes, which she did her best to ignore. A year after his wife's death Santos's oldest daughter, separated from her husband. She and her two teenage daughters promptly moved back in with Santos to her natal tochantlaca.

In 2006 and 2010 I had long interviews with Santos concerning the transitions he was going through, and he quickly noticed my surprise at the abandonment of his fields. This proud elder explained with a smile, "I know, Jay, you must be surprised how easily I gave up being a campesino. Some of my cousins and friends still cling to this path, but with my wife's death and my daughter's coming back home I realized one must adapt to things you never expected to happen."

Women's Changing Roles

One of the most powerful changes in the community has been the coming of new possibilities in the life of women, despite having a cultural system structured to favor male dominance (Ochoa Riviera 2007; Taggart 2007; Wentzell 2013; Susan Kellogg). 📷 Clearly some of the factors related to this have been the reduction of birth rates by more than half and the greater educational and occupational opportunities for women, especially in teaching. In 2003 it was a young woman, with some college education, who opened Amanalco's first Internet café. Yet I was frankly shocked and pleasantly surprised to learn in 2010 about the election of two women to core positions in the community's political governance. This change was also reflected in women beginning to undertake more independent activities in the vital public space of the community's fiesta system.

Such changes follow upon regional and national changes in women's roles that Amanalco's residents are becoming keenly aware of (see Forbis 2003, Marcos 2005). For example, in one of the other nearby indigenous communities a woman was elected to lead the community as a head delegado in the very recent past. Importantly, in November 2012 a woman had been elected to lead Texcoco and serve in the most important political post of the municipality, to which Amanalco is affiliated.

In 2010 I was able to talk with Berta Rojas, Amanalco's recently elected third delegada. I asked her, "In ten years how will Amanalco be different from today?" She told me,

> It is difficult to know. But I hope it is going to be different, and I have the hope that there are more social positions for women. I hope that there exists a water system for the whole community that works fine and that the plaza garden will be remodeled and that there will be a small sign that says Berta Rojas has collaborated in this project. And she worked hard on it but also she values her people and she loved them.

Figure 10.2   Diary entry: Every time I ride into town and see the cell phone tower set behind the long shuddered store of brown weathered adobe brick I can't help remember the nerve wracking day back in 1972 (see introduction to Chapter 4) when I strode into that simple building and introduced myself to some community members for the very first time, June 10, 2010. (Photo by Jay Sokolovsky)

"Never More Campesinos" Within a Multilocal, Globalizing World

It is much too easy to think about the defunct old store and the functioning cell tower (Figure 10.2) or even the texting child (Figure 10.3) to stand in for contrasting traditional and modern cultural landscapes. At the onset of my research in Mexico I puzzled over the contradiction of Amanalco being perceived simultaneously as the most tradition-bound and one of the most modernizing communities in its region. One part of the solution to this seeming paradox was the good fortune of lying close to urban markets but having lost nominal amounts of agricultural, forest, and water resources during the process of colonial domination. In the introductory chapters of the book I noted how this linked with a strong traditional system of cooperative labor grounded in the moral landscape of the fiesta system. This came to be partnered with governmental efforts beginning in the 1960s to foster a modernizing village infrastructure with electricity service, a medical clinic, improved schools, and a better road connecting Amanalco to urban markets. However, by the 1990s an expanding population and rapid decline of a campesino local economy produced new challenges for a decidedly multilocal community, where Amanalco's feature of defiant strength was turned inward by youth in graffiti and gangs. During the first decade of the twenty-first century the cultural constraints that shaped their forms of agrarian life and had once defined people as Indios who pursued a campesino cultural script had exploded their borders. This involved new cultural spaces, the food people eat, the way money is

Figure 10.3   Fieldnotes: I am at the first of two weddings shortly after I arrived back in Amanalco. Walking into the house of the groom's parents I spot a group of 10 young children from about ages 6 to 12. Very quickly the kids scatter into the patio shouting and playing. As the group ran off, I spot a girl of about 9 years sitting quietly behind her older relatives, playing with an uncle's cell phone trying to text her friends who were not at the celebration. June 14, 2010. (Photo by Jay Sokolovsky)

earned, the houses they build, the clothes they dress in, and the flow of authority and emotions across generations.

Between 2006 and 2010 one of the most interesting aspects of cultural space transformation was use of the central plaza and its immediate surrounding area. On the one hand, the surprisingly unkempt condition of the plaza had become a symbol of the collapse of community unity and unquestioned civic labor that had accomplished so much in the 1970s and 1980s. On the other hand, this same cultural space had become a zone of significant sustained commercial and governmental engagement that brought the multilocal world into the spatial heart of Amanalco. During my first Sunday back in 2010 this area was turned into a vibrant covered market that drew not only people from surrounding villages but also urban dwellers from Texcoco and even Mexico City. On that day there was also a federally funded mobile van dispensing free dental care. I had also noticed that along the main street near the plaza were new kinds of stores vending things like hardware, tire repair, and cell phones and that several were owned by individuals from outside Amanalco. The following day, while walking to the center of town, not only did I pass the monthly meeting of the Club of the Third Age but in the plaza itself there were also two large medical vans from Texcoco and nearby a *Policia Preventiva* (prevention police) and two officers, from that city, were watching over the proceedings.

As noted at this chapter's beginning, in 2012 the plaza itself underwent a physical transformation. Ahead of elections to continue controlling Texcoco's municipal government, the party then in power, PRI, had identical new plaza

Figure 10.4   New playground equipment in Amanalco's plaza as part of a plaza renewal program undertaken by Texcoco's municipal government in 2012. Notice the Spider Man figure atop one of the slides. (© Manuel Moreno)

architecture installed in all of the mountain communities. As seen in the Power Point link [P] associated with Figure 10.4, this includes not only a small garden, public toilets, a children's play area with a "Spider Man" image but also exercise equipment for seniors (see Figure 10.4). Importantly, despite this politically motivated largesse, the PRI lost the Texcoco municipal elections in 2012. It was won by a female teacher, Delfina Gomez Alvarez, representing a new political party, *Movimiento Ciudadano* (Citizen's Movement).

Multilocal versus Transnational Globalized Worlds

My McDonald's nightmare described in Chapter 3, though not clairvoyant, previewed some of the things now happening in Amanalco. Throughout the 1990s globalization via consumer products and mass media, especially global music, would invade the consciousness of teens, who formed social groups and gangs with affinities to specific performers and musical styles. By the twenty-first century, music as a preoccupation and sometimes profession affected well over a third of the households, and the community had become a regional center for music competitions and celebrations.

In Amanalco, by 2010, there was widespread use of cell phones and televisions, although still very limited availability of the Internet throughout the community.

These phones were certainly helpful for keeping household members working outside of the community connected to their Amanalco-bound kin and making it easier for me to communicate with people in the community when I was back in Florida. Since 2012, as is happening elsewhere in Mexico, Manuel Moreno reported that telecommunication companies started making a big push to install low-cost satellite dishes and that such structures could be seen on about a third of household roofs. Yet at present the personal engagement of Amanalco with the rest of the world is largely multilocal versus the formation of transnational communities across the national borders of Mexico and the United States. I say that despite encounters such as the following in 2010:

> I am sitting in the new Veracruz-style restaurant chatting with the owner, and at the next table is a group of young men from the community eating and talking. I overhear the word "Florida" float from the conversation and go over to introduce myself. It turns out one of the three had returned from Tampa, Florida [near where I live], six months ago. He worked there for two years installing outdoor wires for a cable company. He had paid $3,000 to be guided across the border by a handler with a pipeline to such jobs. The work dried up, so he decided to return home. (fieldnotes, June 17, 2010)

Migration to the United States from Amanalco is relatively infrequent and very scattered geographically, with Chicago, California, and Arizona being the primary destinations.

Another model of geopolitical interaction is seen three hours north of Amanalco in the Mezquital Valley in the State of Hidalgo, Mexico. Here, among self-identified Hñähñu indigenous communities, since 1980, there has been a significant long-term international migration to Clearwater, Florida, and the formation of a powerful transnational community. Ella Schmidt (2007, 2012), with careful research in both Hidalgo and Clearwater, has documented the impact of money remittances back to Mexico and the creation of support organizations in both nations that promote political and social representation of Hñähñu migrants in both of the transnational communities. Local Hispanic organizations in Clearwater and the Tampa Bay area, in collaboration with the Mexican National Consul in Florida, facilitated teachers and performers from Hidalgo to participate in cultural festivals in Clearwater. Back in Hidalgo there has been the development of bilingual radio programming and a women's collective making use of local resources such as ixtle fiber to produce sponges marketed internationally through the Body Shop. These interactions have reformulated notions of Hñähñu cultural identity and has been a force in indigenous language maintenance. International migration and the remittances that it represents have helped reintroduce traditional technologies and promoted indigenous culture, challenging the assimilationist notions built into Indigenismo. As in the case of Amanalco, engagement with the outside world has helped sustain a transformed indigenous identity in the twenty-first century.

173

"Never More Campesinos" Does Not
Mean Never More Indigenous

Two days before returning to the United States in 2010 I went to Amanalco's high school for what I thought was to be a group interview with some students about their life. Instead, when I arrived I was asked whether I would please give a talk to the entire junior and senior classes about the spiritual realm of the high forest and the powerful beings that inhabit that world. The following week these students would be going to this zone to replant trees. Because many students came from outside the community, it was thought that I, as an anthropologist from the United States, would have the authority to convince them to have sufficient respect and understanding of this special area. After getting over my shock at this change of plans, I was fortunate to learn that they had a computer projector that could be hooked up to my netbook. This allowed me to show video interviews of people talking about this realm and spiritual beings such as the ahuake, discussed in Chapter 9 (see Figure 10.5 below). Some of the students from Texcoco were very dubious, especially about the ahuakes, but several local kids strongly validated my discussion and added examples of their family members' encounters with the mountain dwarfs.

While I returned back home before these students undertook their replanting excursion, Manuel Moreno sent some photos and an audio recording of the ritual that preceded the tree planting. In Figure 10.6 we see the president of Amanalco's

*Figure 10.5   Lecturing to Amanalco's senior high school class about the high forest zone and the **ahuake**, 2010. (© Maria Vesperi)*

*Figures 10.6   Offerings and prayers to Tlaloc by Amanalco's committee of communal
properties. (© Manuel Moreno)*

committee of communal lands lighting copal incense to purify the area. It was
necessary to ask permission of the spiritual guardians of this zone and to leave a
simple offering of fruits. He was dressed in decorated ritual clothing and intoned
first in Nahuatl and then in Spanish the following words: "Tláloc, god of water,
the rain god, who grants us the water that springs from these lands, the rivers that
run through these places that come to puddle where your angels, the ahuakes,
dwell. Let us make this plantation. Making this payment, let us work."

Twenty-First-Century Ethnoscape: Indigenous Without Indigenismo?

In Chapter 6 I emphasized the interaction between the externally created ethnic
notion of indigenismo versus the local shift from Indio to Indigena as a means of
taking control and shaping Amanalco's ethnoscape. This was part of similar efforts
going on in many other parts of Mexico and among indigenous communities
worldwide (Hall and Fenelon 2009). As carefully documented in *Ethnic Identity
in Nahua Mesoamerica* (Berdan et al. 2008), an ethnic identity among Nahua

175

peoples involves a creative act and is typically best understood as a reasonable adaptation to the realities of life (see especially Sandstrom 2008, 158). Part of this response has been recognizing the need to counter the negative subtext of the term Indigenismo by ethnically creative responses "to remedy an intolerable situation and effectively give people a sense of dignity and purpose" (Sandstrom and Berdan 2008, 219).

The forest ritual offering to Tlaloc, noted above, is one aspect of the broader range of ethnically centered ideas and behaviors by which Amanalcanos construct a sense of a contemporary indigenous identity. As noted in earlier chapters, this ethnoscape is embedded in knowledge and myth about this critical environment, magical beings that guard it, and ideas about sorcery, shape-shifting, soul dislocation, and healing. It also includes the Nahuatl language itself, social concepts of respect greetings, core concepts of exchange and mutual support that bolster both the kin construct of the tochantlaca, and the moral imperative of community service.

I believe that one of the cultural gateways for understanding the future of Amanalco's twenty-first-century ethnoscape will be mediated through the contested relationship with the special parts of their environment, especially the mountain forest, with its water springs and sacred landscape of Mount Tlaloc. It is one of the areas of interest and discourse that transcends Amanalco's growing generational divide. I saw this in the keen interest high school students took in the discussion of the forest environment and the need to accept the responsibility of being environmental stewards of this key habitat, which many of my generation have ignored for too long.

It is noteworthy that in 2008 an environmental cleanup project was among the earliest efforts by the Amanalco Pilhuame Ollin group when it began to organize around a modern indigenous identity. One can see this also through a prominent "clean ecology" wall mural put up that same year in a collaboration between the school system and Amanalco's ecology committee (see Figure 10.7). [P]

Reinventing the Future: The Centro Cultural Miyotl

In following the e-mail news from Amanalco I was disappointed to learn both that the Ollin group had recently disbanded and that the hopes of establishing a Nahuatl Cultural Center in Amanalco seemed more distant than ever. However, other things were happening relating to the issue of Nahuatl indigenous identity. For example, in 2012 I began to see web-based reports of Catholic Masses being performed in Nahuatl in Texcoco's cathedral and classes being offered for adults both in Texcoco and in the mountain communities such as Santa Catarina and Amanalco.

Within Amanalco itself, as the Pilhuame Ollin group was fading, a new organization, *Centro Cultural Miyotl* (Rays of Hope Cultural Center), was being created in the center of town. It began slowly in late 2010 through the efforts of

Figure 10.7   A new wall mural by the plaza asks: "What does San Jerónimo prefer, clean or dirty?", 2012. (See this link for the full translation of the sign. P *(© Manuel Moreno)*

a charismatic twenty-seven-year-old man, Miguel Osorio (see the Miyotl Facebook page). ⬆ On the surface Miguel seemed an unlikely candidate to carry out such an endeavor. Although born in Amanalco, his parents separated when he was young, and Miguel shuttled back and forth among Amanalco, Texcoco, and Mexico City. As a teen, he developed problems with drugs, but claims his life was turned around by an urban-based evangelical preacher. He returned to Amanalco with a mission.

In creating the Centro Cultural Miyotl Miguel wanted to establish an educational space where youth could learn occupational and life skills and where elders, especially females, could improve their literacy. It is also his plan to involve older adults in reintroducing some of their knowledge to the young, such as the weaving of cactus fiber, a skill that had almost disappeared by 2010.

Incredibly, by 2013 Miguel had been elected second delegado and managed to convince ten urban teachers to travel to the community and give free lessons in hair styling, various types of craft production, theater, taekwondo, guitar, and even English. Figure 10.8 shows the Centro Cultural Miyotl banner hanging from the delegación building in Amanalco and provides a link to a Power Point P that shows young students learning chess, in an English class, watching a puppet show and elder women overcoming illiteracy. Following this success, on August 1, 2014, although a long-hoped-for Nahuatl Cultural Center still seemed a far-off dream, Amanalco inaugurated its own small, elegant museum within its renovated

*Figure 10.8   Banner for the **Centro Cultural Miyotl**, hanging from the **delegación** building in Amanalco, 2013.* P *(© Manuel Moreno)*

delegación building focusing on local heritage. The entrance is marked by the large beautiful wall mural that adorns this book's cover and was created by a young local man, Sergio Pérez Mendez, who is studying art at a university in Mexico City. In the following added value link you can view videos in sequence, showing the creation of the mural and the opening of the museum.

This was all very exciting to me, and I am eagerly anticipating 2015. Sometime that year I will give this book to the people of Amanalco, hang out with my compadres in Buena Vista, and see how these new developments turn out.

Notes

Chapter One

1. There are 125 *municipios* in Mexico, and they function like counties in the United States.
2. In both cases, despite fierce opposition, Walmarts were built.

Chapter Two

1. The word *milpa* is a Mexican Spanish word but directly connected to the Nahuatl phrase for "to the field." It is derived from the words *milli* (field) and *pa* (toward).
2. Another form of exchange, termed *tlapatlaliztli,* is used for the exchange of food and domestic products that could involve contributing tortillas to a relative for a ritual, or women taking surplus homemade household brushes to another village in exchange for fruit only grown in that area.
3. Coca-Cola bottled in Mexico is sweetened with sugar, whereas the US version is (almost) always made with high-fructose corn syrup.

Chapter Three

1. The enforcement of this legislation in the Texcoco region began in 1537. During this period communities located in the eastern foothills, such as the pre-Hispanic ancestors of Amanalco, were moved to their current town center at an eighty-five hundred-foot elevation, and their prior lands were heavily grazed by sheep that eventually denuded the soil. In 1972, when I first drove by this area, its sole scant plants clung to slightly elevated mounds that marked the house remains of their precolonial ancestors. It is only in the past two decades that there have been successful efforts to reclaim these dead zones once again for agriculture.
2. Article 27 of the 1917 Mexican Constitution calls for land redistribution in the form of ejidos—land parcel grants to communities rather than individuals. Although historical documents show that Amanalco began to request return of their lands as early as 1912, they had to wait until 1930 for the granting of their ejido, giving them back most of their original lands.
3. The people on the Caliente side are also nicknamed *cuerudos* (like cowboys who dress in leather).
4. In other words, you are somewhat most likely to avoid this incest boundary by seeking partners on the opposite side of the village where you were born. This marriage regulation function has been greatly reduced as the population began to expand significantly since the 1990s.
5. The Spanish words *doña* and *don* are titles of respect (for females and males, respectively) often used for persons past age fifty.
6. The Day of the Dead is actually a several-day period now celebrated from October 31 to November 2 and is derived from the Mexica festival dedicated to a goddess called Mictecacihuatl. Originally it was associated with the ninth month of the Mexica calendar, beginning in early August and lasted the entire month. Following the Spanish conquest priests shifted this celebration to the Catholic ritual period of All Saints Day (November 1) and All Souls Day (November 2).
7. The flowers are called *cempoaxochitl in Nahuatl,* and most families will grow them to place on their household altar to create a pleasant setting for the returning spirits of dead children.
8. By 2010 Manuel Moreno counted sixty-seven small diverse establishments, including twenty small general stores; four feed stores; two clothes stores; two medical consultancies; two pharmacies; four papers supply stores, with three having Internet service; four toy stores; two tire repair shops; two cell phone stores; and a Veracruz-style seafood restaurant.

Chapter Four

1. I have also received quite strong comments from a self-described Native American who, in viewing the videos on Archaeology Heritage and Indigenous Identity, wrote such things as, "it's funny how whites kill 95 percent of the Native Americans and then talk about how much more American they are than the so-called Mexicans."

2. More broadly known as the Cambridge University Torres Straits expedition, this late-nineteenth-century research project in the South Pacific was the first such cross-cultural study to employ motion pictures in the field.

Chapter Five

1. Very little is known about preconquest village life and the actual functioning of elders in the context of rural Mexica communities. According to historical sources the elder chief of the highest-ranking clan along with a council composed of other clan elders regulated the distribution of communally owned lands, settled disputes, and saw to the training of warriors and the payment of taxes by the entire community (Soustelle 1961). Aged males and females of any rank had some special roles: men made ritual speeches and prepared corpses, while women arranged marriages and served as midwives. Persons past age seventy also had the privilege of drinking alcohol in public without the severe sanctions imposed on younger individuals who imbibed.

At the household level Aztec-era elders appeared to command filial attention and respect approaching that of the ancient Chinese. Among a child's first lessons were admonitions about showing esteem toward elders (Simmons 1945, 62). Marriage seldom occurred without parental consent, and the father had the power to pawn or sell his children into slavery if his economic situation was severe enough.

2. From the perspective of an adult, the children of your first male-linked cousins are known collectively by the Nahuatl term *inseki,* and these are the children you push your offspring to interact with.

3. Although it does happen, it is exceptionally rare that the girl's parents would not accept "robbing" of their daughter. Once this is accepted, the parents of the couple become compadres to each other, which further cements the bonds between the families.

4. In 1995 the organization of the fiesta system was simplified with a reduction in the number of major fiestas from six to four and the fiscal position no longer having a senior and junior member but now are equal positions, chosen from among men of each side of the community.

Chapter Six

1. It should be noted, however, that according to one of the bilingual teachers there was at least a temporary benefit to the bilingual schools after the concert, as they got some good national publicity and a slight increase in funding.

2. A variety of derogatory slang developed among city dwellers to mock the mountain people by reference to their location in the mountains: *Serrano, Montero,* or *Montesco.* Mention of these terms is based on personal communication with anthropologist Manuel Moreno.

3. In 1948 a law created the Instituto Nacional Indigenista (INI). In 2003 this law was replaced by the Comisión Nacional para el Desarrollo de los Pueblos Indígenas (CDI—Commission for the Development of Indigenous Communities).

4. In should be noted that in 1911 the Mexican government put in effect the Law for Rudimentary Instruction, which prohibited indigenous children from using their maternal languages in school.

5. Since the 1960s in other parts of Mexico there were efforts by bilingual teachers and

promoters of traditional culture to serve as cultural ambassadors in indigenous communities and to prevent this kind of conflict. But this was not the case in Amanalco.

6. In Mexico in the 1960s and 1970s there had developed within both national institutions and independent groups of educators an interest in preserving indigenous languages. This included in 1963 the Promotores Culturales y Maestros Bilingues and, in 1975, an Asociacion de Profesionistas Nahua (OPINAC). Yet it was not until the 1990s that internal and international political pressure would emerge to powerfully promote the interests of communities where those languages still existed.

7. Their proposal for the development of a municipal commission "For the Development of the Nahuatl Culture and Language in the Region of Texcoco, State of Mexico" was submitted to the municipio's president for funding and support. As far as I could find out, as of 2011 no support was provided.

Chapter Seven

1. In 2010 some of the weddings of more prosperous families included some catered food from Texcoco, besides the traditional courses prepared by the members of the tochantlaca.

Chapter Eight

1. It is interesting to note that the signage for this new religious center is both in Spanish and in Nahuatl: "Kajli Kampa Monechi Koaj Iteixpantijkauan Jehová" (House for the Kingdom of the Jehovah's Witnesses).

2. The only fiesta they are not responsible for is that for St. Cecilia, the patron saint of musicians. It is these performers who exclusively organize this event.

3. Apart from the two districts that cooperate in the holidays, Santo Domingo and San Francisco, so do two colonies that also belong to Amanalco, St. Augustine and St. Joseph. However, the colony Guadalupe, although associated with Amanalco, independently runs fiestas and cooperates with the cost of holidays.

4. Important research on the cargo system in Amanalco has been done by Ochoa Riviera (2008).

Chapter Nine

1. Such objects are called *tecunechichiwa* in Nahuatl.

2. Another version of such evil is called *tepalcuatiki,* someone who gives poison or other bad things to cause harm. One infamous suspected female practitioner of this lethal art made fish tamales with scorpions, and people died.

3. It is said in Nahuatl "*nechquaqwaco tlawelpuche*"—a witch came and sucked on me.

4. According to James Taggart, "A more or less composite variant begins when a husband senses his wife getting up in the middle of the night. He watches her remove one of her legs and turn into a bird. She flies out of the house and through the walls of another house where she sucks the blood out of a young child, often a nursing infant. She returns home and vomits the blood into a casserole, fries it in lard, and prepares a concoction that looks like *mole.* The husband tells his mother, and she advises him to burn the wife's leg when she goes after her next victim. He follows his mother's advice, and, the next day, the wife suffers a horrible pain in her leg and dies." (Taggart 2009, 16).

5. This information was acquired August 2012 during an interview with a Mr. Oscar Mokeme, a high-level Igbo healer called an *Nwa-Dibia.* He is also director of the Museum of African Culture in Portland, Maine.

6. They are also known among the other nearby indigenous communities, and in nearby Santa Catarina they are known in Nahuatl as *tioches* but are described in a similar way.

7. See Simon and Hughes (1985) for understanding such illnesses as susto in the context of other culture-bound syndromes.

8. Classic examples of such studies include that of Evans-Pritchard in Africa (1976) and Stewart and Strathern in Papua New Guinea (2004).

References

Aboderin, Isabella. 2006. *Intergenerational Support and Old Age in Africa*. New Brunswick, NJ: Transaction.

Aguilar-Moreno, M. 2007. *Handbook to Life in the Aztec World*. New York: Oxford University Press.

Appadudurai, Arjun. 1996. *Modernity at Large: Cultural Dimensions of Globalization*. Minneapolis: University of Minnesota Press.

Avilés, Paul. 2006. "Seven Ways of Looking at a Mountain: Tetzcotzingo and the Aztec Garden Tradition." *Landscape Journal* 25 (2): 143–157.

Bayles, Bryan, and David Katerndahl. 2009. "Culture-Bound Syndromes in Hispanic Primary Care Patients." *The International Journal of Psychiatry in Medicine Volume* 39 (1): 15–31.

Berdan, Frances F., John K Chance, Alan R. Sandstrom, Barbara Stark, James Taggart, and Emily Umberger. 2008. *Ethnic Identity in Nahua Mesoamerica: The View from Archaeology, Art History, Ethnohistory, and Contemporary Ethnography*. Salt Lake City: University of Utah Press.

Beyene, Yewoubdar. 1989. *From Menarche to Menopause: Reproductive Lives in Peasant Women in Two Cultures*. Albany: State University of New York Press.

Bledsoe, Caroline. 2002. *Contingent Lives. Fertility, Time and Aging in West Africa*. Chicago: University of Chicago Press.

Boehm, Deborah. 2013. *Intimate Migrations Gender, Family, and Illegality Among Transnational Mexicans*. New York: New York University Press.

Brading, David A. 1988. "Manuel Gamio and Official Indigenismo in Mexico Author(s)." *Bulletin of Latin American Research* 7 (1): 75–89.

Brinton, Daniel G. 1896. *Nagualism: A Study in Native American Folk-lore and History*. Philadelphia: Maccalla and Company.

Brulotte, Rhonda. 2009. "'Yo soy nativo de aqui': The Ambiguities of Race and Indigeneity in Oaxacan Craft Tourism." *Journal of Latin American and Caribbean Anthropology* 14 (2): 457–482.

Caple, Erica. 2012. "Witchcraft, Bureaucraft, and the Social Life of (US) AID in Haiti." *Cultural Anthropology* 27 (1): 50–75.

Chick, Garry. 2002. "Cultural and Behavioral Consonance in a Tlaxcalan Festival System." *Field Methods* 14 (1): 26–45.

Cohen, Carl, and Jay Sokolovsky. 1989. *Old Men of the Bowery: Survival Strategies of the Homeless*. New York: Guilford Press.

Cool, Linda, and J. McCabe. 1987. "The 'Scheming Hag' and the 'Dear Old Thing': The Anthropology of Aging Women." In *Growing Old in Different Societies: Cross-Cultural Perspectives*, edited by Jay Sokolovsky, 56–68. Acton, MA: Copley.

Danley, Jason, and Caitrin Lynch. 2013. *Transitions and Transformations: Cultural Perspectives on Aging and the Life Course*. New York: Berghahn Press.

de la Cadena, Marisol, and Orin Starn. 2007. "Introduction." In *Indigenous Experience Today*, edited by M. de la Cadena and O. Starn, 1–30. Oxford: Berg.

del Campo, Edgar Martín. 2009. * The Global Making of a Mexican Vampire: Mesoamerican, European, African, and Twentieth-Century Media Influences on the Teyollohcuani." *History of Religions* 49 (2): 107–140.

Doane, Molly. 2012. *Stealing Shining Rivers: Agrarian Conflict, Market Logic, and Conservation in a Mexican Forest*. Tuscon: University of Arizona Press.

Domosh, Mona. 2010. "The world was never flat: Early global encounters and the messiness of empire." *Progress in Human Geography* 34(4): 419–435.

Douglas, Eduardo. 2010. *In the Palace of Nezahualcoyotl*. Austin: University of Texas Press.

Dow, James W., and Alan. R. Sandstrom, eds. 2001. *Holy Saints and Fiery Preachers: The Anthropology of Protestantism in Mexico and Central America*. Westport, CT: Praeger.

Earle, Rebecca. 2007. *The Return of the Native*. Durham, NC: Duke University Press.

El Observador en el Estado de Mexico. 2014. Texcoco Celebra el Dia Del Adulto. https://feyiyi1.word press.com/2014/08/30/texcoco-celebra-el-dia-del-adulto-mayor/ (accessed September 9, 2014).

El Universal. 2011. "La cantera de la musica de viento." In *El Newspaper*, August 28, 2011 http://www.eluniversal.com.mx/cultura/66229.html (accessed July 1, 2013).

Ennis-McMillan, Michael. 2006. *A Precious Liquid: Drinking Water and Culture in the Valley of Mexico*. Stamford, CT: Cengage.

Evans-Pritchard, E. E. 1976. *Witchcraft, Oracles, and Magic Among the Azande*. Oxford: Oxford University Press.

Everett, Margaret, and Josef Wieland. 2013. "Diabetes Among Oaxaca's Transnational Population: an Emerging Syndemic," *Annals of Anthropological Practice*, 36:2: 295–311.

Forbis, Melissa M. 2003. "Hacía la Autonomía: Zapatista Women Developing a New World." In *Women of Chiapas: Making History in Times of Struggle and Hope*, edited by Christine Eber and Christine Kovic, 231–252. New York and London: Routledge.

Foster, George M. 1965. "Peasant Society and the Image of Limited Good." *American Anthropologist* 67: 293–315.

Friedman, Thomas. 2005. *The World Is Flat: A Brief History of the Twenty-first Century*. New York: Farrar, Straus, and Giroux.

Galinier, Jacques. 2004. *The World Below: Body and Cosmos in Otomi Indian Ritual*. Boulder: University of Colorado Press.

Gamio, Manuel. 1979 [1922] *La población del Valle de Teotihuacan*. Mexico City: INI.

Geschiere, Peter. 2012. "Sociality and Its Dangers: Witchcraft, Intimacy and Trust." In *Sociality: New Directions*, edited by Nicholas J. Long and Henrietta L. Moore, 61–82. New York: Berghahn Books.

Giraudo, Laura, and Stephen E. Lewis. 2012. "Pan-American Indigenismo (1940–1970): New Approaches to an Ongoing Debate." *Latin American Perspectives* 39: 3–11.

Glazer, Mark, Roberta D. Baer, Susan C. Weller, Javier Eduardo Garcia de Alba, and Stephen W. Liebowitz. 2004. "Susto and Soul Loss in Mexicans and Mexican Americans." *Cross-Cultural Research* 38 (3): 270–288.

Good, Catherine. 2011. "My Thirty Years in Mexican Anthropology." *Anthropology and Humanism* 36 (1): 36–46.

Gross, T. 2009. "Farewell to Fiestas and Saints? Changing Catholic Practices in Contemporary Rural Oaxaca." *Journal of Ethnology and Folkloristics* 3 (1): 3–19.

Hall, Thomas, and James Fenelon. 2009. "Indigenous Peoples and Globalization: Resistance and Revitalization." In *Indigenous Mexico: Globalization and Resistance*, edited by Glen Kuecker, 63–90. Boulder, CO: Paradigm.

Harvey, David. 1989. *The Conditions of Postmodernity*. Oxford: Blackwell.

Inda, Jonathan, and Renato Rosaldo. 2002. *The Anthropology of Globalization: A Reader*. Oxford: Blackwell.

Ingham, John. 1986. "Mary, Michael and Lucifer: Folk Catholicism in Central Mexico." Austin: University of Texas Press.

Ixtlilxóchitl, Alva. 1965. *Obras Historicas*. México, D.F: Editora Nacional.

Knab, Timothy 2009. *The Dialogue of Earth and Sky: Dreams, Souls, Curing, and the Modern Aztec underworld*. Tuscon: University of Arizona Press.

Lastra, Y., D. Sherzer, and J. Sherzer. 2009. *Adoring the Saints: Fiestas in Central Mexico*. Austin: University of Texas Press.

Lewis, Oscar. 1960. *Tepoztlan: Village in Mexico*. New York: Holt.

Lorente Fernández, David. 2009. "Nociones de etnometeorología nahua: el complejo ahuaquesgranicero en la Sierra de Texcoco, México." *Revista Española de Antropología Americana* 39 (1): 97–118.

———. 2010. "El Agua de Tláloc: el mundo Serrano de los graniceros y los dioses de la lluvia." In *Texcoco en el nuevo milenio: Cambio y continuidad en una región periurbana del Valle de México,* edited by Roger Magazine and Tomas Martinez Saldana, 335–360. México, D.F.: Universidad Iberoamericana.

Madsen, William. 1960. *The Virgin's Children: Life in an Aztec Village Today.* Austin: University of Texas Press.

Magazine, Roger. 2012. *The Village Is Like a Wheel: Rethinking Cargos, Family and Ethnicity in Highland Mexico.* Tuscon: University of Arizona Press.

Magazine, Roger, and Tomas Martínez Saldana, eds. 2010. *Texcoco en el Nuevo milenio: Cambio y continuidad en una region periurbana del Valle de Mexico.* Mexico, D.F.: Universidad Iberoamericana.

Marcos, Sylvia. 2005. "The Borders Within: The Indigenous Women's Movement and Feminism in Mexico." In *Dialogue and Difference: Feminisms Challenge Globalization,* edited by Sylvia Marcos, 81–112. New York: Palgrave Macmillan.

Martin, JoAnn. 2005. *Tepoztlán and the Transformation of the Mexican State: The Politics of Loose Connections.* Tuscon: University of Arizona Press.

Mehta, Kalyani. 1997. "Cultural Scripts and the Social Integration of Older People." *Ageing and Society* 17: 253–275.

Mexico D. F., ATN, "Amanalco," 1912. Archivos de Terrenos Nacional. "Amanalco," Expediente 81, 1.24 (12h.2E8).

Millard, Anne. 1985. "Child mortality and economic variation among rural Mexican households." *Social Science & Medicine* 20(6): 589–599.

Mindek, D. 1994. "No Nos Sobra, Pero Gracias a Dios, Tampoco Nos Falta, Crecimiento Demographico y Modernizacion en San Jerónimo Amanalco." Master's thesis, Universidad Iberoamericana.

Moreno, Jose Manuel. 2010. "La continuidad de lo indígena en una sociedad desindianizada: el caso de San Jerónimo Amanalco, Estado de México." Master's thesis: Universidad Iberoamericana.

Moreno-Brid, Juan Carlos, Juan Ernesto Pardinas Carpizo, and Jaime Ros Bosch. 2009. "Economic Development and Social Policies in Mexico." *Economy and Society* 38 (1): 154–176.

Najera-Ramirez, Olga. 1997. *La Fiesta de Los Tastoanes: Critical Encounters in Festival Performance.* Albuquerque: University of New Mexico Press.

Newton, Lisa. 1999. "Truth Is the Daughter of Time: The Real Story of the Nestle Case." *Business and Society Review* 104 (4): 367–395.

Nutini, Hugo G., and John M. Roberts. 1993. *Blood-Sucking Witchcraft: An Epistemological Study of Anthropomorphic Supernaturalism in Rural Tlaxcala.* Tucson: University of Arizona Press.

Obermeyer, C., and L. Sievert. 2007. "Cross-Cultural Comparisons: Midlife, Aging and Menopause." *Menopause* 14 (4): 663–667.

Ochoa Riviera, Teresa. 2007. "La dominación masculina en el sistema tradicional de cargos: el caso de San Jerónimo Amanalco, municipio de Texcoco, México." *Otoño.* Tomo 4 (1): 1–19. http://www.uia.mx/actividades/publicaciones/iberoforum/4/pdf/teresao.pdf (accessed April 28, 2013).

———. 2008. "La dominación masculina en el sistema tradicional de cargos: el caso de San Jerónimo Amanalco, municipio de Texcoco, México." *Primavera* 4(1): 1–19.

———. 2011. *Representación de Persona. Una mirada a través de la salud-enfermedad, alimentación y gordura en San Jerónimo Amanalco, Estado de México.* Doctoral thesis, Universidad Iberoamericana.

Peralta Ramirez, Valentín. 1995. "Achikoli-Nezahualcóyotl. Remembranzas de un pasado, literatura y filosofía en la comunidad de Amanalco, Tezcoco, Edo. de México." *Amerindia: Revue d'ethnolinguistique Amérindienn* 19/20: 341–349.

Pérez Lizaur, Marisol. 1977. *Población y sociedad: cuatro comunidades del Acolhuacan.* México, D.F.: Centro de Investigación Superior, Instituto Nacional de Antropología e Historia.

Pomar, Juan Buatista. 1941. *Relaciones de Texcoco y de la Nueva Espana.* México, D.F.: S. Chavez Hayhoe.

Quinlan, Marsh. 2010. "Ethnomedicine and Ethnobotany of Fright: A Caribbean Culture-Bound Psychiatric Syndrome." *Journal of Ethnobiology and Ethnomedicine* 6 (9): 2–18.

Radford, Benjamin. 2011. *Tracking the Chupacabra: The Vampire Beast in Fact, Fiction, and Folklore.* Albuquerque: University of New Mexico Press.

Redfield, Robert. 1930. *Tepoztlan, a Mexican Village: A Study of Folk Life.* Chicago: University of Chicago Press.

Reich, Robert. 2007. *Supercapitalism: The Transformation of Business, Democracy and Everyday Life.* New York: Knopf.

Robichaux, David. 2005. "Familias Nahuas en la Edad Industrial: Cambios y Permanencias en la Estructura y Organización Domésticas en Tlaxcala." In *Familia y Parentesco en México y Mesoamérica. Unas Miradas Antropológicas,* edited by David Robichaux, 117–150. México: Universidad Iberoamericana.

Roseberry, William. 1993. "Beyond the Agrarian Question in Latin America." In *Confronting Historical Paradigms: Peasants, Labor, and the Capitalist World System in Africa and Latin America,* edited by Frederick Cooper, Allen Isaacman, Florenica Mallon, William Rosebery, and Steve J. Stern, 318–370. Madison: University of Wisconsin Press.

Rosenberg, Harriet. 2009. "Complaint Discourse, Aging and Caregiving Among the Ju/'hoansi of Botswana." In *The Cultural Context of Aging: World-Wide Perspectives,* 3rd ed., edited by Jay Sokolovsky, 30–52. Westport, CT: Greenwood Press.

Ross, Norbert, Catherine Timura, and Jonathan Maupin. 2012. "The Case of Curers, Noncurers, and Biomedical Expersts in Pichátaro, Mexico." *Medical Anthropology Quarterly* 26 (2): 159–181.

Rothstein, Frances. 2007. *Globalization in Rural Mexico: Three Decades of Change.* Austin: University of Texas Press.

Rubel, Arthur, Carl O'Nell, and Rolando Collado-Ardon. 1991. *Susto: A Folk Illness.* Berkeley: University of California Press.

Rubel, Arthur, and Carmella Moore. 2001. "The Contribution of Medical Anthropology to a Comparative Study of Culture: Susto and Tuberculosis." *Medical Anthropology Quarterly* 15 (4): 440–454.

Ruby, Jay. 1991. Speaking for, Speaking with, or Speaking Alongside: An Anthropological and documentary Dilemna. *Visual Anthropology Review* 7 (2): 50–67.

Sandstrom, Alan. 2008. "Blood Sacrifice, Curing, and Ethnic Identity Among Contemporary Nahua of Northern Veracruz, Mexico." In *Ethnic Identity in Nahua Mesoamerica: The View from Archaeology, Art History, Ethnohistory, and Contemporary Ethnography,* edited by Frances F. Berdan, John K. Chance, Alan R. Sandstrom, Barbara Stark, James Taggart, and Emily Umberger, 150–182. Salt Lake City: University of Utah Press.

Sandstrom, Alan, and Frances Berdan. 2008. "Some Finishing Thoughts and Unfinished Business." In *Ethnic Identity in Nahua Mesoamerica: The View from Archaeology, Art History, Ethnohistory, and Contemporary Ethnography,* edited by Frances F. Berdan, John K. Chance, Alan R. Sandstrom, Barbara Stark, James Taggart, and Emily Umberger, 204–220. Salt Lake City: University of Utah Press.

Sandstrom, Alan, and Pamela Sandstrom. 2010. "Respuestas de la religión huasteca nahua a la globalización y la invasión protestante." In *San Juan Diego y la Pachamama: Nuevas vías delCcatolicismo y de la Religiosidad Indígena en América Latina,* edited by Félix Báez-Jorge, and Alessandro Lupo, 158–195. Xalapa, Mexico: Editora de Gobierno del Estado de Veracruz.

Sanjek, Roger. 1990. *Fieldnotes: The Makings of Anthropology.* Ithaca, NY: Cornell University Press.

Savage, M., G. Bagnall, and B. Longhurst. 2005. *Globalization and Belonging.* London: Sage.

Scheper-Hughes, Nancy. 1981. *Saints, Scholars, and Schizophrenics*. Berkeley: University of California Press.
———. 2000. "Ire in Ireland." *Ethnography* 1 (1): 117–140.
Schmidt, Ella. 2007. "Whose Culture? Globalism, Localism, and the Expansion of Tradition: the Case of the Hñähñu of Hidalgo, Mexico and Clearwater, Florida." In *Cultures of Globalization: Coherence, Hybridity, and Contestation*, edited by Kevin Archer, 101–114. Ann Arbor, MI: Routledge.
———. 2012. "Citizenship from Below: Hñähñu Heritage in a Transnational World." *Latino Studies* 10 (1–2): 196–219.
Schnegg, Michael, and Douglas White. 2008. "Getting Connected: Kinship and Compadrazgo in Rural Tlaxcala, Mexico." In *Networks, Resources and Economic Action: Ethnographic Case Studies in Honor of Hartmut Lang*, edited by Glemens Greiner and Waltraud Kokot. Berlin: Verlag. http://intersci.ss.uci.edu/wiki/pub/FS_HLSchneggWhite_Dec_12_08_BW.pdf (accessed July 1, 2013).
Sievert, L. 2006. *Menopause: A Biocultural Perspective*. New Brunswick, NJ: Rutgers University Press.
Simmons, Leo W. 1945. *The Role of the Aged in Primitive Society*. New Haven, CT: Archon Books.
Simon, R. C., and C. C. Hughes. 1985. *The Culture-Bound Syndromes: Folk Illnesses of Psychiatric and Anthropological Interest*. Dordrecht, the Netherlands: D. Reidel.
Smith, Robert. 2006. *Mexican New York: Transnational Lives of New Immigrants*. Berkeley: University of California Press.
Sokolovsky, Jay. 2002. "Living Arrangements of Older Persons and Family Support in Less Developed Countries." *Population Bulletin of the United Nations* Nos. 42/43: 162–192.
———. (ed). 2009. *The Cultural Context of Aging: World-Wide Perspectives*, 3rd ed. Westport, CT: Greenwood Press.
———. (ed). Forthcoming. *The Cultural Context of Aging: World-Wide Perspectives*, 4th ed. Connecticut: Greenwood Press.
Soustelle, Jacques. 1961. *Daily Life of the Aztecs on the Eve of the Spanish Conquest*. Stanford, CA: Stanford University Press.
Stavans, Ilan. 2010. *Quinceanera*. Santa Barbara, CA: ABC-CLIO.
Stephen, Lynn. 1996. "The Creation and Re-creation of Ethnicity: Lessons from the Zapotec and Mixtec of Oaxaca." *Latin American Perspectives* 23 (2): 17–37.
———. 2013. *We Are the Face of Oaxaca: Testimony and Social Movements*. Durham, NC: Duke University Press.
Stewart, Pamela, and Andrew Strathern. 2004. *Witchcraft, Sorcery, Rumors, and Gossip*. Cambridge: Cambridge University Press.
Stresser-Péan, Guy. 2009. *The Sun God and the Savior: The Christianization of the Nahua and Totonac in the Sierra Norte de Puebla, Mexico*. Boulder: University Press of Colorado.
Taggart, James. 2007. *Remembering Victoria: A Tragic Nahuat Love Story*. Austin: University of Texas Press.
———. 2008. "Nahuatl Ethnicity in a Time of Agrarian Conflict." In *Ethnic Identity in Indigenous Mesoamerica: The View from Archaeology, Ethnohistory, and Contemporary Ethnography*, edited by Frances F. Berdan, John K. Chance, Alan R. Sandstrom, James Taggart, and Emily Umberger, 183–203. Salt Lake City: University of Utah Press.
Taggart, James, and Alan Sandstrom. 2011. "Special Issue: Long-Term Fieldwork." *Anthropology and Humanism* 36 (1): 36–46.
Torres, Guillermo. 2006. "Los jóvenes de San Jerónimo Amanalco." Master's thesis: Universidad Iberoamericana.
Underberg, Natalie, and Elayne Zorn. 2013. *Digital Ethnography: Anthropology, Narrative, and New Media*. Austin: University of Texas Press.
Weller, S. C., R. D. Baer, and J. M. García de Alba. 2008. "Susto and Nervios: Expressions for Stress and Depression." *Culture, Medicine and Psychiatry* 32 (3):406–420.

187

Wentzell, Emily. 2013. *Maturing Masculinities: Aging, Chronic Illness, and Viagra in Mexico.* Durham, N.C.: Duke University Press.

Whiteford, Michael. 1999. "Homeopathic Medicine in the City of Oaxaca, Mexico: Patients' Perspectives and Observations." *Medical Anthropology Quarterly* 13 (1): 69–78.

Wolf, Eric R. 1955. "Types of Latin American Peasantry: A Preliminary Discussion." *American Anthropologist* 57: 452–471.

———. 1966. *Peasants.* Englewood Cliffs, NJ: Prentice Hall.

———. 1982. *Europe and the People Without History.* Berkeley: University of California Press.

———. 1986. "The Vicissitudes of the Closed Corporate Peasant Community." *American Ethnologist* 13 (2): 325–329.

Worthham, Erica. 2013. *Indigenous Media in Mexico: Culture, Community and the State.* Durham, NC: Duke University Press.

WHO (World Health Organization). 2011. World Health Rankings. http://apps.who.int/gho/data/node.main.688?lang=en (accessed September 9, 2014).

Yoshioka, Hirotoshi. 2010. "Indigenous Language Usage and Maintenance Patterns Among Indigenous People in the Era of Neoliberal Multiculturalism in Mexico and Guatemala." *Latin American Research Review* 45 (3): 5–34.

Index

Authors Index

About the Author

Jay Sokolovsky, Ph.D., is Professor of Anthropology in the Department of Society, Culture and Language at the University of South Florida St. Petersburg. He is a cultural anthropologist with specialties in the globalization of indigenous Mexico, the anthropology of aging, urban anthropology, and video documentation. Jay was the 2013 recipient of the Textor Award for Anticipatory Anthropology awarded by the American Anthropological Association. He is the author of numerous articles and five books including the award-winning volume, *The Cultural Context of Aging*.

His research has been done in a Mexican indigenous community, New York City, Florida's Tampa Bay region, the new town of Columbia, Maryland and in urban neighborhoods in England and Croatia. His latest ethnographic video, *Urban Garden: Fighting for Life and Beauty*, documents the community garden movement in New York City.